DESCARTES
AND THE
POSSIBILITY OF SCIENCE

Also by Peter A. Schouls

Reasoned Freedom: John Locke and Enlightenment
Descartes and the Enlightenment
The Imposition of Method: A Study of Descartes and Locke

DESCARTES

and the

POSSIBILITY OF SCIENCE

PETER A. SCHOULS

CORNELL UNIVERSITY PRESS

ITHACA AND LONDON

First published 2000 by Cornell University Press

Printed in the United States of America

Library of Congress Cataloging-in-Publication Data

Schouls, Peter A.
   Descartes and the possibility of science / Peter A. Schouls.
     p. cm.
   Includes bibliographical references and index.
   ISBN 0-8014-3775-X (cloth)
   1. Descartes, René, 1596–1650.   2. Science—Philosophy.   I. Title.
B1875 S368 2000
194—dc21

                           00-024021

Cornell University Press strives to use environmentally responsible suppliers and materials to the fullest extent possible in the publishing of its books. Such materials include vegetable-based, low-VOC inks, and acid-free papers that are recycled, totally chlorine-free, or partly composed of nonwood fibers. Books that bear the logo of the FSC (Forest Stewardship Council) use paper taken from forests that have been inspected and certified as meeting the highest standards for environmental and social responsibility. For further information, visit our website at www.cornellpress.cornell.edu.

Cloth printing   10 9 8 7 6 5 4 3 2 1

FSC FSC Trademark © 1996 Forest Stewardship Council A.C.
     SW-COC-098

To Jeanette

for the sense of adventure shared during

our sojourns in Canada, England, Scotland,

Holland, and New Zealand.

Contents

Preface

Descartes believed that the world and humanity exist in a relationship which makes it possible for humanity to improve its state through manipulating the world. This manipulation is by means of developing and applying science. Science applied is to enable humankind to walk the path of ever-continuing progress through increases in freedom from the drudgery of labor, from the suffering of illness, and from the anxiety of interpersonal and international quarrels.

What must human nature be like for humanity to be capable of developing and applying the required sciences and so of accomplishing this ambitious program of improving the human condition? It is Descartes's answer to the first part of this question, that concerning human nature and the possibility of science, which I trace in this study. The answer (in my second through fifth chapters) reveals the importance of a mental power which Descartes believes we possess and is absolutely crucial to the development of science. It is the power of intellectual imagination—an aspect of Descartes's thought until recently almost entirely neglected by commentators.

Is humanity really capable of developing and applying the requisite sciences? Descartes's answer to this question (introduced in the first and developed in greater depth in the sixth chapter) reveals the equally neglected relationship between the role he ascribes to human freedom and the Cartesian Archimedean point. Along the way some interesting additional insights present themselves; for example, in spite of the modern divide between arts and sciences that is part of our Cartesian legacy, these two sides nevertheless have a common root in Descartes' view (and use) of imagination (see chapter 4).

When discussing human nature in relation to science, I draw on chapter 3, parts 3 and 4, of my *The Imposition of Method: A Study of Descartes and Locke*, where I first articulated aspects of what I take to be Descartes's "logic of discovery." Although I have changed position on some of the details there presented, on the whole I believe that earlier articulation to be adequate as far as it went. Hence I have incorporated some of it in the first three parts of my third chapter. A version of my work on human nature and metaphysics in parts 2 and 3 of my sixth chapter was first published as chapter 8 of *Reason, Will and Sensation: Studies in Descartes's Metaphysics*, edited by John Cottingham. Both these books were published by Oxford University Press. I am grateful for their permission to draw on this material. A version of the material presented in chapter 4, part 2, and chapter 5, parts 2 and 3, is forthcoming as "Descartes: From Sparks of Truth to the Glow of Possibility," which is a chapter in *Descartes' Natural Philosophy*, edited by Stephen Gaukroger, John Schuster, and John Sutton (Routledge, 2000).

A research grant awarded by the Social Sciences and Humanities Research Council of Canada (1992–95) while I was at the University of Alberta made it possible for me to engage in some of the research and draft parts of some chapters for this study. It also allowed me to secure the services of graduate student Elzbièta Szymanska-Swiatek; what turned out to be chapter 5, parts 2 and 3, have benefited much from her assistance. My move to New Zealand's Massey University in 1996 and the administrative tasks it entailed postponed completion of this study, but, especially through most pleasant and efficient secretarial assistance in the person of Sharon Cox, it also provided the ambience in which it could be finished. I am grateful to the two universities, to the Council, to Elzbièta, and to Sharon for their various ways of support of my work.

This book could not have been written apart from the extensive conversations with colleagues worldwide, whether face-to-face or through their publications; wherever I was conscious of their influence I have acknowledged this in footnotes and bibliography. Helpful comments from the Press's reader have clarified the exposition in various chapters. As ever the presence of Jeanette, my friend and spouse, was of inestimable worth.

PETER A. SCHOULS

New Zealand

DESCARTES
AND THE
POSSIBILITY OF SCIENCE

1

Setting the Context

Descartes's Methodology and Metaphysics

1. INTRODUCTION

The *Discourse on the Method* must be the starting place for any discussion of Descartes's view on how science is to be developed, for in it he tells us how reason goes about its successful pursuit of truth in any area in which truth is accessible to the human mind. The *Discourse*, in other words, presents a functional definition of reason, where I use 'reason' in its broadest sense as the human ability to intuit, deduce, and in the context of these processes to make proper use of imagination, sensation, and memory. Following closely in importance is the *Meditations*, for there we encounter Descartes's attempt to provide the metaphysical justification for his account of the mind's abilities which make correct scientific procedure possible. This chapter's discussion of Descartes's methodology and metaphysics therefore serves as the framework for my following chapters. In particular, it sets the stage for the upcoming account of intellectual imagination.

One measure of a book's importance is the extent to which it is taken seriously by the author's contemporaries. Descartes's *Meditations* was taken very seriously indeed. Published in 1641, it was accompanied by responses from some of the most eminent thinkers of the day, among them Thomas Hobbes and Antoine Arnauld. The *Meditations* has exerted formative influence over Western thought and action ever since.

The willingness of a philosopher such as Hobbes and a theologian-logician like Arnauld to be involved in this venture of the *Meditations'* publication was no doubt related to the impact of Descartes's *Discourse on the Method*, published four years earlier. The *Discourse* is one of the seventeenth-century works most responsible for changing the nature of the Western intellectual world. Its doctrine called for a rejection of whatever has not been authorized for acceptance by the individual's reason, a rejection which readers of the *Meditations* are to carry out for themselves through the very act of reading and (re)thinking of the *Meditations'* arguments.

Because such a rejection in effect amounts to a shift in the location of the foundation for all knowledge and goodness, it demands a dismissal of crucial aspects of some two thousand years of philosophical tradition. For a philosopher like Plato, the foundation for both thought and action consisted in norms such as those for truth, justice, and goodness, which were taken to exist in a timeless manner in a world apart from that revealed to human beings through their senses, and to hold for all times and all human beings if they are to live a truly human life. For Christian philosophers such as Augustine and Aquinas, the ground of all truth and goodness was, ultimately, God. Descartes rejects these external beings as grounds and finds the ground (the "Archimedean point") for all systematic (philosophic and scientific) thinking, and hence for all genuinely human action, within the consciousness of each individual thinker.

It is no doubt true that in his self-conscious attempt to reject tradition Descartes was responding to a shift in point of view already well in progress. The *Discourse* was therefore both symptomatic of a change in the making[1] and a major catalyst in making this change acceptable, even commonsensical and commonplace. By the time Descartes started to write, Galileo had provided firm support for Copernicus's work in astronomy, which placed human beings in a more peripheral position in the universe than that to which they had been long accustomed, thus at least relativizing an important aspect of "the tradition" and in the process attracting the wrath of its guardians, the church's Inquisition. Thomas Hobbes had already accepted a method not unlike that advocated in the *Discourse* just prior to the latter's publication and was beginning to apply it in his work on optics as well as in political philosophy.[2] In bits and pieces, with respect to various limited subject matters, what came to be known as "the Cartesian method" was in the air. Descartes, however, made it very clear

---

[1] As John Cottingham has recently written, we need a sense "of the arbitrariness and artificiality of standard historiographical boundaries . . . [and to] realize just how protracted and gradual was the parturition of the 'modern age'." See Roger Ariew, John Cottingham, and Tom Sorell, eds., *Descartes' Meditations: Background Source Materials* (Cambridge, Eng., 1998), 8.

[2] I do not mean to imply that Hobbes employed a single scientific method in his writings on political and physical science. As Quentin Skinner has argued, the form of Hobbes's political writings was at least in part the result of his negative reaction to the rhetorical tradition of classical and Renaissance humanism. See Skinner's " '*Scientia civilis*' in Classical Rhetoric and in the Early Hobbes," in *Political Discourse in Early Modern Britain*, ed. Nicholas Phillipson and Quentin Skinner (Cambridge, Eng., 1993), 67–93.

that he aimed to reject not this or that aspect of tradition but *all* of it. This was because, unlike his contemporaries, he universalized method, making it apply to all objects of thought; and this method, as we shall see more clearly later, dictates initial rejection of that to which it is applied.

This wholesale rejection, coupled with the attempt to find the foundation and starting point for thought and action within the individual thinker, marks the beginning of modern (that is, postmedieval, post-Renaissance) philosophy. In a sense, Descartes is the father not just of modern philosophy but, in important respects, of modern culture—of modern Western culture and later, through export of its ideas, of much of modern world culture.[3] Descartes's endeavor announces modern philosophy's determination to rise above tradition, above the particularity of any historical circumstances, and so, purified of historical contingency by rejecting it as prejudice, to speak only what he took to be the absolutely trustworthy and universally valid language of reason.

One further measure of a position's influence is the opposition it calls into being. Galileo was called on the carpet by the Inquisition for teachings about astronomy which Descartes, too, was about to publish. Had he not recanted, Galileo might have been executed; even his recantation earned him no better than house arrest for the remainder of his life. When Descartes heard about Galileo's troubles he decided not to publish a work then in its final stages of revision[4] and resolved that life in liberal

---

[3] That Descartes was the first consistently revolutionary thinker in the modern sense of this term I argued in *Descartes and the Enlightenment* (Edinburgh and Montreal, 1989), passim. That he developed and riveted to the Western mind a sophisticated form of the modern notion of progress is the point of my "Descartes and the Idea of Progress" (*History of Philosophy Quarterly* 4, no. 4 [1987]: 423–33; republished in *René Descartes: Critical Assessments* [New York, 1991], 50–60). *Revolution* and *progress* are only two of the ideas through which Descartes helped to structure the modern mind. In *John Locke and the Ethics of Belief* (Cambridge, Eng., 1996), Nicholas Wolterstorff argues that it is Locke rather than Descartes who takes the place of preeminent influence in Western thought (see especially his third chapter); although he presents an interesting case, I believe Wolterstorff to be wrong on this point and have argued so in "Locke, 'the Father of Modernity'?" in *Philosophia Reformata* 61, no. 2 (1996): 175–95.

[4] This was *The World or Treatise on Light*, published posthumously in 1664, although Descartes incorporated parts of its doctrine in the *Discourse*. At the end of November 1633 Descartes wrote to Marin Mersenne: "I had intended to send you my *World*. . . . But I have to say that in the meantime I took the trouble to inquire . . . whether Galileo's *World System* was available . . . . I was told that it had indeed been published but that all the copies had immediately been burnt at Rome, and that Galileo had been convicted and fined. . . . I must admit that if [his] view is false, so too are the entire foundations of my philosophy, for it can be demonstrated from them quite clearly. . . . so I preferred to suppress it" (AT 1:270–1; CSMK 3:40–41; *The World* is printed at AT 9:3–48; CSM 1:81–98). Whenever possible, all references to Descartes's writings will be given in the text, with the first reference to the Adam and Tannery edition of Descartes's *Oeuvres* (11 vols. vols. 8 and 9 in two parts [Paris, 1965-75]); the second to one of the volumes of *The Philosophical Writings of Descartes*,

Protestant Holland might be safer than that in his home country, Catholic France. So in 1628 he moved to Holland, where he remained until 1649, the year before his death. (His last year he spent in Sweden as Queen Christina's private tutor—an occupation which probably hastened his death.)[5] During his two decades in Holland he wrote and published all his major works. But in both Holland and beyond, opposition was not long in coming.

At first, influential theologians and philosophers at major Dutch universities adopted and enthusiastically taught Cartesian doctrines. But this acceptance was short-lived. At the University of Utrecht it was forbidden to teach Cartesianism within two years of the publication of the *Meditations*, and, two years after that, Utrecht's city council pronounced a formal ban on all discussion of Descartes in print. Soon after, the University of Leiden followed suit. In both places Cartesianism was seen as anti-Christian, in part because of its assertion of the limitlessness of human freedom.[6] In Rome, Descartes's works were placed on the *Index* in 1663, and in 1671 French universities were forbidden to teach Descartes by royal decree.[7]

It was, however, too late to recall what had by now become a widespread attitude not just in philosophy but also in the mathematical sciences, in physics, and even in ethical and political theory (the French Revolution, a century and a half after the publication of the *Discourse*, was hardly unrelated to Cartesian modes of thought).[8] The major doctrines responsible for this new stance concern (i) methodology and epistemology as well as (ii) metaphysics. I shall devote the rest of this chapter to an introductory state-

---

edited in the case of the first two volumes by John Cottingham, Robert Stoothoff, and Dugald Murdoch [Cambridge, Eng., 1985] and in the case of the third volume by these three editors joined by Anthony Kenny [Cambridge, Eng., 1991].)

5   For a brief account of Descartes's winter in Sweden and of his last days, see pages 415–16 of Stephen Gaukroger's *Descartes: An Intellectual Biography* (Oxford, 1995). For a more extensive account, see the final chapter of Geneviève Rodis-Lewis, *Descartes: His Life and Thought*, trans. Jane Marie Todd (Ithaca, 1998).

6   Some influential Christian thinkers championed Descartes as defender of the faith. Chief among these was Antoine Arnauld. However, a good case can be made for the position that Augustinian Arnauld believed Cartesianism could be incorporated into Christian traditional thought only because he failed to understand its radical novelty. See my "Arnauld and the Modern Mind (the *Fourth Objections* as Indicative of Both Arnauld's Openness to and His Distance from Descartes)," in *Interpreting Arnauld*, ed. Elmar Kremer (Toronto, 1996), chap. 3.

7   See Nicholas Jolley, "The Reception of Descartes' Philosophy," in *The Cambridge Companion to Descartes*, ed. John Cottingham (Cambridge, Eng., 1992), 393–423. See also Enrique Chávez-Arvizo, "The Utrecht Controversy and the Descartes-Regius Affair: A Historical Note," *British Society for the History of Philosophy Newsletter*, n.s. 3, no. 1 (1998): 1–5.

8   I gave grounds for this judgment in *Descartes and the Enlightenment*, particularly in its closing chapter.

ment of these doctrines. For the first of these I will, in this chapter, largely confine myself to the *Discourse*, for the second to the *Meditations*.

2. METHODOLOGY AND EPISTEMOLOGY

Underlying the *Discourse* there is an ancient assumption (held throughout the Middle Ages) as well as a new perspective (which is one of the significant ways in which Descartes breaks with medieval thought). The ancient assumption is that there is a rational God who has created a world which operates on rational laws or principles, as well as human beings in this world whose nature it is to be rational and free.[9] The new perspective

[9]   This is a doctrine which, in one way or another, finds its expression in patristic and medieval philosophy. In Augustine, we meet it in his view that "Philosophy by itself had come to know the intelligible world that had been revealed in the gospel as the eternal Word of God, but without recognizing it as such." Anselm accepts "God as the light of minds, and sense-experience as requisite for the image from which the mind gave birth to the human concept." Bonaventure, "though rejecting an explanation of cognition solely in terms of causal influx . . . tended to align it with the divine concurrence in human actions." For Aquinas, "both cognitional and real being were authentic ways of existing. Existence was understood in various senses, all genuine, but in the order of primary and secondary instances. Primary was the thing's existence in God, secondary its existence in itself; dependent on both was its existence in human cognition." These quotations are all from Joseph Owen's "Faith, Ideas, Illumination, and Experience," which is chapter 21 in *The Cambridge History of Later Medieval Philosophy*, ed. Norman Kretzmann, Anthony Kenny, and Jan Pinborg (Cambridge, Eng., 1982), 441, 444, 451, and 453, respectively. It is a docrine which, in addition to Descartes's works, surfaces in various writings of the seventeenth century, for example, in that of the Cambridge Platonists. As John Rogers has remarked with respect to one of these, "[I]t was the supremacy of the rational intellect in man, God and the universe that Cudworth saw as the supreme truth which could account for the world as we find it" (G. A. J. Rogers, *Locke's Enlightenment: Aspects of the Origin, Nature, and Impact of His Philosophy* [Zurich and New York, 1998], 161). This doctrine underlies the shift in the relationship between epistemology and ontology which Kenneth Barber has called the shift from the *Weak Model* to the *Strong Model*, a shift he takes to be completed in Descartes's *Meditations*. In the first, "epistemological concerns are subordinate or at best parallel to ontological concerns" and "existents . . . are given as are the categories available for their analysis." In the second, "epistemological considerations serve as criteria for the adequacy of an ontological system: putative candidates for inclusion in the catalogue of existents must first pass a test for knowability and, once included, their classification of categorial features must again meet the same rigorous standard. Failure to pass these tests is . . . sufficient reason for discarding . . . the ontology in question, no matter how firmly entrenched the latter may have been in a philosophical tradition." The shift from the *Weak* to the *Strong Model* Barber takes to be that from the medieval to the Cartesian position. As long as it is recognized that underlying this shift in perspective there is this ancient assumption, I believe Barber to be right. Perceptively, he adds that, from the medieval perspective, the Cartesian shift "would have been regarded not as an indication of philosophical acumen but rather as a potential source of heresy." See Kenneth F. Barber and Jorge J. E. Gracia, eds., *Individuation and Identity in Early Modern Philosophy: Descartes to Kant* (New York, 1994). My quotations are from Barber's introduction, pp. 4–5.

is that rational human beings should be able to *use* this world to make it work for them through the sciences of "mechanics" (no more sweat in the provision of daily needs), "medicine" (no more pain and indefinite postponement of death), and "morals" (no more anxiety resulting from interpersonal and international quarrels).[10] This new perspective is one which rejects preoccupation with a paradise lost in a distant past or paradise to be regained in a non-earthly future through the grace of God, and which accepts as a challenge the use of human rationality and "generosity"[11] to create on earth the good life of freedom from labor, illness, and anxiety. It is an attitude which makes the world of "nature" an object of instrumental value (it exists primarily to serve human needs and aspirations), and which firmly plants the idea of indefinite progress in the Western mind.

For Descartes, the ancient assumption and the new outlook put together give rise to troubling questions. If, as rational beings, we are equipped to understand the world and make it work for us to free us from labor, pain, and anxiety, why are we in the condition in which we find ourselves? We sweat to procure our precarious daily bread, we die at an early age after a life often filled with bodily suffering, and (as persons and nations) we kill for both physical things like property and intellectual matters such as religious dogma. And this has been going on for generations, from time immemorial. Is this the result of rational beings acting rationally in a rational world created by a rational God?

Descartes's answer to the last of these questions is an emphatic "No!" It is, he believes, the result of rational beings acting *irrationally* in a rational world created by a rational God. Hence his response to the first question is that it is irrational action which lands and keeps us in this perilous state. We act irrationally, says Descartes, because we do not know what reason is, that is, we do not know how reason works. If we knew how reason goes about its business when it gets us at the truth, and if we then firmly committed ourselves to following reason's ways and acting on the results so obtained, progress toward a life free from drudgery, pain, and anxiety would be guaranteed. The very fact that we find ourselves not to be on this path of progress should tell us, says Descartes, that we are ignorant of reason's manner of operation—which is to say that we are ignorant of the proper *method* to be used in acquiring truth which will be *useful* in this life. In the *Discourse* Descartes presents us with this method.

---

[10]   The assumption that Descartes had no moral theory has been convincingly rejected in John Marshall's *Descartes's Moral Theory* (Ithaca, 1998).

[11]   *The Passions of the Soul*, article 153, states that "true generosity . . . has only two components. The first consists in his knowing that nothing truly belongs to him but this freedom to dispose his volitions, and that he ought to be praised or blamed for no other reason than using this freedom well or badly. The second consists in his feeling within himself a firm and constant resolution to use it well—that is, never to lack the will to undertake and carry out whatever he judges to be best. To do that is to pursue virtue in a perfect manner."

In the *Meditations* he shows both its and reason's absolute trustworthiness. Because Descartes's method is in effect his functional definition of reason, the *Meditations* accomplishes this task not as a double but as a single assignment.

Descartes succinctly states his method in the "four rules" of the second part of the *Discourse* (AT 6:18–19; CSM 1:120). The *first rule* forbids acceptance of primary givens, that is, of whatever one initially encounters in one's experience, whether through sensation or from tradition, unless the individual who accepts them recognizes these givens as clear and distinct, in which case there is no occasion to doubt them. If there is no occasion for doubt, then there is certainty. That which is certain is, for Descartes, knowledge rather than belief or prejudice. Clarity and distinctness are, therefore, Descartes's criteria of knowledge. For something to be clear, *all of it* must be grasped by the individual's mind; for it to be distinct, *nothing but what pertains to that clear item only* may be grasped by the individual's mind (see *The Principles of Philosophy* 1:45 [AT 8A:21–2; CSM 1:207]). The position here articulated is one of individual epistemic autonomy: each individual determines by her- or himself what is or is not an item of knowledge. Given "clarity and distinctness" as the criteria of knowledge, for this position the object of knowledge is, fundamentally, contextless. Since primary givens are always bound up in a context, we can already see that they can never be grasped as clear and distinct to begin with; whatever one experiences to begin with would become a prejudice if it were to be accepted as true or good just on the basis of such experience. For Descartes, such acceptance is irrational action. Whatever one experiences must be made subject to doubt if it is to become an item of knowledge. Hence, in Descartes's own words, the first rule is "never to accept anything as true if I did not have evident knowledge of its truth; that is, carefully to avoid precipitate conclusions and preconceptions, and to include nothing more in my judgments than what presented itself to my mind so clearly and so distinctly that I had no occasion to doubt it."

Mention of "doubt" leads to the *second rule*: "to divide each of the difficulties I examined into as many parts as possible and as may be required in order to resolve them better." The doubt in question is methodological in the sense that it enables the thinker to divide (or, to mention other terms which Descartes uses to describe this process, to resolve, decompose, or analyze) the complex primary givens until no further division is possible. At that stage, the end result(s) of this analysis may still be obscure rather than clear and distinct to the intellect, and one then recognizes that the matter is beyond the intellect's grasp (and most likely of no theoretical importance). Alternatively, the end result(s) may be clear and distinct, hence known with the kind of certainty which no longer calls for doubt. In that case, the thinker has reached the "foundation" for this field of knowledge and is ready to implement the next rule.

This *third rule* allows for creation of intelligible complexity through putting together the results achieved by analysis. It governs the process Descartes calls composition or synthesis or deduction (where he uses "deduction" in a nonsyllogistic sense), a process which exhibits a certain order in that it always moves from the simple or less complex to the more complex. Sometimes, it is not clear to the intellect which simple (or simpler) items to connect. This does not necessarily bring the deduction to a halt, for in that case one is to "[suppose] some order even among objects that have no natural order of precedence"—phrases through which Descartes introduces the activity of hypotheses-generating imagination in the development of theory. This activity, of crucial importance for Descartes in the development of both philosophy and science, is that of intellectual, not corporeal, imagination. (Until recently, it has been almost entirely neglected by commentators on Descartes's work; I will give it considerable attention in all of the following chapters.) Descartes's complete statement of this rule is, "to direct my thoughts in an orderly manner, by beginning with the simplest and most easily known objects in order to ascend little by little, step by step, to knowledge of the most complex, and by supposing some order even among objects that have no natural order of precedence."

The *fourth rule* is, "throughout to make enumerations so complete, and reviews so comprehensive, that I could be sure of leaving nothing out." That is, at the beginning of the process of analysis and throughout that of deduction, one must make sure that all the aspects relevant to the issue at hand have been introduced—this Descartes calls "enumeration" or preview. "Reviews" occur at the end of the process of deduction, when one is to run through the argument again and again until the entire process is firmly, clearly, and distinctly in mind and the role of intrinsically fallible memory is as much as possible curtailed.

We can now see that this statement of the method is meant to be an account of how reason works, that it is a functional definition of reason. Through analysis (implementation of the first two rules), reason attempts to gain an intuitive grasp of the simplest aspects of whatever it tries to understand. Synthesis or deduction is reason's activity of generating intelligible (that is, clear and distinct) complexity. Analysis and synthesis express the essence of reasoning. Since the results of the combined processes of analysis and synthesis are to be clear and distinct, they are to be accepted as beyond doubt, as absolutely certain knowledge. Reason, in other words, is for Descartes infallible; it can only give us truth. If, therefore, we use reason and determine ourselves to act on the results reason gives, we act rationally. Through rational action we can "make ourselves, as it were, the lords and masters of nature" (AT 6:62; CSM 1:142–43) since it places us on the path of progress toward ever greater freedom from drudgery, pain, and anxiety.

As an introductory statement about Descartes's methodology and epistemology, the account of this section is complete but for one point. In all of his works, Descartes speaks of more than "reason" when he deals with the theory of knowledge. He speaks of *mind as distinct from body*. "Mind" then includes reason, but it also includes the human ability to imagine ("imagination"), to be aware of one's surroundings ("sense" or "sensation"), and to remember ("memory"). However, he stresses again and again that it is reason only which determines what is and what is not characterized by certainty, what is or is not clear and distinct, hence absolutely certain and true. When sensation, memory, and especially imagination receive attention in the following chapters, we shall see that they play crucially important roles but never have ultimate say. The final word is to be spoken by *reason*.

3. METAPHYSICS: *The Meditations*

Descartes believes that for centuries we were unable to make progress in philosophy and the sciences because, not knowing how reason worked, we did not have the right method. Without the right method we remained ignorant of the true principles of philosophy and without these principles could not satisfactorily develop mathematics or pure physics, let alone the sciences based thereon, mechanics, medicine, and morals. Ignorant of these sciences, we remained incapable of achieving mastery, hence we are still in the precarious situation in which we have always been.[12] Now that the *Discourse* reveals what Descartes takes to be reason's procedure, he believes we can begin to implement the method and start our journey on the path of indefinite progress.

But Descartes anticipates objections, along lines like these: Why do you think you can succeed where Plato, Aristotle, and the entire tradition of the Schools have (so you say) failed? What proof can you give that your method is efficacious, that your idea of the workings of reason is the right idea of reasoning? Can you show us that the results obtained through what you call reason are indeed absolutely trustworthy?

Descartes takes this skeptical attitude seriously. Since he wants absolute certainty, he will have to be able to show that his position is beyond doubt, impervious to all skeptical attacks. He therefore writes his *Meditations* with the skeptic firmly in mind. As he says in the synopsis of the First Meditation, he wants to establish the truth about knowledge, about the human ability to attain knowledge as well as about the ability to

---

[12]   See, for example, this statement from the preface to the French edition of the *Principles*: "[T]he best way of proving the falsity of Aristotle's principles is to point out that they have not enabled any progress to be made in all the many centuries in which they have been followed" (AT 9B:18; CSM 1:189).

recognize knowledge when it has been attained; if this exercise turns out to be successful, it will "make it impossible for us to have any further doubts about what we subsequently discover to be true" (AT 7:12; CSM 2:9). Will that be impossible even for the skeptic? Yes, says Descartes in the Seventh Set of Objections and Replies: in my *Meditations* I gave "arguments by means of which I became the first philosopher ever to overturn the doubt of the skeptics" (AT 7:550; CSM 2:376).

What tactic could one adopt to silence the skeptic? Descartes's answer is to ask questions so universal in their scope that no skeptic could ask questions more skeptical. Descartes's tactic is that of stretching methodological doubt beyond its usual limits to become *metaphysical* doubt. This, then, is his aim in the *Meditations*: by means of metaphysical doubt (the most extreme doubt imaginable) to reach metaphysical certainty (the most assured truth achievable). As he writes in its opening paragraph, "I will devote myself sincerely and without reservation to the general demolition of my opinions"; the outcome hoped for from this exercise is that he will be able "to start again right from the foundations" and so occupy the required position "if I wanted to establish anything at all in the sciences that was stable and likely to last." The *Meditations* is, therefore, meant to be heuristic in nature; it is instrumental in making scientific progress possible.

I will now offer an overview of what I take to be the *Meditations'* mainline argument. By "mainline argument" I mean that which serves to "establish the sciences" so that they are "stable and likely to last." Most of its no doubt interesting side spurs (such as the Third Meditation's discussion of material falsity, the Fifth Meditation's proof for the existence of God, and other spurs to be indicated on the excursion along the main line) will be left untraveled.[13] I determine what is main line and what is spur through the question: *Does this part of the argument concern human nature as it relates to the possibility of progress in science?* Only if the answer is strongly positive will that part of the argument be included. The overview that results through implementing this criterion will be a coherent picture composed of preliminary sketches of the nature of, and relations among, mind, matter, reason, imagination, sensation, memory, doubt, free will, God, and Archimedean point. This particular itinerary will be an introduction, often through short but sometimes through longer stops along the way, to important features of the Cartesian landscape, some of which

[13]   Many of the issues which I leave unexplored or which will be allowed to detain us only briefly are dealt with in detail in various recent studies. Especially interesting and useful are Georges Dicker's *Descartes: An Analytical and Historical Introduction* (New York and Oxford, 1993), and *Reason, Will, and Sensation: Studies in Descartes's Metaphysics*, ed. John Cottingham (Oxford, 1994); I have attempted to avoid duplication of their details as much as the theme of my study allows.

will be explored more thoroughly in chapters 4 and 6. At the start of this journey, three preliminary notes are in order.

1. The journey will be an interpretive one, that is, as we travel I will, at certain points, describe the landscape in ways which go beyond what immediately meets the eye. There will be no justification for these extrapolations beyond that provided by the coherence of the resulting experience.

2. Since it is Descartes's belief that anyone who wants to know will have to know for her- or himself (his epistemology calls for individual epistemic autonomy), he intends for each of us to make this journey by ourselves. That is, each must read the *Meditations'* arguments as if individually developing them. My overview will therefore be in first-person-singular language. Since this is also primarily Descartes's mode of writing in the *Meditations*, one benefit of adopting it is that it will facilitate the use of exact quotations.

3. Throughout the *Meditations*, I shall identify the origin of quotations and of various (parts of the) arguments by reference to the paragraph(s) in which they occur; references like (1, 1) or (3, 5) or (6, 4) then respectively refer to the First Meditation's first paragraph, the Third Meditation's fifth paragraph, the Sixth Meditation's fourth paragraph.

I begin the journey with the realization that since I know that some of what I used to take as truth turned out to be false, for all I know any one of my current beliefs is false. Since I do not know which of them are true or false, I shall reject them all "and start again right from the foundations" (1, 1). My question to begin with is, then: Do, or can, I know anything, and can I know that I know it?

I cannot possibly examine all my beliefs individually—an endless task—but that is not required. I need only scrutinize "the basic principles on which all my former beliefs rested" (1, 2), where I use "principle" with the meaning of "origin." If I can trust the origin(s) of my beliefs, I may be able to accept these beliefs as true (1, 2). If I find any ground to doubt the trustworthiness of these origins, I will doubt whatever they purport to give me as knowledge. To doubt, in this case, will mean to attempt rejecting such givens as false.

To enumerate (1, 3–9): The origins I can think of are the senses, the senses and reason combined, and reason alone. I cannot think of any other origins, for the imagination by definition gives me what I know to be imaginary rather than real or true; and memory is not a source of knowledge but at best a storehouse for knowledge obtained through sensation or reason. This enumeration is, therefore, complete. I shall now divide the question (do, or can, I know anything, and can I know that I know it?) into its parts. Thus I shall deal in turn with whether sensation, sensation and reason combined, and reason alone, give me indubitable items which I can recognize as knowledge.

Can I trust the givens of sensation (1, 4–6)? I know the senses sometimes deceive me, e.g., distant square towers look round to me and distant large objects look small (6, 7). But are there no sensations of which I am absolutely certain? What if I take that set of sensations which give me my current spatiotemporal location: that I am now at this particular location reading this particular book? Is not this a set of sensations which I always trust?

But is there anything in my present experience which tells me that I am not dreaming that I am where I am, doing what I am doing? I must stress that this is a question about *my present experience*, for I am concerned with those sensations which I have so far taken as most trustworthy, namely, those telling me of my current spatiotemporal location and activity. It will not do to say: I know I am not dreaming because, compared with earlier experiences, this does not feel like a dream; or, I will know later whether I am now dreaming because then I will know whether this current experience fits coherently into my day. This will not do because it goes beyond the set of sensations which give me my spatiotemporal location and my current activity, and my question is simpler than one which would introduce comparisons of present with past or anticipated experiences. In any case, such comparisons would require the introduction of memory, and I know I cannot give absolute trust to my memory, for from the outset of my journey it holds that what I used to remember as true I now believe quite possibly to be false. So not only is the introduction of memory illegitimate, but it would abort the journey if I placed trust in that of which I must now say that it "tells me lies" (2, 2).[14] Therefore, for all I know, I may now be dreaming, for internal to my present experience "there are never any sure signs by means of which being awake can be distinguished from being asleep" (1, 5).

So I conclude that I cannot absolutely trust even the set of sensations in which I have always put my greatest trust. If I can doubt these sensations, I can doubt whether any particular sensation gives me knowledge. I will therefore reject all claims to knowledge based on sensuous experience. But I used to believe that, through sensation, I get to know that there is an external world. Does this mean I cannot be sure there exists an external world?

This conclusion would be drawn too hastily, for (1, 6–7) if I dream, I must dream about something. Even if my experience is as "unreal" as the Satyr which I believe I drew yesterday, that is, has nothing exactly corresponding to it objectively or apart from myself, there must be something

[14]   In this Second Meditation verdict on memory, Descartes implicitly anticipates an argument like Bertrand Russell's (*The Analysis of Mind* [London, 1921], 159 ff.; and *Human Knowledge: Its Scope and Limits* [New York, 1948], 189 ff.): a deceitful God may have given me memories about a past which never existed. This argument is implicit in Descartes as follows. My memories are about my sensuous experience and / or my reasoning and / or my imaginings. If nothing corresponds to the ideas of sense, if I cannot trust the conclusions of reason, and given the nature of imagination, then there is no ground for saying that any of my memories, or an entire apparently coherent set of memories, is veridical. In spite of what all my memories tell me, the world (in Russell's words) "may have come into being just now" complete with the "memories" I in fact have.

out of which it is made (just as to draw the Satyr I needed pencil, paper, and ideas of men and goats). What could this be? Physical reality in general, with its properties such as shape, size, location, duration, etc.? But I can only sense particulars, I cannot sense reality *in general*.

I can, however, *reason* about reality in general. So, *what if I combine sensation and reason, can I trust that team to give me knowledge?* If I think about falling objects in general, about suns, moons, and stars in general, about human bodies in general, can I trust to have knowledge of the kind called physics, astronomy, medicine? But to obtain these generalizations must I not begin with particulars? Or, at the least, am I not bound to particulars for testing my judgments about objects in general? I must see objects fall for me to be able to think of, and certainly to test, the law of gravity; and I must dissect bodies to get at the truth about the circulation of blood. So the generality of the knowledge of the sciences in which reason deals with physical objects is based on particular sense experiences. Since I cannot trust sense experience, I cannot accept these sciences as indubitable knowledge. And what I can doubt, I will reject, taking it to be false. Must I now conclude that I know nothing at all? Again, that would be premature.

For perhaps *reason alone* can give me absolutely certain knowledge (1, 7–9). Surely, to say that "two and three added together are five, and a square has no more than four sides" would seem to be an articulation of truths so "transparent" that it would be "impossible" that they "should incur any suspicion of being false"? May I not, therefore, call arithmetic and geometry pure sciences—pure in the sense that their truth does not depend on the senses at all? Certainly the argument from dreaming—the argument that overthrew my trust in the senses—does not apply here, for "whether I am awake or asleep, two and three added together are five."

But let me use my imagination, untrustworthy though it may be. Just imagine that the ancient assumption I have always accepted—the one about there being a rational God who created a rational universe with me as rational being in it—is a false assumption. Suppose this God is not as I believed him to be, which is infinitely good, but instead is capable of evil. This is only a new assumption, but that is not a ground for it to be dismissed. Thus what if, whenever I add two and three, this evil God manipulates it so that I always get a result of five, but this is the wrong result? In that case, there is something wrong with my deductive power of reason— it is unable to discover the truth about rational relationships and I cannot then trust it to develop knowledge even of the pure scientific kind. Moreover, suppose this evil God deceives me with respect to "some even simpler matter" than the addition of two and three? What if I am wrong about the foundations of such judgments, foundations like my knowledge of (what I took to be) self-evident concepts such as *unity* or *equality*? In that case, there is something wrong with the intuitive power of my rea-

son. What I then take myself to know as foundational to science I do not
really know; the item intuited may then not be an item of knowledge.
Thus I would have no rational foundation even for the pure sciences.[15]
Even if there then existed a rational universe, I would not be in it as a *rational* creature.

I began with an enumeration of the three possible sources of knowledge: sensation, sensation combined with reason, and reason alone. I now
know that accepting these as sources of knowledge was buying into assumptions, that skeptical questions are possible about each of them, so
that I am "compelled to admit that there is not one of my former beliefs
about which a doubt may not properly be raised" (1, 10). And since I cannot as yet see how to refute the skeptic, the skeptic may be right: perhaps
I have no knowledge at all, and even if I did, I would not know that I did.
As long as the skeptic might be right, I have no absolute certainty. So (1,
11) let me adopt this as a new assumption to "counter-balance" the weight
of the long-held assumptions of the trustworthiness of sensation and reason. I shall assume that sensation and reason are fallacious. With the old
and new assumptions balancing each other, perhaps I can keep free from
error even if I cannot reach the truth. This position of "balance" then em-
powers me to "guard against assenting to any falsehoods, so that the deceiver, however powerful and cunning he may be, will be unable to im-
pose on me in the slightest degree" (1, 12).

My withdrawal of trust from both sensation and reason makes me feel
as if "I have fallen unexpectedly into a deep whirlpool which tumbles me
around" (2, 1), so that I have no firm place to stand. For all I know, "body,
shape, extension, movement and place are chimeras. So what remains
true? Perhaps just the fact that nothing is certain" (2, 2). In the past (if
there was a past), I was persuaded of their existence; now I am half persuaded to the contrary, for I may be the victim of an omnipotent God's
wholesale deception (2, 3).

If, however, "there is a deceiver of supreme power and cunning who is
deliberately and constantly deceiving me," then "I too undoubtedly exist
if he is deceiving me" (2, 3). For thinking that I am being deceived is a
really-existing act of thought. This I know without a doubt, in spite of the
best efforts of an omnipotent and evil God directed against me. And so I
have come to my first certainty, a certainty coinciding with truth: it is that
even if there is no truth to any of my beliefs about the world or about science, it cannot be the case that there is no truth at all, for it remains true

15   In his discussion of "The Deceiver Argument" Dicker (29–34) takes this to be "intended
to show that the *senses* provide no certainty" (29). Although it is true that this argument
clinches the doubtfulness of the senses, it does much more, in that it calls into question the
trustworthiness of any human ability. This is the assumption guiding my exposition in this
chapter; I shall offer grounds for it in my final chapter.

that I am, as thinking, doubting, wondering, exploring being. I have reached my Archimedean point: "*I am, I exist*, is necessarily true whenever it is put forward by me or conceived in my mind" (2, 3).

Knowledge of my own existence "is the most certain and evident of all" the knowledge I have had hitherto (2, 4). It is a truth known without reference to other truths—for all I know there are no other truths. It is an item known without context, self-evidently, hence intuitively. As far as I can now see, it implies nothing at all about the trustworthiness of sensation or of reason in its deductive function. All I have is one instance of the trustworthiness of reason functioning intuitively.

If, in order to get beyond this stage of my knowledge, I were now to use either sensation or deductive reasoning, I would regress to the earlier assumptions that sensation and deductive reason are trustworthy, and that would put me back into the realm of prejudice where I am vulnerable to the skeptic. If sensation and / or deduction are going to be used legitimately, their trustworthiness will first have to be established. And all I have, so far, to help me in this task is reason functioning intuitively in the single instance concerning my own existence.

There is, however, something else which I can articulate about this truth: "I am, I exist—this is certain. But for how long? For as long as I am thinking" (2, 6). That is, attentively focusing intuitively on what I already know makes me recognize the *contingency* or *limitation* or *finitude* of the thinking-that-is-going-on. And I recognize something else, namely, "I am . . . a *thing* that thinks; that is, I am a mind, or intelligence or intellect, or reason," "a *thing* which is real and which truly exists" (2, 6). For if there is an action (like thinking), then there must be an actor (in this case, a thinker); if there is a quality or property, then there must be a subject or substance to which this property belongs or in which it inheres.

If I now (3, 1–2) review "everything I truly know, or at least everything I have so far discovered that I know," and if I use my intuitive power of reason to examine this knowledge "more carefully," perhaps I may find "other things within me which I have not yet noticed." And I do. It is this. It may be false that there exists "the earth, sky, stars and everything else that I [believed I] apprehended with the senses" (3, 3), and it may be false that two plus three makes five. It is nevertheless true that I have ideas like these. And "even now I am not denying that these ideas occur within me" (3, 3). I now recognize that if there is thinking-going-on, then there must necessarily be something thought about. I cannot have contentless thoughts, and the content of my thinking, that of which I am immediately aware whenever I think, is what I call an *idea*. Thus the question is not whether I have ideas but whether there corresponds something to the ideas I have, whether when I think I see a hand there is an actual spatial hand corresponding to this idea of mine, or whether when I cannot help but think that two plus three makes five there is actually truth to this relation I have just drawn among these ideas. Metaphysical doubt does not do away with the fact that I think; it only requires me to question whether there is any *truth* to the ideas I have.

In order to silence the skeptic once and for all and place myself in the position where I can legitimately begin to build on my foundation, I cannot avoid this metaphysical doubt. I cannot now simply dismiss the idea of a deceiving God by saying that it is just an idea; I can only legitimately dismiss it if I can beyond any doubt show that there exists no such being. This, then, will have to be my next task: "I must examine whether there is a God, and, if there is, whether he can be a deceiver" (3, 4).

All I know as trustworthy so far is reason functioning intuitively in its grasping the truth that if I think then I exist as a finite substance conscious of ideas. But intuitively I also understand that a cause of something must be as great as or greater than its effect, for if it were not, then something would have come from nothing, and I intuitively understand that to be impossible (3, 14). Now relate this knowledge to the *ideas* I possess and, using only intuitive reasoning, ask about their *cause*. I know that I exist as finite thinking substance. I also know that I have so far been unable to pass beyond this stage of knowledge because of the supposition of the existence of an omnipotent deceiving God. Where do these connected ideas of the existence of a deceiving God come from? What is their cause?

Let me use an example to help me at this stage (AT 7:14, 103–4; CSM 2:10–11, 75–76). It is the case that I am not sufficiently technically inclined to be able to construct "a very perfect machine." If my life depended on it, I would not be able even to begin to explain its workings—I simply have *no idea*. Now suppose that some time later I find I have the idea of "a very perfect machine," and that I know a good deal about the way it works. How would I have obtained this idea? Not from myself, for only a short time ago I was quite incapable of explaining it, and I remain insufficiently technically gifted to have developed to the stage where I would be able to do so unaided. Since I now really understand this machine, this idea is itself a reality in my mind. Since it cannot have derived its reality from my own mind, someone or something else must, therefore, have informed me about it, must (as it were) have put this idea into my mind. That is, I can only explain the existence of this idea in my mind by reference to something beyond my mind. Since, on its own, my mind was incapable of creating something as great as this idea of the machine, there must exist something greater than my mind, something great enough to create the idea of this machine and impart it to me. Now the idea of God (3, 22) is the idea of an infinite substance to which belong all possible perfections. I intuitively know that I am finite substance, and that the finite cannot produce the infinite even at the level of ideas. Hence "the more carefully I concentrate on" the idea of God, "the less possible it seems that the idea I have" of God as a being possessing all possible perfections "could have originated from me alone. So from what has been said it must be concluded that God necessarily exists." This idea of infinite substance "has been put into me by some substance which is truly infinite." Moreover since the idea of God is the idea of a being possessing all possible perfections, "it is clear enough . . . that he cannot be a deceiver," for I intuitively know "that all fraud and deception depend on some defect" (3, 38).

I realized early on that my existence is contingent, that for all I know it is nothing but the activity of thinking actually going on, and that this activity need not necessarily go on. But this implies that I was aware of necessary existence, of the infinite and perfect. "For how could I understand that I doubted . . . and that I was not wholly perfect, unless there were in me some idea of a more perfect being which enabled me to recognize my own defects by comparison?" (3, 23). I could not even have grasped the idea of my self had there not all along been immediately related to it the idea of God. Thus, by attentively intuitively focusing on the idea of my own existence, I come to understand intuitively that God exists.

Earlier in the argument it became clear to me that not all intuitive awareness could be tampered with even by an omnipotent deceiver, for this deceiver could not make it be true that I did not exist if I thought I did (or if I thought anything at all). Intuitive attention focused on myself as existing finite thinking substance has now dispelled the existence of an evil God and established the existence of a good God. But it was only the supposed existence of an evil God which made me doubt the trustworthiness of both intuitive and deductive reasoning and of the criterion of clarity and distinctness, the telltale mark which indicated that the results of such reasoning were really indubitable, absolutely certain, knowledge. Since I now know that no evil God exists, there are no grounds whatsoever to doubt the trustworthiness of reason. Reason is infallibly correct, the products of reasoning are absolutely certain knowledge, and the criterion of clarity and distinctness—characterizing both intuitive and deductive knowledge—is fully dependable. No skeptic will ever be able effectively to cast doubt on any of this again.

I have now used reason in its intuitive functioning to establish the absolute trustworthiness of reason functioning deductively and may now legitimately hold that reasoning always leads to the truth on matters in which truth is achievable for the human mind. Since whatever reason offers is always clear and distinct, I can accept clarity and distinctness as the criterion of knowledge. The ancient assumption that human beings are rational beings in a rational universe created by a good and rational God is firmly reestablished with respect to the existence of myself and of God. To this extent, it is no longer a prejudice: it is a rationally established fact. I can now employ all of my reasoning power to try to determine whether I can trust the senses. As long as I do not know whether I can trust the senses, I do not know whether anything exists apart from myself and from God. But before I do so, I will interpose a question and an activity. The question is: If reason is infallible, where do my mistakes come from, both in theory and in practice, both as error and as evil?[16] This is the question to be answered next; it occupies the Fourth Meditation.

The answer relates to an aspect of what went before to which I have not drawn much attention so far, to the fact that I am not only rational, I am also free. Freewill is involved in my existence just as much as is thinking, and it played its role in the argument in tandem with reason. I clearly understand this when I reflect on the following details. I reached the cogito through doubting, and doubting is an act of will. Following that achievement, nothing much happened unless I paid careful attention to the results of this act of doubting, and paying attention is, again, an act of will. I did not have to doubt had I chosen not to, and I could have refused to pay attention had I wanted to do so. Thus my ability to show reason to be trustworthy depends as much on my persistent employment of my freewill as on my use of the intuitive function of reason. The "I" whose existence I established is that of a *willing* thinking finite being: "But what then am I? A thing that thinks. What is that? A thing that doubts, understands, affirms, denies, is willing . . . " (2, 8).[17]

Now the finitude which characterizes the "I" clearly attaches to reason, but in a sense not to the will. I cannot know everything, but I can will whatever I like, and so, in a sense, freedom of the will is infinite. I say "in a sense" because, though I can will whatever I like, I cannot accomplish whatever I will. I can will to fly, but that does not make me able to fly. Still, I can will whatever I like. It is this combination in me of finite reason and infinite will which provides the answer to the problem of error and evil.[18] I must make a firm resolution never to will to act on that which I do not understand, always to let my will be guided by my reason, always to act on what I clearly and distinctly know to be well-considered reasons.

The upshot is that to err or not to err, to sin or not to sin are really in my

---

16   There remains ongoing debate about whether Descartes meant to deal with sin in the Fourth Meditation. In spite of his disclaimer in its synopsis—"I do not deal at all with sin, i.e. the error which is committed in pursuing good and evil, but only with the error that occurs in distinguishing truth from falsehood"—I believe he does. See my "Arnauld and the Modern Mind," 38–40.

17   In my final chapter, I shall develop and discuss the often-neglected role of the will in the early Meditations.

18   Descartes's concept of freedom and its relation to reason is complex and not free from inner tension. I have dealt with it at length in chapters 4 and 5 of *Descartes and the Enlightenment*.

own hands. If I err or sin, I certainly cannot blame anyone else for it, least of all God who has created me with both free will and reason and with the ability to use them well. Would I have been a better creature if God had made it impossible for me to go against what I know to be true or good? Would it have been better not to have free will? No, for that would have deprived me of a power in which I most resemble God, the power to be self-determined or autonomous.

The activity in which I want to engage before I turn to the question about the trustworthiness of the senses is an exercise of my now-known-to-be-trustworthy reason, particularly its deductive function. So, let me focus on some of the ideas I have, specifically those about a physical world.[19] If it exists, a material world will be like what the ideas I now believe I have of this world tell me of it, *to the extent that these ideas are clear and distinct*. For the clarity and distinctness of anything indicate the truth of that thing (5, 5), and as the indicators of truth they are the indicators of rationality. Thus, if there is anything clear and distinct about the ideas I possess and which I believe to be about the external world, then, if there is such a world, the rational properties conveyed to me through these ideas will be characteristic of the real properties of that world. "For there is no doubt that God is capable of creating everything that I am capable of perceiving in this manner," that is, "clearly and distinctly" (6, 1). In fact, "everything which I clearly and distinctly understand is capable of being created by God *so as to correspond exactly with my understanding of it*" (6, 9).

The ideas I have of the world are of a world extended in space. They are also of a world of various colors, odors, temperatures, sounds, and tastes. Now I "distinctly imagine the extension of the quantity (or rather of the thing which is quantified) in length, breadth and depth. I also enumerate various parts of the thing, and to these parts I assign various sizes, shapes, positions . . . " (5, 3). In fact, I have an entire clear and distinct science dealing with such quantitative aspects, namely, the science of geometry. Therefore to the extent that I can conceive of the world in terms of these quantitative aspects, I conceive of it as it essentially is, if it exists.

I cannot say the same for the qualitative characteristics which my ideas of the world would make me accept if I were not sufficiently careful. Ideas of these characteristics are not clear and distinct. Take, for example, the idea of heat (6, 15). Suppose a world exists, suppose I am in it in bodily form, suppose I am cold, and suppose there is a fire. Then, at first, since I feel cold, I

[19]   The Fifth Meditation has a main topic in addition to the one on which I focus, in that it presents a deductive (as distinct from the Third Meditation's intuitive) argument for the existence of God. Given the confines of my theme, I take this argument as a side spur and will therefore neglect it.

will be tempted to say that it is cold here. Then, as I walk up to the fire and I feel warmth, I will be tempted to say that the fire is warm. As I come closer to the fire I will feel heat and will be tempted to say that the fire is hot. Finally, as I step too close to the fire, I will feel pain—but now I am not tempted to say that the fire is pain or that there is pain in the fire. I take pain to be a subjective experience. Why should I not take the feelings of cold, warmth, and heat as equally subjective? Why should I ascribe these qualities to objects outside of me? It is not at all clear that I should do so. Therefore, I should not do so. (This, again, is no more than acting in accordance with the first methodological precept of the *Discourse*.) And I can say the same about ideas of color, odor, sound, and taste. Take the last of these. After I have eaten a slice of lemon, a slice of orange tastes sweet; after I have eaten a lump of sugar, a slice from that same orange tastes sour. So it seems to be the case that taste depends on my subjective states, on my peculiar circumstances.

My conclusion is that "the certainty and truth of all [nonintuitive] knowledge depends uniquely on my knowledge of the true God, to such an extent that I was incapable of perfect [systematic] knowledge about anything else until I knew him" (5, 16). This reiterates the position I had reached at the end of the Third Meditation. In the meantime, I have made progress. Not only is it clear to me that I can trust deductive reason, but I now also know how to avoid error, and that if I exist in a material world, that world is in essence a rational world. But is there a world corresponding to the ideas I have of a world? Or are there "bodies which produced the ideas" which are "the immediate objects of my sensory awareness"? (6, 6). And does this world (among many other things) contain what I believe it contains, namely, a "body which by some special right I called 'mine' "? (6, 6). A positive answer to both presupposes the trustworthiness of the senses.

In order to establish "the existence of material things" apart from me I must begin with what I experience as part of me, for it is this "I" of whose existence I am now certain. Among the things I experience is that I have the ability to imagine things, to present myself with mental pictures such as those of a winged horse (5, 9) or a triangle (6, 2). Of a triangle, for example, "I do not merely understand that it is a figure bounded by three lines, but at the same time I also see the three lines with my mind's eye as if they were present before me . . . " (6, 2). I also have the ability to sense or perceive things, as I now have perceptions of this room and of various things it contains, of their "colours, sounds, tastes . . . and so on" (6, 4). These abilities can not exist apart from me, for both of them are "modes of thinking" (6, 4) and as such "include an intellectual act in their essential definition" which, as I already saw much earlier (at 2, 6), entails they have "an intellectual substance to inhere in" (6, 10).

I know I am the source of the pictures of my imagination, for I am aware of the fact that I give them to myself. I am not aware of the fact that I give myself the ideas coming to me through perception.[20] To the contrary, perception seems to be a "passive faculty" (6, 10). Its ideas "come to me quite without my consent," and are "more lively and vivid . . . than any of those which I deliberately formed" (6, 6). Does this give me grounds to conclude that "the things which are perceived by means of that mode of thinking which I call 'sensory perception' provide me with any sure argument for the existence of corporeal things"? (6, 4). Since I am not aware of giving these ideas to myself, and since I cannot help having them, they must be given to me by something else, something great enough to produce them in me. This something else must be either physical reality, or God.

Is this too hasty a conclusion, or, if not, can I eliminate God as their source so that I can determine that a physical world exists? The conclusion might be too hastily drawn, for even if "the perceptions of the senses were not dependent on my will," it need not follow "that they proceeded from things distinct from myself, since I might perhaps have a faculty not yet known to me which produced them" (6, 7). God, the omniscient and omnipotent being, could have given me such a faculty. Alternatively, and without any difference in the final outcome, God could, without the intermediary of such a faculty, give me ideas of a world which I sense as external to me while there is no world external to me. Perhaps either scenario could be effected in such a way that I would never know that no external world exists, for in either case all my perceptual experiences would indicate that there is such a world. But in either case God would be deceiving me, not, this time, by tinkering with my intellect but by—indirectly or directly—imposing on my senses. However, since "God has given me no faculty at all for recognizing any such source for these ideas" but has, instead, "given me a great propensity to believe that they are produced by corporeal things" (6, 10), and since I have already shown conclusively that God cannot be a deceiver, I must conclude that he is not deceiving me mediately through an unknown faculty of mine or immediately through manipulating my senses. From all of this "it follows that corporeal things exist" (6, 10). This is saying no less than that I can trust my senses.

There is, however, a restriction to be placed on this trust. For I already know (through considering the ideas of heat and of pain in relation to the idea of fire) that the physical objects whose existence is revealed to me through my senses "may not all exist in a way that exactly corresponds with my sensory grasp of them, for in many cases the grasp of the senses is very obscure and confused" (6, 10). Nevertheless, I can now legitimately take as standpoint the position that these objects "at least possess

[20] These two sentences involve assumptions. The first assumes that I am active when I experience myself to be so, the second that I am passive when I experience myself to be so. Both assumptions will receive minimal justification in this chapter but will be more adequately justified in my final chapter.

all the properties which I clearly and distinctly understand, that is, all those which, viewed in general terms, are comprised within the subject-matter of pure mathematics" (6, 10). In short, the world revealed through perception really exists and really has the quantitative properties which perception clearly and distinctly reveals it to possess.

Is there no more to the objective world than what pure mathematics can tell me about it? This is the last of the questions to be raised in the project of gathering and relating methodological and metaphysical foundational items relevant to a consideration of human nature in connection with the idea of the possibility of science. Its answer requires consideration of a very special set of perceptions, namely, the perceptions which tell me that I am more than a thinking thing, that I also have a body.

From the Second Meditation on I knew with certainty what I now reiterate, "that absolutely nothing else belongs to my nature or essence except that I am a thinking thing" (6, 9). But I also "have a distinct idea of body, in so far as this is simply an extended, non-thinking thing" (6, 9). Putting these two together I can now conclude that, although it is true that sensation reveals to me a "body which . . . I called 'mine' " (6, 6), it is also true "that I am really distinct from my body, and can exist without it"; for what I can conceive as distinct (nonthinking extended body as distinct from nonextended thinking mind), God can certainly create and maintain as separate entities (6, 9).

But do I exist without a body? Now that I can trust the senses, I believe I must deny that I do. For "there is nothing that my own nature teaches me more vividly than that I have a body, and that when I feel pain there is something wrong with the body, and that when I am hungry or thirsty the body needs food and drink" (6, 12). Moreover, my experience tells me that I do not just lodge in this body, as a pilot might be in a ship. To the contrary, through sensations such as those of pain and thirst "nature . . . teaches me . . . that I am very closely joined and, as it were, intermingled with it, so that I and the body form a unit" (6, 13).

This union is of two substances with quite different properties: of a thinking willing mind, and of extended matter. That there is such a union I experience most intimately and immediately from moment to moment. Since, throughout these experiences of this substantial union, I continue to conceive of mind as distinct from matter, these experiences do not tempt me to reduce mind to matter or matter to mind.

I can now answer the question whether there is more to the objectively existing world than those properties which can be dealt with geometrically. For (6, 14) "from the fact that I perceive by my senses a great variety of colours, sounds, smells and tastes, as well as differences in heat, hardness and the like," I rightly conclude "that the bodies which are the source of these various sensory perceptions possess differences corresponding to them," corresponding, that is, to the different properties in colors, sounds, smells, and so on—although, for example, given the lack of clarity with respect to ideas of warmth, heat, pain, and fire, such properties do not "resemble" what is in objects, so that I should probably continue to say that I know that the warmth is in me, not in the fire. Nevertheless, there must be something in the fire which produces warmth, or pain, in me. Warmth and pain are "in" the fire at least in the sense that fire *causes* me to feel warmth or pain (6, 15).

The colors, tastes, feels, smells, etc., "of" objects are therefore "in" objects in the sense that objects possess the powers to produce these sensations in me. Since God created me "as a combination of mind and body," God has also given me the ability to discern what is good for or detrimental to my being as a union of these substances. Take, again, the case of fire. The pleasurable feeling of warmth leads to my well-being, while too much coldness makes me experience the pain of freezing, and too much heat makes me feel the pain of burning. Both freezing and burning lead to my destruction. It is the same with other sensations of this kind. Objects possess the powers to make me feel pleasure or pain, delight or disgust, attraction or repulsion, in order to teach me what is good or bad for me as a being composed of mind and body. If, as a human being, as a person, I pursue what is pleasurable, delightful, attractive, then, on the whole, I act for the well-being of this particular substantial union which is the person I am. Similarly, on the whole, with respect to avoidance of pains and of what disgusts or repels me. So, although I doubt whether such properties are in the objects in the way I experience them, at least I know that objects have the power to make me experience such properties, and that objects have such powers for my well-being. I shall call these perceptions "teachings of nature." They are not teachings of reason, for they are not clear and distinct. Nevertheless, "there is no doubt that everything that I am taught by nature contains some truth" (6, 11); and my experience tells me that these teachings are useful, even necessary, for me to heed, given that I exist in this world as a substantial union of mind and matter (6, 24).

I think I have now sufficiently considered all the relevant issues. I began by asking whether I had any knowledge, and if I did, whether I could know that I did. I tried to answer these questions through looking at the "principles" or sources of knowledge: sensation, sensation and reason combined, and reason alone. I introduced the most extreme doubt I could possibly conceive in the form of a deceiving God. The outcome is that I know I can absolutely trust my reason. And I can trust my senses to the extent that what they tell me about objects is clear and distinct, and even to a degree when they convey to me the "teachings of nature." Moreover, I have a criterion for knowledge: if something is an item of knowledge for me then it must be clear and distinct to me.

Could I be dreaming all of this? No, for with the trustworthiness of sensation and reason I now also possess a criterion through which I can distinguish between waking and dreaming experiences. It is the criterion of *coherence*. If my memory tells me that an experience, fits coherently with the rest of my experiences then it is not a dream; if it disrupts this coherence, then that experience is probably a dream.[21]

[21] A question commentators tend to ignore is whether this dismissal of the argument from dreaming in a way which has recourse to memory raises questions which remain unanswered. Among these would be the following. Does not this argument presuppose an argument for the trustworthiness of memory? Even with a trustworthy God on the scene, memory is fallible, that is, particular memories don't come to us with THIS IS THE TRUTH stamped on them—and even if they did, what would we be able to infer from that characteristic? Is there a criterion which can be applied to ostensible memories to test their veracity? If so, what is it? Descartes talks about *coherence*, but the coherence (or lack of coherence) he means is that of dreams with the rest of reality—a coherence (or lack of coherence) which memory is to reveal to us. However, as long as there is no criterion which indicates which ostensible memories are really memories and which are not, does this beg the question? But perhaps there is more to Descartes's final point than meets the eye in a superficial glance? I will return to the issue of the trustworthiness of memory in chapter 4, section 3.

2

Mind Out of Nature

1. DESCARTES'S DUALISM

One of the characteristic features of Descartes's philosophy is its dualism: mind and body, the thinking soul and extended matter, are taken to be distinct from one another in a sense which includes the possibility of separate existence and action. This doctrine is conspicuous in the full title of the *Meditations*: *Meditations on First Philosophy, in which are demonstrated the existence of God and the distinction between the human soul and the body.* Within the *Meditations* it is articulated at several points, most explicitly in Meditation 6:

> ... I know that everything which I clearly and distinctly understand is capable of being created by God so as to correspond exactly with my understanding of it. Hence the fact that I can clearly and distinctly understand one thing apart from another is enough to make me certain that the two things are distinct, since they are capable of being separated, at least by God. ... Thus, simply by knowing that I exist and seeing at the same time that absolutely nothing else belongs to my nature or essence except that I am a thinking thing, I can infer correctly that my essence consists solely in the fact that I am a thinking thing. It is true that I may have (or, to anticipate, that I certainly have) a body that is very closely joined to me. But nevertheless, on the one hand I have a clear and distinct idea of myself, in so far as I am simply a thinking, non-extended thing; and on the other hand I have a distinct idea of body, in so far as this is simply an extended, non-thinking thing. And accordingly, it is certain that I am really distinct from my body, and can exist without it. (AT 7:78; CSM 2:54)

This doctrine functions not only in Descartes's metaphysical works but also in those concerned primarily with the theory of knowledge and methodology. It is crucial to Descartes's thought from at least the

Discourse on[1] and plays a significant role in each of my following chapters. Answering the question "What was Descartes's main reason for his insistence on the doctrine?" will place me in the position to enunciate the theme of my study in a way which shows why this doctrine is essential to it; and indicating the doctrine's pervasiveness in Descartes's ("mature") works allows preliminary statements of its implications relevant to my theme.

Descartes hints at one of the principal reasons for his need of the doctrine in the *Discourse on the Method* as well as in the preface to the French edition of *The Principles of Philosophy*. In the *Discourse* he writes that because the human or "the rational soul . . . cannot be derived in any way from the potentiality of matter," therefore it must have been "specially created." The implied dual nature of human beings contrasts with the mere corporeality of beasts: it is not as if "beasts have less reason than men," for "they have no reason at all." And if we insist on speaking of the "souls" of animals (as Descartes himself does in this passage), then we must recognize that such "souls" are "completely different in nature from ours" (AT 6:58–59; CSM 1:140–41).[2] In the *Principles* Descartes makes explicit the importance of this distinction between human and animal nature:

> [W]e should consider that it is . . . philosophy alone which distinguishes us from the most savage and barbarous peoples, and that a nation's civilization and refinement depends on the superiority of the philosophy which is

[1] Beginning with "Descartes and the Eclipse of Imagination, 1618–1630" (*Journal of the History of Philosophy* 27, no. 3 [1989]: 379–403), Dennis L. Sepper argues that the *ingenium* of the *Regulae* bridges body and mind through the co-presence in it of an "image-making" function and a "poetic-cognitive power," and that this "imagination-*ingenium* that had bridged body and mind was irreparably sundered" in Descartes's mature writings, with the image-making power assigned to body while the *res cogitans* became the power which, although "not itself imaginal, yet . . . contained within itself the cognitive principle of all image—formation" (397–98 and 400–401). Sepper's work—in addition to the article quoted, there is his "Ingenium, Memory Art, and the Unity of Imaginative Knowing in the Early Descartes" in *Essays on the Philosophy and Science of Rene Descartes*, ed. Stephen Voss (New York and Oxford, 1993), 142–61, and his *Descartes's Imagination: Proportion, Images, and the Activity of Thinking* (Berkeley, 1996)—provides the most interesting sustained discussion on imagination in Descartes. I shall have occasion to draw upon it at various later points. Commentators such as Emily Grosholz see this "mature doctrine" present in the *Regulae*. She writes that in rule 12 (at AT 10:410–17; CSM 1:39–43) "Descartes asserts that the imagination is an indispensable aid to the understanding in mathematical investigations, even though the former is a corporeal faculty and the latter alone capable of perceiving the truth." See her "Descartes' Unification of Algebra and Geometry" in *Descartes: Philosophy, Mathematics and Physics*, ed. Stephen Gaukroger (Brighton, Sussex, and Totowa, New Jersey, 1980), 160.
[2] This quotation is from Descartes's summary of his argument in *The World*. I am treating this summary as an integral part of the *Discourse*.

practised there. . . . The brute beasts, who have only their bodies to pre-serve, are continually occupied in looking for food to nourish them; but hu-man beings, whose most important part is the mind, should devote their main efforts to the search for wisdom . . . a higher good than all those that they already possess. Now this supreme good, considered by natural rea-son without the light of faith, is nothing other than the knowledge of the truth through its first causes, that is to say wisdom, of which philosophy is the study. (AT 9B:3–4; CSM 1:180–81)

These statements imply that the distinction between mind and matter is necessary for Descartes given his desire that humanity should not be pre-occupied with immediate natural needs. Humanity's goal differs from that of brute beasts: human beings ought to achieve mastery over nature through establishing freedom from the drudgery of physical labour, free-dom from the pain of physical illness, and freedom from the anxiety of in-terpersonal and international quarrels. This mastery requires physical na-ture (including the human body) to be a mechanistic system which we are capable of understanding through science. We will not be able to relate to nature in the requisite way unless we decide to do so. That decision, as well as its persistent application, requires acts of will, that is, presupposes that human beings are essentially free. Human essence must therefore be taken as distinct from that of mechanistic nature so that, in crucial respects, there is no limitation of *res cogitans* by *res extensa*. The only way to increase freedom is through progress in science. But for science to be possible, hu-man nature must be characterized not just as rational but, equally impor-tant, as free. This is one ground for Descartes's insistence on the doctrine of absolute distinctness in essence of human being and mere natural being.[3]

The mind must have some degree of freedom to begin with if science is to be possible, and development of science is necessary if increased free-dom is to be achieved. Since gain in freedom is the ongoing actualization of human potential, such actualization depends on progress in science—on developments requiring the involvement of all of the mind's powers: of the understanding or reason, of imagination, of sensation, and of memory.

---

[3] Another reason is that this distinction allows for the soul's survival of the body's death. Often, this is taken to be Descartes's main reason for this doctrine, as for example in George Graham, *Philosophy of Mind: An Introduction* ([Oxford, Eng., and Cambridge, Mass., 1993], 19), which echoes Richard Watson, "What Moves the Mind: An Excursion in Cartesian Dualism," *American Philosophical Quarterly* 19 (1982): 73. Which of the two rea-sons was the more important one for Descartes is mainly a matter of biographical specula-tion (although see note 6 below). It is less speculative to say that the nontheological or hu-manistic reason was the more important one historically speaking, for it helped to create the dualism of freedom and nature, a dualism which came to dominate Western thought irrespective of the presence or absence of theological aspirations of later thinkers.

But sensation, and (at least important forms of) imagination and memory, are, for Descartes, body-based. When he speaks of sensation (or, as he often calls it, of "sense"), he intends what we refer to when we speak of seeing, hearing, tasting, touching, smelling. He frequently refers to the corporeal imagination. And the process of memory he explains in terms of brain traces. Memory, imagination, and sense are necessary for developing science. No science is developed at all except through the free activity of the mind. Although the realm of freedom is supposed to be the realm of the mental and that of determinism the realm of the corporeal, we now see that three of the four mental functions necessary for the development of science depend on the realm of the corporeal. It therefore appears as if Descartes has serious problems. For does not the corporeality of imagination, memory, and sensation preclude the mental freedom necessary for the very possibility of science? And if "mind" or "soul" is the essence of the human being, how can this essence be said to be quite distinct and separate from that of corporeal nature if three of the four aspects of "mind" are themselves corporeal? Answers to these questions—answers which will reveal the problems I just articulated to be only apparent rather than real for Descartes—may be found through exploring a further question.

This is the question which, in the first chapter, came to the fore as the leitmotif for my study, and answers to which will become articulated and gain in plausibility through its course: What must Descartes's concept of human nature be in order for it to make possible advancements in science? The first step toward an answer requires awareness of the pervasiveness of Descartes's dualism. Statements of this doctrine in a variety of his works add both nuance and relief to the picture so far presented.

In rule 12 of the *Regulae* we read that "the power through which we know things in the strict sense is purely spiritual, and is no less distinct from the whole body than blood is distinct from bone, or the hand from the eye" and "nothing quite like this power is to be found in corporeal things" (AT 10:415; CSM 1:42). Later on in the same rule Descartes states this distinction to be a logically necessary one: "[T]here are many instances of things which are necessarily conjoined . . . for example the proposition . . . 'I understand, therefore I have a mind distinct from my body' " (At 10:422–23; CSM 1:46).

In the *Discourse on the Method* Descartes informs his readers of this doctrine's presence in *The World*, the earlier treatise (composed in the early 1630s) which he had had ready for publication but had suppressed when he heard of the Church's condemnation of Galileo for teachings which he judged no more radical than those he had been about to present. *The World*'s story as retold in part 5 of the *Discourse* is a hypothetical account of God's creation of our world. In this account the doctrine that mind is not an aspect of physical nature looms large (see especially the second half of part 5, AT 6:55–59; CSM 1:139–41). "Thought," "mind," or "soul" pertains peculiarly to human beings; it is their essence, an essence which is "entirely independent of the body" (AT 6:59; CSM 1:141). In contrast, the human body is entirely material, hence nothing but a particular modification of physical nature; it is said to function with the same necessity as a clock. Beginning with this earlier work Descartes regularly uses clockwork imagery in writing about corporeal nature. The ground given for it in this part of *The World / Discourse* 5 is that nature is geometrical extension subject to motion and so "the laws of mechanics . . . are identical with the laws of nature" (AT 6:54; CSM 1:139). This passage continues with the statements that machines made in all respects like the body of a monkey would be such that "we should have no means of knowing that they did not possess entirely the same nature as these animals." Contrariwise, we should be able to distinguish between human beings and machines which "bore a resemblance to our bodies and imitated our actions as closely as possible for all practical purposes," for machines would not be able to respond as human bodies can simply because machines are not "joined and united with" reason. It is therefore only in "the contingencies of life" in which "our reason makes us to act" that we express ourselves as human beings. All other events in which we partake or to which we are subject are to be explained mechanistically, exactly as we would explain the workings of these machines or the behaviour of animals, in which there is "no intelligence at all" and in which "it is nature which acts . . . according to the disposition of their organs [hence just as] a clock . . . " (AT 6:59; CSM 1:141).

Descartes never abandoned this doctrine, and some of these formulations from *The World* reappear almost verbatim twenty years later in *The Passions of the Soul*, the last of the works which he prepared for publication. It will, however, suffice to limit ourselves and draw attention once more to Descartes's best-known works, the *Discourse* passages which do not duplicate *The World*, and the *Meditations*; in each of these this doctrine occupies an important position.

In the *Discourse* we meet it immediately after Descartes for the first time presents his "Archimedean point." On his statement, "[O]bserving that this truth '*I am thinking, therefore I exist*' was so firm and sure that all the most extravagant suppositions of the sceptics were incapable of shaking it, I decided that I could accept it without scruple as the first principle of the philosophy I was seeking," there follows:

> Now I examined attentively what I was. I saw that while I could pretend that
> I had no body and that there was no world and no place for me to be in, I could
> not for all that pretend that I did not exist. I saw on the contrary that from the

mere fact that I thought of doubting the truth of other things, it followed quite evidently and certainly that I existed; whereas if I had merely ceased thinking, even if everything else I had ever imagined had been true, I should have had no reason to believe that I existed. From this I knew I was a substance whose whole essence or nature is simply to think, and which does not require any place, or depend on any material thing, in order to exist. Accordingly the 'I'— that is, the soul by which I am what I am—is entirely distinct from the body, and indeed is easier to know than the body, and would not fail to be whatever it is, even if the body did not exist. (AT 6:32–33; CSM 1:127)

In a sense the entire Second Meditation serves to lead the reader to reestablish this conclusion of the *Discourse*. As its synopsis has it, "[T]he mind . . . supposes the non-existence of all the things about whose existence it can have even the slightest doubt; and in so doing the mind notices that it is impossible that it should not itself exist during this time" (AT 7:12; CSM 2:9). Among those things of whose existence it has a slight doubt is all of corporeal nature. Hence, while the mind exists, nature can be taken not to exist. One consequence of "this exercise" is therefore that "it enables the mind to distinguish without difficulty what belongs to itself, i.e. to an intellectual nature, from what belongs to the body" (ibid). This is a conclusion which many have taken not to follow from the argument, while others have attempted to provide grounds for its validity.[4] It is not necessary to attempt to adjudicate this point, important though it is for philosophical interests different from those central to my study. My concern is with what Descartes proceeds to build upon what he believed he had established in the *Meditations*, specifically, that mind and body are two wholly different entities, that body or matter or nature consists of extension characterized by shape and motion and that mind consists of thought characterized by "the perception of the intellect and the operation

---

[4]   From Arnauld's Fourth Objections (AT 7:201 f.; CSM 2:141 f.), to Margaret Dauler Wilson's *Descartes* ([Boston, 1978], 190 f.), Bernard Williams's *Descartes: The Project of Pure Enquiry* ([Hassocks, Sussex, 1978], chap. 4), and John Cottingham's *The Rationalists* ([Don Mills, Ont., and New York, 1988], 117 f.), it has been maintained that this is at best the conclusion of an invalid argument or of an argument from ignorance, and at worst a mere assertion. By way of contrast, in *Descartes: His Moral Philosophy and Psychology* ([Hassocks, Sussex, 1978], 60–67), John J. Blom, drawing on aspects of Descartes's argument not all of which are made explicit in the *Meditations*, argues that Descartes can conclude mind not to be a material thing "just because the mind can be known to exist without yet knowing whether any material thing exists." The most pointed brief defense of Descartes's position is Robert Imlay's, in his review of Cottingham's *The Rationalists* in *Canadian Philosophical Reviews* 10, no. 1 (1990): 7. A more extensive recent defense upholding Descartes's conclusion of "the logical possibility of the mind's existing without the body, and its consequent nonidentity with the body" is the fifth chapter of Georges Dicker's *Descartes: An Analytical and Historical Introduction*; the quoted phrases are from page 233. Dicker's nuanced account makes the further point that, even for Descartes, this nonidentity did not establish the soul's immortality. This is a point relevant to the matter I raise in note 6 below.

of the will,"[5] and that therefore (quoting again the Second Meditation's synopsis) "the natures of mind and body are not only different, but in some way opposite." This opposition Descartes here illustrates in terms of the divisibility of the human body and the indivisibility of mind. But it would have been equally apt to elucidate it in terms of the causal determination of matter and the freedom of mind, for it is the difference and opposition of matter and mind in this latter respect which is a condition for the development of science.[6] In this statement "science" is to be taken in its broad sense, to include metaphysics, mathematics or "pure" or "theoretical" physics, and those sciences for which the latter is the immediate foundation and which Descartes calls mechanics, medicine, and morals.[7] But before I deal with developing science, more must be said about that which helps make this development possible to begin with, namely, this opposition between the causal determination of nature and the freedom of the mind.[8]

2. Freedom and Nature

Freedom and Nature: Descartes needs the two poles of this opposition. For a science of nature to be possible it is necessary that nature be the

---

[5]   This formulation is from the *Principles* 1:32.
[6]   In these sentences, the two main reasons for Descartes's dualism—the theological and the humanistic one—are juxtaposed. Perhaps there are grounds here for saying that the second is the most important reason. Descartes is quite clear about the *Meditations'* different achievements: whereas its arguments are "enough to give mortals the hope of an afterlife" (AT 7:13; CSM 2:10), they—in part through establishing the non-identity of mind and body—*realize* the hope for a stable and lasting foundation for the sciences. On this, in turn, depends the possibility of translating the hope of an afterlife into firm knowledge: "the premises which lead to the conclusion that the soul is immortal depend on an account of the whole of physics" (ibid.). See Dicker, 231–33.
[7]   It is plausible enough that physics is the immediate foundation for mechanics and medicine, for both of these are said to be about "machines," the first about the machine of the world and the second about the machine of the body. The reason why, for Descartes, "morals" also depends on physics is that without a knowledge of physics the mind will not be able to master the body-based passions and without such mastery the passions will tend to lead human beings away from rather than toward what is good for them and so will tend to preclude a life of moral uprightness and happiness. I have dealt with this aspect of Descartes's position in chapter 7 of *Descartes and the Enlightenment*. For a fuller account, see John Marshall's *Descartes's Moral Theory*.
[8]   Before I leave this introductory statement about Descartes's dualism, I should draw attention to a number of commentators who argue that it is an incoherent position (and, so some continue the argument, Descartes became well aware of this). Among these are John Cottingham (see the second half of chapter 5 of his *Descartes* [Oxford, 1986]) who, because of "Cartesian dualism and its problems," particularly because of the place of "sensation and imagination" in Descartes's thought, argues that this dualism should be replaced with

realm of causal determination and it is necessary that the mind be free. Notwithstanding this opposition, there is an intrinsic connection between these two poles, not between nature and the mind's freedom but between nature and the mind's activity of intellection or reasoning. However, because there is no reasoning, hence no science of any kind, except through the exercise of free will, it is now important that we recall some of what we met as Cartesian doctrine about freedom in the first chapter. Particularly relevant is what Descartes's methodological and metaphysical grounds for science preclude on the one hand and require on the other. Following this recapitulation we will be ready to consider the intrinsic connection between nature and reasoning.

Descartes's methodological and metaphysical grounds for science preclude that thinkers start with accepting as true that with which their cultural and natural contexts immediately present them. They demand that, to begin with, thinkers appraise these givens to be obscure and therefore suspend judgment about their truth or falsity until they have achieved clarity and distinctness with respect to them. Initially, all such experiences are characterized by obscurity because they are complex and the human mind is incapable of immediately perceiving whether such givens are, or allow for, true judgments. Suspension of judgment followed by analysis of these given complexities prepares the ground for synthesis into clear and distinct complex wholes. If these wholes turn out to be identical with those which one initially found in one's experience, then one is in the position to pronounce such givens as being, or as allowing for, true judgments. Suspension of judgment, analysis of the complex items given in experience, paying attention to the simple results of such analysis, synthesis

a "Cartesian 'trialism.' " In addition to Cottingham's, the best know of those who argue for "incoherence" are probably Daisie Radner, "Descartes' Notion of the Union of Mind and Body," *Journal of the History of Philosophy* 9 (1971): 159–70; Janet Broughton and Ruth Mattern,"Reinterpreting Descartes on the Notion of the Union of Mind and Body," *Journal of the History of Philosophy* 16 (1978): 23–32; and Daniel Garber ("Understanding Interaction: What Descartes Should Have Told Elizabeth," *Southern Journal of Philosophy* 21, Supplement [1983]: 15–32). In a recent article David Yandell argues against these (and others) that although Descartes makes the substantial union of mind and body to be "the essential attribute of the human being"—of what I call the person—he should "not be read as conceding any contradiction in thinking of mind and body as distinct and as in union." Yandell argues convincingly "that it was a legitimate position for Descartes to take" that "we have a primitive notion of mind-body union, on a par with those of mind and of body," and that "the various aspects—the mental, the physical, and the interrelation—of the world in general, and of humans in particular, can be classified in terms of them." See David Yandell, "What Descartes Really Told Elizabeth: Mind-Body Union as a Primitive Notion," *British Journal of the History of Philosophy* 5, no. 2 (1997): 250 and 273. Less interesting because less novel (though far lengthier and more complex) is the recent account by Gordon Baker and Katherine J. Morris in their book *Descartes' Dualism* (New York, 1996).

of these simple items and comparison of the results of such synthesis with that which was at first experienced—all of these are possible only as exercises of one's freedom. Unless one *wills* to suspend judgment, analyze, pay attention, synthesize, and compare, none of these activities are carried out.

Later on, I shall focus especially on acts of synthesis, for it is through them that science is *developed* on the foundations given through analysis. We shall see that without free will there can be no synthesis, if only because synthesis requires the use of imagination in the introduction of hypotheses, and there cannot be the relevant imaginative activity except through acts of will. Since similar statements pertain to the relevant uses of memory and sense, we can begin to see how this discussion of the development of science is bound up with that of a human nature including more than its basic modes of "perception of the intellect" and "operation of the will." It will require discussion of what Descartes takes to be a *person*, that is, a being in which there is *unity* of mind and body. We already had some inkling of this when I mentioned that corporeal memory and imagination may appear to be problems for the Cartesian position.

At this point, however, it is not the union of soul and body but the opposition of mind and nature, an opposition in terms of freedom versus causal determination, which needs to be considered. Against the background of this recapitulation of aspects of free will, we must now consider the fact that the opposition between will and nature in terms of freedom and determinism nevertheless does not preclude a connection, one which is as much a condition for the possibility of science as is the opposition. This connection is between nature and the other mode of mind, the perception of the intellect or the operation of reason. Brief consideration of it will reveal an important aspect which underlies Descartes's thought and whose presence I presuppose throughout this study; and it will naturally lead us back to the distinction between mind and nature in terms of freedom and determinism.

One belief which (as we saw in the first chapter) Descartes takes his *Meditations* to legitimate is that human beings can come to know nature because reason's order corresponds to nature's order.[9] For Descartes, intelligible propositions are such as can be reduced or analyzed into epistemic atoms—clear and distinct simple items which are knowable per se. They can be so reduced because they have themselves been composed out of these epistemic atoms obtained through analysis. Not all acts of analy-

---

[9] This issue arose in the first chapter, page 7, in the context of the criterion of clarity and distinctness and its connection with the essence of the possibly existing physical world.

sis are of intelligible concepts and propositions. Although all complex givens of one's experience are to be analyzed, these givens may include what turn out to be clear concepts and true propositions, but will also include propositions which cannot be reduced to clear and distinct items, and will certainly initially include givens not in propositional form, as when we sense objects (about which we then entertain propositions).[10] As our journey through the Fifth Meditation revealed, if we take nature to be geometrically determined matter subject to motion, then we take it as the kind of object which reason can come to know.

That Descartes believes nature to be geometrical matter subject to motion is implicit in his clockwork imagery. He makes the point explicitly in various places additional to the Fifth Meditation, as in this passage from the Sixth Set of Objections and Replies: "I observed . . . that nothing whatever belongs to the concept of body except the fact that it is something which has length, breadth and depth and is capable of various shapes and motions" and "that heaviness and hardness and . . . all the other qualities which we experience in bodies, consists solely in the motion of bodies, or its absence, and the configuration and situation of their parts" (AT 7:440; CSM 2:297).[11]

Explanations in terms of size, shape, and local motion are mechanistic ones; it is these which Descartes takes to explain nature and whatever transpires in it. Hence the statement from the *Discourse* which we met earlier, that "the laws of mechanics . . . are identical with the laws of nature." It is Descartes's view of reasoning, and his belief about the relation which holds between reason and nature, which make him take nature as the realm of causal determination. For the order of nature is an order demanded by reason if reason is to be able to give a scientific account of nature. After the *Meditations* Descartes believes it to be beyond doubt both that reason can give such an account and, in view of how he takes reason

[10]   It is the *order* of reason which demands this analysis followed by synthesis, which is to say that it is a demand imposed by Descartes's method. This is clear from, e.g., the headings of rules 4 and 5 of the *Rules for the Direction of the Mind*: "We need a method [*necessaria est methodus*] if we are to investigate the truth of things" and "The whole method consists entirely in the ordering and arranging of the objects on which we must concentrate our mind's eye if we are to discover some truth. We shall be following this method exactly if we first reduce complicated and obscure propositions step by step to simpler ones, and then, starting with the intuition of the simplest ones of all, try to ascend through the same steps to a knowledge of all the rest." This reduction or analysis is to lead us to the simplicity and clarity and distinctness which characterize its end results, the epistemic atoms; the ascending or composition or synthesis is to give us our intelligible complexity in the forms of complex concepts and propositions. In his "Cartesian Epistemics and Descartes' *Regulae*" (*History of Philosophy Quarterly* 13, no. 4 [1996]), Bruce M. Thomas aptly characterizes this part of Cartesian doctrine as a "regulative" or "normative epistemology" (434 ff.) to which "Cartesians can take a 'nondefensive' stance" if they adopt "modest epistemic goals" and fortify "their theories with higher-order epistemic norms" (446).
[11]   For similar statements see, e.g., *Principles* 4:204, 205, and 206.

to operate—explaining complex wholes by means of the epistemic atoms which are supposed to compose intelligible judgments about them—that the only kind of account it can give of whatever is corporeal is a mechanistic one.[12]

This returns us to the other mode of mental activity. For one consequence of this conception of nature is that, if freedom is to be preserved and if science is to be possible, then human essence must be located on the side of mind and mind must be taken as quite separate from body or nature. In the realm of nature there is no room for freedom.[13] But since without freedom neither science nor further actualization of human potential is possible, therefore to allow for these possibilities Descartes's conception of nature needs alongside it the conception of mind as separate from, independent of, opposed to, nature.

There are, thus, two related statements, both of which we must keep before us if we are to do justice to Descartes's position. The one is that mind is to be taken as separate from nature in order that we may deal with nature mechanistically. The other is that anything "natural" is to be taken as utterly distinct from mind in order that the freedom of mind can be guaranteed.

Because it leads us to a more fundamental truth than the first, the second statement is in a sense the more important one. For if, like the human body, the mind is a part of nature, then not only can we neither begin nor develop science, but we would not even have a conception of nature as we now do and would, in fact, not be human. Whatever would then be left would be indistinguishable from "the brute beasts." Without the will to activate reason, reason does not function, that is, does not actually exist. Or in Descartes's terms, without "the operation of the will," there is no "perception of the intellect."

However, if will and intellect (in the sense of "reason") were all there is

---

[12]   To Descartes's epistemic atomism there does not correspond a physical atomism (this in contrast to the position of Descartes's late contemporary, Isaac Newton). For Descartes there are no "indivisibles" in nature. Ultimate are "vortices," which are points of force, foci of matter in motion. The account of the relationships between and among these vortices is a purely mechanistic one, and—except for its epistemic foundationalistic atomism—this account reflects at the level of intellect what holds at the level of nature.

[13]   I do not mean that Descartes holds the mind or will to be incapable of affecting nature—a view quite contrary to Descartes's intent. It is precisely for the sake of "affecting" nature that science is to be developed. This is one of the important distinctions between the Cartesian position on the one hand, and Greek and medieval philosophy on the other: for Descartes knowledge has instrumental value only; science is to serve the cause of human progress; and the stance of contemplation is to be exchanged for that of manipulation. In this respect Descartes is not just the father of modern Western philosophy, but the progenitor of modern culture. It is both these assertions of the preceding sentence which are denied by Nicholas Wolterstorff in his *John Locke and the Ethics of Belief* and whose denial I have argued to be mistaken in "Locke, 'The Father of Modernity'?"

to the mind, then we could have neither our metaphysics, pure mathematics, or physics, nor the sciences that are to allow us our mastery in the practical affairs of life. For the former we need as well an intellectual memory and intellectual imagination; for the latter, we require the body-based or corporeal memory and imagination, and sense perception. But unless mind is first separated from body, the latter three hinder rather than help, with as a result that, instead of freely developing "foundations" for the applied sciences, the intellect gets caught in confused ways of thinking through determination by contingent experience.

In the remainder of this section, I continue my focus on the need for this confusion-avoiding separation; and I shall begin to provide grounds for the need of intellectual memory and intellectual imagination in the section following it. I shall then conclude this chapter with separate discussions of memory and imagination. Various uses of corporeal memory, corporeal imagination, and sensation as required for specific purposes in particular sciences will be taken up in later chapters.

To help set the stage for the discussions remaining for this chapter, consider a passage from rule 8 of the *Regulae*. Here Descartes speaks of mind as capable of developing scientific knowledge but not of mind as entirely independent of material substance when he includes in it intellect or understanding, (corporeal) imagination, sense perception, and memory. Only the first three of these Descartes then calls "modes of knowing"; for although "there can be no truth or falsity in the strict sense except in the intellect alone," they "often originate from the other two modes of knowing," from corporeal imagination and sense perception (AT 10:396; CSM 1:30). Because memory obtains its "contents" from understanding, imagination, and sensation, it is not really an "origin" of knowledge and is therefore excluded from being a mode of cognition. The intellect or understanding is here said to contain nothing corporeal and so to be entirely on the side of "mind" as an independent substance. Knowledge can "originate" from sensation or from the corporeal imagination but the understanding need not derive it from these sources, although it does so "often." And when it does not, it derives knowledge entirely from ideas or principles which it itself produces and thus acts in total independence of the body. The knowledge it then possesses Descartes calls "innate," so that, in this context, an innate idea or principle is one which has no source except the intellect itself.[14]

Also this doctrine of innate knowledge and of what Descartes here calls "the pure intellect" (understanding functioning apart from body whether modified as sensation or as corporeal imagination) recurs throughout his

[14] The qualification "in this context" is meant to limit discussion on the extent of innate knowledge. Sometimes, as in the Third Meditation, Descartes restricts innate knowledge to

works.[15] In the Sixth Meditation he speaks of such ideas or principles "that belong to the mind alone" when he writes of "my perception that what is done cannot be undone" as a representative example of "all other things that are known by the natural light"—to which the French edition adds "without any help from the body" (AT 7:82; CSM 2:57). Among these "things" are concepts like those of substance, duration, number, extension, and motion, as well as principles such as the causal principle. The intellect's ability to produce such concepts and principles "without any help from the body" is one part of the explanation of how pure science is possible. Other parts are the existence of intellectual memory and intellectual imagination.

Sensation can by definition never be independent of the body. Although it is true that "in no case are the ideas of things presented to us by the senses just as we form them in our own thinking," it is just as true that only through the intermediary of the senses can we know that certain ideas are "of" extramental things because when we sense them "these things . . . transmit something which, at exactly that moment, gives the mind occasion to form these ideas by means of the faculty innate in it" (AT 8B:358–59; CSM 1:304). But sensation is only an intermediary, dependent for its functioning on extraneous things, extraneous always to the mind and often to the body to which the mind is joined. And as their very names reveal, neither the corporeal memory nor the corporeal imagination can be independent of body.

Through sensation, corporeal imagination, and corporeal memory, mind and body are "intermingled." We know that although for the development of applied sciences we must make use of this intermingling, no pure science can be developed if we start with the intermingled state. But because of the dependence of the applied on the pure sciences, no science at all can be developed, or at least not developed very far, as long as there is this intermingling. Initially, science must be developed by the mind operating independently from sensation, corporeal imagination, and corporeal memory. If it does not, the result is confusion and at best a chancing on truth through "haphazard studies and obscure reflections" which, "lucky" though they may appear, nevertheless only "blur the natural light

what the mind can know apart from the body; at other times, as in the *Comments on a Certain Broadsheet*, he speaks of all knowledge as innate—"with the sole exception of those circumstances which relate to experience, such as the fact that we judge that this or that idea which we now have immediately before our mind refers to a certain thing situated outside us" (AT 8B:358–59; CSM 1:304).

15   For examples, see the third from the last paragraph of the Third Meditation, as well as both the Second and Third Set of Objections and Replies (AT 7:133 and 189; CSM 2:96 and 132) and *Comments on a Certain Broadsheet* (AT 8B:357–58; CSM 1:303).

and blind our intelligence" (AT 10:371; CSM 1:16). These quotations from the *Regulae* express Descartes's considered opinion about sensation, imagination, and memory.[16] It is not difficult to validate this judgment with respect to each of these in turn.

If we begin with accepting as true what the senses offer, then we take as true what is at best confused but often what the intellect would reveal to be false. The reasons I have adduced for this belief were methodological and the examples were general rather than specific and related to more than sensation. In the following paragraph, methodological concerns are as relevant as they were before, but will be more implicit than explicit; and the examples will be specific and all strictly from the realm of sense perception.

It is not just the "sensations of hunger, thirst, pain, and so on" which "are nothing but confused modes of thinking which arise from the union and, as it were, intermingling of the mind with the body" (AT 7:81; CSM 2:56). Equally confused thoughts produced by the same source are opinions about heat, color and size, opinions like "stars and towers and other distant bodies have the same size and shape which they present to my senses" (AT 7:82; CSM 2:56–57). Acting on such confused beliefs about nature may compound confusion and so is often not conducive to extension of our freedom in the practical affairs of life. The "rules" so derived from sensation differ from the "principles" which reason provides. I "misuse" the givens obtained through "sensory perceptions" if I use them "as reliable touchstones[17] for immediate judgements about the essential nature of the bodies located outside us," for "this is an area where they provide only very obscure information" (AT 7:83; CSM 2:57–58). Hence "knowledge of the truth about such things seems to belong to the mind alone, not to the combination of mind and body" (AT 7:82–83; CSM 2:57). Whatever practical wisdom is gained from noticing and remembering what gives pain or pleasure (and thus avoiding or pursuing such things and situations in the future) is a wisdom akin to that of the provisional morality by which we must live until we have one founded on the secure basis of

---

[16] Since I take this view to be Descartes's considered opinion which remains unchanged throughout his later writings, it does not matter if the *Regulae* was one of Descartes's early works much of which he had abandoned by 1630 (as Sepper holds in "Descartes and the Eclipse of Imagination"). The part in question would then be one of the retained parts—on Sepper's view, one of the few.

[17] "Reliable touchstones" translates *regulis certis* (AT 7:83; CSM 2:57). It seems to me that the Haldane and Ross translation ("absolute rules"), though almost equally imprecise as a literal rendering, makes Descartes's intent clearer than does CSM. See E. S. Haldane and G. R. T. Ross, *The Philosophical Works of Descartes*, vols. 1 and 2 (Cambridge, Eng., 1911). The passage in question is at 1:194.

metaphysics and physics.[18] Both this practical wisdom and provisional morality require us to adopt as guides for action merely probable opinions which we follow as second best. In the case of this practical wisdom, these are guides inductively derived from only partially understood contingent occurrences. They at the very best allow us only to get by in a daily life of which they temporarily sanction the status quo, and are thus very different from the principles of wisdom which Descartes expects to gain from the power-bestowing knowledge properly called "science." *That* knowledge is clear rather than confused because, though not developed in its applied form without involvement of the body, it is ultimately founded on intellectual items known per se which allow for development of "purely rational schemes" if such development is guided by the light of nature.

Understanding intermingled with corporeal imagination does not get us very far either. Like sense perception, corporeal imagination is necessary in the applied sciences, but it throws us off the right track if used too soon, before the proper rational schemes have been developed. The applied sciences rest on pure physics; and pure physics, in turn, cannot be developed apart from pure mathematics.[19] And although, as we shall see later, corporeal imagination is required even in the development of mathematics, again, if used too soon, it prevents the flourishing of the perception of the understanding in that field. This was precisely Descartes's complaint about arithmetic and geometry as these sciences were taught from the period of the Greeks to that of his own day (see AT 10:374–75; CSM 1:17–18). Because they employed corporeal imagination, mathematicians before Descartes's day could not get beyond concepts like a, a^2, and a^3 with their corresponding entities of lines, squares, and cubes. That which could not be pictured in the imagination or could not be constructed by ruler and compass did not exist. Relations and proportions like a^4 or a^5, because not picturable, were unintelligible as mathematical entities. Dependence on the imagination here inhibited the perception of the intellect to such an extent that it made them "get out of the habit of using [their] reason." Hence Descartes's charge that too early a use of the corporeal imagination closed off the proper development of the mathematical sciences. Descartes's counterposition, which allowed him to invent analytic geometry, will occupy center stage in my fifth chapter.

Whatever else needs to be introduced about corporeal imagination

---

[18]   See *Principles* 1:3; as well as the *Discourse*, part 3.
[19]   In chapter 5 we shall see that, to an extent, pure physics and mathematics are in fact identical for Descartes, namely, when mathematics takes the form of geometry.

must also be said about corporeal memory. I shall therefore now turn to the latter as well, and so deal with these together.

Both corporeal imagination and corporeal memory depend on "traces," "folds," or "impressions" in the brain. These are established through sensation.[20] For our purposes we need not consider Descartes's mechanistic account of how these traces become fixed in the brain. Instead, it is important to understand his doctrine that corporeal imagination and corporeal memory tend to lock us into the kind of habit which keeps the understanding from developing science. This tendency is an important ground for the separation of mind from body at the beginning of the scientific enterprise.

Brain traces result from the body's interaction with its environment. Repeated exposure to similar circumstances fixes brain traces in ways such that these circumstances are easily recalled, or usual combinations of them easily imagined. What is then recalled or imagined is dependent on the contingent succession of experiences in our past. What we recall is what we regularly happened to experience; what we imagine is what we regularly found to be imaginatively associated with what we experienced. Patterns impressed through fortuitous experience lead us to anticipate future events as resembling the past, and we then near automatically order our experience to fit these expectations. And so corporeal memory and imagination lock us into habits.

Whatever pattern there is to such habitual behavior is, for Descartes, a contingent pattern. To the extent, therefore, that we live by corporeal memory and imagination, no science is developed, because the associations then made by the mind when it draws imaginatively on its store of ideas in the memory are not dictated by the necessity of rational connections. Such rational connections reveal themselves to the mind only in "a comparison between two or more things" (AT 10:440; CSM 1:57) when the mind places before itself the second "or more" of the "two or more things" drawing on the resources of memory through its imagination. But this allows for *rational* connections only if both imagination and memory here function in ways free from the constraint of habit but disciplined by the rule of reason. Full development of these statements constitutes the next three chapters. At this point it is important to introduce only the following remarks.

It would be a mistake to say that the difference between the right and

<hr/>

[20]   See, e.g. Descartes's letters to Mersenne of 1 April 1640 (AT 3:48; CSMK 3:145–46) and of 6 August 1640 (AT 3:143–44; CSMK 3:151); to Hyperaspistes, August 1641 (AT 3:433; CSMK 3:196); and to Elizabeth, 6 October 1645 (AT 4:310; CSMK 3:270). In the fifth chapter we will see that the intellect, and not just sensation, plays an important role in some instances of creating these "impressions".

wrong uses of the imagination and memory lies in the presence or absence of associations. The difference, instead, lies in the *kind* of associations: associations determined by habit resulting from regularity in fortuitous experience versus associations determined by rational or necessary connections. The first come to mind "automatically"; the second call for the exercise of free will in the use of the imagination disciplined by reason. The first tends to reduce one's action to the level of beasts or automatons; the second allows for the rational activity which actualizes additional freedom.

In order to actualize the freedom potentially available to human beings, we must gain mastery over the vicissitudes of daily life. To that end we must develop science, for we need "absolute rules" by which to make "judgments about the essential nature of the bodies located outside us" (AT 7:83; CSM 2:57–58) No "confused modes of thinking" ever qualify as science. But "confused modes of thinking . . . arise from the union and, as it were, intermingling of the mind with the body" (AT 7:81; CSM 2:56), intermingling of the understanding on the one hand and sensation, corporeal imagination, and corporeal memory on the other. Once mind and body have been separated, the mind can without any help from the body develop metaphysics, mathematics and theoretical physics, that is, a system of absolute rules required as foundation for developing true judgments about the essential nature of the human body and of external objects. The absolute rules thus developed are, however, only about potential bodies and objects.

These rules, being absolute, hold for any possible world, including the world in which I find myself; but in their generality they do not tell me enough about the particularity which pertains to *my* body and *my* world. What I want to know is how to construct efficient labor-saving devices, how to avert or cure illness and perhaps even prevent aging,[21] how to forestall or dispel the anxiety which clings to my daily acts and even penetrates my sleep.[22] I want a mechanics, medicine, and morals for *my* world. That too can be attained, but only subsequent to the separation of mind and body. For once, during this period of separation, I have developed my purely rational foundations in metaphysics, mathematics, and theoretical physics, I am again free to make use of the "union" and "inter-

---

[21] See the *Discourse*, the opening paragraphs of part 6, especially AT 6:62–63; CSM 1:143.
[22] Descartes claims that through freely using his reason he has been able to dispel the anxieties which often afflict one in dreams. As he writes to Elizabeth: "For each person wants to make himself happy; but many people do not know how to, and often a bodily indisposition prevents their will from being free. This happens too when we are asleep; because nobody, however philosophical, can prevent himself having bad dreams when his bodily disposition so disposes him. Experience, however, shows that if one has often had a certain thought while one's mind was at liberty, it returns later on, however indisposed

mingling" of mind and body. I am then free "to think with the body",[23] that is, to use corporeal imagination and sensation to construct models and conduct experiments on this purely rational foundation. I am then in the position to increase my mastery over nature and so work at the continued actualization of my freedom through development of the applied sciences.

Various of the important aspects pertinent to Descartes's dualism can now be stated succinctly. There will be no progress in achieving greater freedom unless there are developments in science. No applied science can be developed unless on the foundations of metaphysics and physics. No such foundations can be constructed unless the mind be taken as separate from nature. Dualism, therefore, is a necessary condition for the possibility of science. It is the desire for progress in the actualization of human potential, and for the sake of that cause progress in all the sciences, which helps shape the details of Descartes's dualism on the side of both nature and mind.

The essence of nature may be seen as determined by the facts that reason is assumed to be able to gain scientific knowledge of it and that reason is taken to function in a manner which demands that its nonmental object be of a mechanistic kind. The essence of mind may be seen as determined by the desire to preserve and extend freedom through development of science. In its initial stages this development demands that anything corporeal be separated from mind, but it also requires that mind be characterized as possessing both an intellectual memory and an intellectual imagination.[24]

My claim is not that it is the desire for progress which consciously led Descartes to establish his dualism.[25] Instead, it is that the conviction of the

one's body may be. Thus I can tell you that my own dreams never portray anything distressing . . . " (1 September 1645, AT 4:282; CSMK 3:262–63).

[23] This phrase is an adaptation of the title of one of Amélie Oksenberg Rorty's articles, "Descartes on Thinking with the Body" in Cottingham, *Cambridge Companion*, 371–92.

[24] The question "What must nature and mind be like for human progress to be possible?" is not one which, in this form, Descartes himself poses. For some readers it may sound too Kantian. But when carefully handled it will lead to illuminating answers. And there is more than one good precedent for this procedure, perhaps the best of the more recent ones Amélie Oksenberg Rorty's: "What must the body be like, so that its contribution to thinking is reliable, and perhaps even useful? What nonepistemic benefits does the body bring to the mind? Although Descartes did not himself ask these questions in just these terms, answering them is central to the success of his enterprise" (371).

[25] I agree, therefore, with Rozemond's statement that "It is unlikely that Descartes's scientific preoccupations moved him to adopt it," where "it" refers to what Rozemond calls "the Independence Thesis," i.e., "the view that intellect is an operation of the mind alone." See Marleen Rozemond, "The Role of the Intellect in Descartes's Case for the Incorporeity

possibility of such progress helped shape aspects of this dualism's two poles.[26]

There are two doctrines, relevant at various points in this and the preceding section, which demand a moment's further attention. The *first* of these concerns the implication that an uncompromising dualism of mind and body is necessary to the possibility of science. It is an implication which subsequent developments in philosophy and science have proven to be mistaken. Drawing attention to it now will allow me to leave it to the side for the rest of this study. The *second* concerns what might be called the relationship between the "utility of science" and the "truth about nature." It is a doctrine about which the statements in this chapter may appear to be too strong once my account develops in later chapters. For as we shall then see, there are nuances Descartes introduces which in some respects bring him close to, for example, classical pragmatism on the matter of this relationship. Although I will draw attention to this doctrine now, its relevant details will be given sharper contours as my picture becomes more complete.

First. There are various aspects to Descartes's position on human nature and the possibility of science which I believe to be of lasting importance for our continued reflection on human ability and scientific possibility. Not the least of these is what we will come to recognize as

---

of the Mind," in Voss, 97–114, specifically 98–99. But that does not preclude the content of the dualism from being at least in part determined by "Descartes' scientific preoccupations."

[26] Although dualistic positions had dominated the philosophical scene for centuries prior to the advent of Descartes, I would conjecture that, had it suited his purposes, Descartes would have been quite capable also of "uprooting from [his] mind" (AT 6:28; CSM 1:125) the dualistic tradition. In a sense he did uproot it and replaced it with a type of dualism quite different from that inherited from Aristotle. For Aristotle, "matter" was on anything but an equal footing with "mind." For Descartes, "matter" and "mind" are on an equal footing at least to the extent that each is a "substance." Several decades ago, Aram Vartanian wrote that establishing a Cartesian-type dualism was not just a novelty but a revolutionary act, a move which "was itself the first great step towards naturalism." Parts of Vartanian's argument in support of this conclusion are that a Cartesian-type substance "gets on better alone than in pairs" and that the criterion of clarity and distinctness precludes the "formal demonstration" of the union of these two substances in "their concrete mutual functioning in man." One of these substances would therefore be bound to relinquish its place as independent entity on an equal footing with the other. And so, Vartanian concludes, the development of Cartesianism led to naturalism once "mind" gave place to "matter." See Aram Vartanian, *Diderot and Descartes: A Study of Scientific Naturalism in the Enlightenment* (Princeton, 1953), 10–11. Vartanian's argument, in part echoed and in part extended by Georges Dicker (see pages 69–70 of the latter's *Descartes*), is plausible but at best tells only half the story. For on the same grounds Descartes's position can then also be seen to lead to post-Enlightenment idealism through the development in which "matter" or "nature" relinquishes its place to "mind," "reason," or "freedom."

Descartes's doctrine about the nature and role of imagination, especially as related to the function of hypotheses. However, the implication that in order to be able to develop science at all we must adopt a dualistic, nonnaturalistic position is one which history has proven to be wrong. One might argue that Descartes already had more than an inkling about this. For on the one hand he insists on a thoroughgoing dualism which allows him both to characterize human beings as essentially free and to characterize nature as causally determined. And on the other hand he insists on what we shall come to recognize in later chapters as the crucial role of corporeal imagination and sensation in the scientist's work. The transition from the corporeal to the intellectual, and vice versa, remains problematic and full of tension in Descartes's work. When, already in the seventeenth century, this tension was "suspended" through Locke's agnosticism about the essence of both mind and matter or, in the eighteenth and nineteenth centuries, was "resolved" in favor of "nature" by materialists and naturalists or in favor of "freedom" by idealists, developments in science hardly ground to a halt. The least of the morals to be drawn from these historical developments is that no metaphysics totally determines the possibility (or impossibility) of developments in science.

Second. Looming large, but not always given its proper weight by commentators, is the emphasis Descartes places on the utility of his doctrines. This, too, is a stance which pervades all of his mature works. So in the *Discourse* Descartes tells us that, were he not to publish his thoughts, he "would be sinning gravely against the law which obliges us to do all in our power to secure the general welfare of mankind"—for his work constitutes "a practical philosophy" which places us in the position to "make ourselves, as it were, the lords and masters of nature" (AT 6:61–62; CSM 1:142). The *Meditations* is essentially heuristic. Its purpose is to establish the legitimacy of our absolute trust in reason and its aids (when the latter are used properly). And Descartes takes the work to have established this legitimacy once and for all: in words from the opening paragraph of its synopsis, "[T]he usefulness of such extensive doubt . . . lies in freeing us from all our preconceived opinions," so that it becomes "impossible for us to have any further doubts about what we subsequently discover to be true." So, after the *Meditations*, we can leave metaphysics behind and concentrate on the sciences which promise dividends for the improvement of everyday life.

Again, history has shown that those who stress the utility of science do not necessarily worry overly much about whether useful scientific doctrine also in some deep sense gives us insight into the nature of the universe. For pragmatists, for example, questions about metaphysical or epistemic realism are of little concern. But for Descartes, the *Meditations* makes legitimate the belief that human beings can come to know nature because nature's order corresponds to reason's order. One might therefore be inclined to expect Descartes to be a rigorous epistemic realist, with the truth of science strictly corresponding to the truth of the state of affairs the scientist investigates. And the formulations I have advanced in this section would provide support for such an interpretation of Cartesian doctrine. But as we shall see, Descartes is interested in giving *a*, but not necessarily *the*, scientific truth; that is, he does not pretend to a "God's eye view." In the end, utility looms larger than absolute correspondence of the truth of science and the truth of nature. Thus even Descartes will be seen as capable of introducing a measure of agnosticism about the "fit" between scientific theory and the nature of reality, while at the same time advocating a strong conviction about the utility of science. But for this claim to become fully plausible without denying the validity of the formulations about reason's and nature's order earlier introduced, we need to have seen a good deal more of Descartes's position than we have now before us.

3. Intellectual Memory and Imagination

A single preliminary argument may be advanced to make plausible the statement that the Cartesian mind is in part characterized by the functions of intellectual memory and intellectual imagination. This argument has strict limitations, for it demonstrates no more than that, given Descartes's dualism and his views on how science is to be developed, his position requires both intellectual memory and intellectual imagination. The next two sections of this chapter will present a case for Descartes's conscious use of these powers.

Science, in the peculiarly Cartesian sense of that word, is *deductive* argumentation.[27] All deduction requires memory, for without memory there is

---

[27] From the first chapter we already know that "deduction" for Descartes is quite different from "syllogistic deduction"; whereas the latter only explains, the former "discovers" or "invents." When he writes of "finding the deductive inferences that will help us attain . . . knowledge" the phrase for "finding deductive inferences" is *deductiones inveniendae sint* (AT 10:372; CSM 1:16). The *Regulae* is one place where he argues the need for memory (in rules 7 and 11) and imagination (in rule 10) for this activity. The next chapter will expand on the brief account which follows.

no store of ideas upon which to draw, no awareness of what preceded the present stage of the argument, and consequently no notion of the next possibly relevant move to be made. Neither can there be deductive argument without the imagination, since no "links" can be added to the deductive "chain" except through proposing hypotheses, and no hypotheses can be introduced except by the imagination. But if science can be developed in spite of action in keeping with the supposition that nothing corporeal exists and that therefore nothing bodily can be used in its development, then there must be noncorporeal memory and imagination. For Descartes, the *Meditations* and *Principles* (parts 1 and 2) are ample proof for the correctness of his belief that science can be developed while the supposition of the nonexistence of anything corporeal is in force. For under that stricture he produces his metaphysics in the former, and metaphysics and theoretical physics in the latter. When we saw him comment on this practice in the closing paragraphs of the Fifth Meditation, we saw him state explicitly that, before we know anything about the existence of the material world, we can develop both these sciences. Such statements commit him to the existence of both a noncorporeal memory and a noncorporeal imagination.

Even if we lifted the restriction which rules nature to be nonexistent, the outcome would be the same. With nature (and hence the human body) in place, memory might be nothing but a function of brain traces. In that case, at least to the extent that their behavior depended on memory, human beings would be creatures of such freedom-precluding habits as can be explained mechanistically through the causally determined effects of contingent past experiences on, and processes in, the body. Similarly, the requisite freedom of imagination would be lacking if the imaginative processes determining our experiential expectations were to be explained entirely through habitual association of ideas which uncritically accepted sensuous experience has forged together in our minds. Developing science requires the freedom of memory to select ideas from its store and the freedom of imagination to propose hypotheses through their free combination. To put this negatively: It demands that neither memory nor imagination be bound by the rules of association which belong to the machine of nature. Since Descartes believes that science is possible, he can limit neither memory nor imagination to the mechanism of bodily functions. Thus, given his views on what is required for science to be possible, Descartes needs both intellectual memory and intellectual imagination.

Now it is striking that commentators have paid little if any attention to the presence and role of either of these intellectual powers in Descartes's system. Perhaps this is because Descartes hardly ever referred by name to the first, and never to the second (or, at least, not by use of the phrase "intellectual imagination"). He may have been frugal in his explicit references precisely because it was so clear to him that both are necessarily involved. He explicitly named memory and imagination as corporeal. That was perhaps not because he considered them more important than their intellectual counterparts, but because they are potentially a liability for developing science. Hence it is vital to be clear about their existence and limitations, lest we would allow them to play their roles at inappropriate moments and so become stymied in metaphysics (as we would have, for example, in the Second Meditation's seventh paragraph)[28] or in mathematics (like the early Greeks). But since memory and imagination in their *corporeal* form are used so frequently and Descartes so often flags their functions, his response is one indicating surprise when his correspondents do not seem to be aware of the *intellectual* memory's presence in his work. In the following section of this chapter we will see that, when he is asked about memory, his response is something like: But of course there is an intellectual memory, how else can we explain . . . ! It is likely that, had he been asked about intellectual imagination, there would have been a similar response.

It may be argued that, although their presence in Descartes's works is clear enough to us, it was not at all clear to Descartes himself. This is the position adopted by Alan White with respect to philosophers until recent times.[29] White believes that for almost all of them the actual use of imagination contradicts what they say about imagination. Their *theory* is in terms of what Descartes called corporeal imagination, the mode of imagining bound up with images; but their *practice* includes imagining what cannot be pictured—such as arguments—or imagining what, why, how, and that.[30]

White claims that the reason for this difference in theory and practice rests on an assumption all these philosophers shared: they always conceived of ideas as images.[31] This claim does not hold for Descartes.[32] True,

---

[28] This is one point in the argument where Descartes attempts to gain knowledge beyond that initially revealed in the cogito. He then makes clear that we cannot gain such knowledge if we rely on (presumed to be nonexistent) body-based powers, like corporeal imagination. I shall develop this part of the argument in my fourth chapter.

[29] Alan R. White, *The Language of Imagination* (Oxford, 1990).

[30] On this difference between what philosophers have said about imagination and how they in fact used it, see White, 6, 13, 29, 42, 83–84, 176; with respect particularly to Descartes, see 20–24, 43, 176.

[31] White, 43.

[32] Although White is well aware of this (see page 22) and points to passages such as follow in my text, he seems to forget about his earlier insight later in his study: "It was 'a way

he writes (in the Third Meditation) that "the ideas in me are like <pictures, or> images".[33] But on the same page he states that "Among my ideas, apart from the idea which gives me a representation of myself, which cannot present any difficulty in this context, there are ideas which variously represent God, corporeal and inanimate things . . . " (AT 7:42; CSM 2:29). We know it to be Descartes's position that, whereas the idea of a corporeal thing may be spoken of as "image" in the sense of "picture," the idea of God is not (like) a picture at all. To have an idea of God is to apprehend God's attributes. "By 'God' I mean the very being the idea of whom is within me, that is, the possessor of all the perfections which I cannot grasp, but can somehow reach in my thought." These perfections are of a "substance that is infinite, <eternal, immutable,> independent, supremely intelligent, supremely powerful" (AT 7:52; CSM 2:35, and AT 7:45; CSM 2:31). None of these concepts can be imaged or pictured; it is their intellectual apprehension which gives us the idea. Hobbes (who *does* conceive of ideas as images) objects to this part of the Third Meditation's argument in the words "[W]e have no idea or image corresponding to the sacred name of God. . . . It seems, then, that there is no idea of God in us" (AT 7:180; CSM 2:127). Descartes's reply is unambiguous:

> Here my critic wants the term 'idea' to be taken to refer simply to the images of material things which are depicted in the corporeal imagination; and if this is granted, it is easy for him to prove that there can be no proper idea of an angel or of God. But I make it quite clear in several places throughout the book, and in this passage in particular, that I am taking the word 'idea' to refer to whatever is immediately perceived by the mind. For example, when I want something, or am afraid of something, I simultaneously perceive that I want, or am afraid; and this is why I count volition and fear among my ideas. (AT 7:181; CSM 2:127)

Descartes speaks of images or ideas coming from the senses, memory, and imagination. He also speaks of ideas which cannot be assimilated to images, ideas such as those of God, of volition, of fear. The sequel will make it clear that to this class of ideas belong some of the ideas of memory and imagination. There is then, for Descartes, imageless memory and imageless imagination. That is (since both corporeal memory and corporeal imagination are characterized by the presence of imagery), there is an intellectual or noncorporeal memory and imagination.

In White's interpretation, Descartes conceives of all ideas of imagina-

---

of ideas, conceived of as images' as old as Aristotle and continuing through Descartes . . . " (43).
[33] In my use of "< . . . >" I follow the CSM convention to indicate French additions to the *Meditation*'s Latin original.

tion as images.[34] White then applies to Descartes a claim he makes about David Hume,[35] namely, that this conception "undermined his theory of imagination" in that it became "at variance with his own practice" when, in that practice, he regularly depended on imageless imagining, on nonsensory imagination. Once we give full play to the fact that Descartes does not conceive of all ideas as images, White's conclusion need not follow. The worst case is then not a situation in which practice undermines theory, but a situation in which there is a stated theory about corporeal imagination and an unstated—but clearly and consistently practiced—theory about intellectual imagination. That the two are different need not (and in Descartes's case does not) undermine either theory or practice. Moreover, a case will emerge from this study to the effect that the practiced theory about intellectual imagination is not without its corresponding statement.

4. MEMORY

Sometimes Descartes uses the phrases "intellectual memory" and "corporeal memory" in explicit juxtaposition, but more often he names only the second of these. Consideration of statements about corporeal memory can lead us to his doctrine of intellectual memory, for instance, when we read that the very possibility of corporeal memory requires the copresence of both these forms of memory.

References to corporeal memory are scattered throughout Descartes's writings. With respect to the Second Meditation, Pierre Gassendi asked: If it is true that the soul always thinks and can presumably remember its thoughts, why is it that we have no recollection of the thoughts we had while "in the womb" or "during deep sleep" (AT 7:264; CSM 2:184)? Since

---

[34] He writes that "Descartes . . . is quite clear that to imagine is to have an image" and that "it is in vain to 'try to imagine a thing which is not imageable' " (23). But this is only part of Descartes's doctrine, the part pertaining to corporeal imagination. White himself adduces evidence for the latter claim, but, in order not to jeopardize the coherence of his own interpretation, he ascribes incoherence to Descartes. A passage in question is that in which White discusses the position that what is impossible is unimaginable because unimageable. "An apparent exception to this occurs, especially among the classical philosophers, not when these philosophers are discussing the imaginable and the possible, but when they are actually using them. Thus, Descartes allows that writers of fables imagine what is not possible, and both he and Berkeley and Hume on occasion accuse their opponents of imagining what is impossible, e.g. that there can be indivisible atoms or no God, or matter or abstract ideas, or changeless time. Of course, on many topics, including that of imagination, philosophers' theories about concepts are often at variance with their actual use of those concepts" (176).

[35] Page 43. Even about Hume there are indications that White may be on thin ice, as when he admits that "In fact, Hume inconsistently with his general views about imagination, at times seems to allow that we can imagine, and not only feign or suppose, what we cannot have an image of."

Gassendi's query is posed within the framework of the union of mind and body, Descartes's reply is in terms of bodily modifications: "For the recollection of the thoughts which the mind has had during the period of its union with the body, it is necessary for certain traces of them to be impressed on the brain; and turning and applying itself to these the mind remembers" (AT 7:357; CSM 2:247). In article 42 of the *Passions* Descartes expands on this theory by adding to the terminology of brain traces (which he also calls "folds" or "pores" in the brain) that of the pineal gland and of "animal spirits." All these terms (including the word "spirits" in the phrase "animal spirits") refer to parts or modifications of the body. In this expansion two further points are introduced. The first is that the corporeal memory is in an important respect unlike other phenomena which witness to the "intermingling" of mind and body, phenomena like hunger, cold, or pain. One is aware of hunger only when hungry, and if there is no actual hunger, one's then willing the experience never suffices to bring it about. One can however will to remember something, and often the mere willing of it gives the desired recollection. As Descartes puts it in this article: "[W]hen the soul wants to remember something, this volition makes the [pineal] gland lean first to one side and then to another, thus driving the [animal] spirits toward different regions of the brain until they come upon the one containing traces left by the object we want to remember." So, although remembering is not always a matter of will (there are unwilled memories which come to mind through contingent association), the will can play its part, and when it does there are more than bodily factors (in addition to that of the will) involved in the explanation of corporeal memory—a doctrine alluded to in article 42 as well.

This doctrine (which is the second point to be introduced) is implicit in the last phrases of the final sentence of article 42: "And so the spirits enter into these pores more easily when they come upon them, thereby producing in the gland that special movement which represents the same object to the soul, and makes it recognize the object as the one it wanted to remember." This statement Descartes intends to be taken as an explanation of "How we find in our memory the things we want to remember" (as the heading of this article puts it). The implicit point is that, for instances of corporeal memory to occur, the presence of noncorporeal factors is essential. The following considerations will help to make this doctrine explicit.

Even if we were to have no difficulty with Descartes's mechanistic account—with its brain traces, animal spirits, and special role for the pineal gland—there are still major problems with this explanation of memory knowledge. One is that for Descartes, knowing is always a function of the understanding and never of the body, not even of a "special movement" of the pineal gland. For its solution Descartes falls back on the doctrine of occasionalism. But even if we grant him that a "special movement" "in the gland" "represents the same object," it is still the case that this "move-ment" cannot make the understanding "recognize the object as the one it wanted to remember." The (bodily) representation and—here the doc-trine of occasionalism enters—its accompanying (mental) knowledge of an "object" are one thing, the knowledge that this is the object one wanted to have presented is quite another.

Descartes is well aware of the fact that a theory in terms of corporeal as-pects, even if supplemented with a doctrine of occasionalism, is insuffi-cient to account for what is essential to remembering, to knowing some-thing as *the same again*. He holds that knowledge of *the same again* cannot be explained through considerations about corporeal movement, that memory acts of a noncorporeal kind must accompany acts of the corpo-real memory for the latter to occur at all. In a letter to Arnauld of 29 July 1648, written some two years after the composition of the *Passions,* he is quite explicit about this. The relevant passages (which are the origin of all quotations in the two following paragraphs) are at AT 5:220–21; CSMK 3:356–57.

> If we are to remember something, it is not sufficient that the thing should previously have been before our mind and have left some traces in the brain which give occasion for it to come into our thoughts again; it is neces-sary in addition that we should recognize, when it comes the second time, that this is happening because it has already been perceived by us earlier.

When something remembered "comes into our thoughts," Descartes calls it "direct thought." No "direct thought" can occur without "traces in the brain which give occasion for it." Both it and the traces are necessary conditions for instances of corporeal memory. Another necessary condi-tion is the occurrence of what he here calls "reflective thoughts"; they are of the kind which make us "recognize" that "it . . . come[s] into our thoughts *again*." This "second perception" or "reflection" Descartes then attributes "to the intellect alone."

I have adapted the argument of this letter for my particular use here. Actually, Descartes relates "direct thoughts" and "reflective thoughts" not only to the moment of recollection but also to the moment at which the brain traces which are destined to become memory traces are first made. This is how that passage reads:

> From this it is clear that it is not sufficient for memory that there should be traces left in the brain by preceding thoughts. The traces have to be of such a kind that the mind recognizes that they have not always been present in us, but were at some time newly impressed. Now for the mind to recognize this, I think that when these traces were first made it must have made use of

pure intellect to notice that the thing which was then presented to it was new and had not been presented before; for there cannot be any corporeal trace of this novelty.

Recognition of this "newness," both at the time when the traces were first made and at the time of recollection, Descartes calls "reflective thought." Because, just as with the recognition of *the same again*, "there cannot be any corporeal trace of" it, these statements implicate something noncorporeal. It is therefore Descartes's position that no complete account of corporeal memory can be given without recourse to an essential noncorporeal factor; this factor is the "second perception" which, when it includes knowledge of *the same again*, is an instance of intellectual memory.

The passages in which Descartes identifies intellectual memory by name leave no doubt that he intends a memory which involves no corporeal aspects whatsoever. In two letters to Marin Mersenne there is an explicit juxtaposition of corporeal and intellectual memory; and since both letters were written in 1640, it is clear that this is not a doctrine on which Descartes hit only in the final years of his life; it was firmly in his mind during the time he worked on the *Meditations*. The first letter states that "besides this memory, which depends on the body, I believe there is also another one, entirely intellectual, which depends on the soul alone" (1 April 1640, AT 3:48; CSMK 3:146). The second is more explicit and makes a further point: "Moreover, in addition to the corporeal memory, whose impressions can be explained by these folds in the brain, I believe there is also in our intellect another sort of memory, which is altogether spiritual, and is not found in animals. It is this that we mainly use" (6 August 1640, AT 3:143; CSMK 3:151). The "we" who "mainly use" this "spiritual" memory here are rational beings to the extent they act rationally, particularly, scientists engaged in their scientific pursuits.

A letter from the following year (to Hyperaspistes, AT 3:425; CSMK 3:190) may at first sight seem a retreat from this position of there being a purely intellectual memory:

> [W]hen the mind joined to a body thinks of a corporeal thing, certain particles in the brain are set in motion. Sometimes this results from the action of external objects on the sense-organs, sometimes from the ascent of animal spirits from the heart to the brain, and sometimes from the mind's own action, when it is impelled simply of its own free will to a certain thought. The motion of these brain particles leaves behind the traces on which memory depends. But where purely intellectual things are concerned, memory in the strict sense is not involved; they are thought of just as readily irrespective of whether it is the first or second time that they come to mind—unless,

as often happens, they are associated with certain names, in which case, since the latter are corporeal, we do indeed remember them.

To the notion of remembering names of purely intellectual things I shall return in a moment, when I introduce a later passage which sheds light on it. Of first concern is the statement that "where purely intellectual things are concerned, memory in the strict sense is not involved," the ground for this statement being that "they are thought of just as readily . . . the first or second time that they come to mind." Initial appearances to the contrary, this is not a denial of intellectual memory; it is an assertion of its difference from corporeal memory. When purely intellectual things come to mind a second time as items of memory knowledge, then they are still "purely intellectual," and everything corporeal—corpuscular motions, brain particles, brain traces—is excluded. Hence "they are thought of just as readily . . . the . . . second time that they come to mind"—and this in contrast to what often happens in corporeal memory. In the latter case, if the original stimulus was not a very strong one, or if the time passed between original stimulus and moment of memory is very long, then the brain trace is slight, the animal spirits do not easily find passage there, and the issue in question is not "thought of just as readily" as it was the first time. The statement that memory of purely intellectual things "involves" no "memory in the strict sense" occurs in the context of a discussion of corporeal memory. The conclusion to be drawn is not that there is no intellectual memory but that intellectual memory is not to be discussed in terms relevant to corporeal memory.

This reading is supported by a letter to Mesland written three years later (2 May 1644, AT 4:114; CSMK 3:233):

> As for memory, I think that the memory of material things depends on the traces which remain in the brain after an image has been imprinted on it; and that the memory of intellectual things depends on some other traces which remain in the mind itself. But the latter are of a wholly different kind from the former, and I cannot explain them by any illustration drawn from corporeal things without a great deal of qualification. The traces in the brain, on the other hand, dispose it to move the soul in the same way as it moved before, and thus to make it remember something. It is rather as the folds in a piece of paper or cloth make it easier to fold again in that way than it would be if it had never been so folded before.

Thus memory of intellectual things is not memory "in the strict sense" to the extent that we speak of memory in terms of brain traces. For, in the "strict sense" of "traces" as "brain traces," there are not any: the "traces" of intellectual memory "are of a wholly different kind."

Finally, in the *Conversation with Burman* both the memory of "purely intellectual things" and that of "names" come to the fore when Burman reports Descartes as saying:

> I do not refuse to admit intellectual memory: it does exist. When, for example, on hearing that the word 'K-I-N-G' signifies supreme power, I commit this to my memory and then subsequently recall the meaning by means of the memory, it must be the intellectual memory that makes this possible. For there is certainly no relationship between the four letters (K-I-N-G) and their meaning, which would enable me to derive the meaning from the letters. It is the intellectual memory that enables me to recall what the letters stand for.[36]

Hearing the word "king" is hearing a sound or name. Hearing this sound causes a modification or "trace" in the brain. Hearing the significance of this word similarly causes such a modification. But neither of these modifications is a thought. Thus Descartes draws a distinction between the trace and the sound or name as the cause of the trace, and of the causal relationship between the two he offers a mechanistic account. He also draws a distinction between sound and trace on the one hand, and knowledge as well as subsequent remembering of the meaning of the sound, of our possession of the concept, on the other. There is no explanation of how we go from sound or trace to meaning or concept apart from the doctrines of occasionalism and innatism. But these doctrines are themselves (re)statements rather than explanations of the mind-body dualism.

We know that because it allows for freedom this dualism is a condition for the development of science. But science demands as well a memory wholly on the mind side of this dualism. How Descartes believes this memory to function in the context of his dualism is no clearer than his doctrine of the mind's "intermingling" with the body. But that he holds

---

[36] AT 5:150; CSMK 3:336–37. Although these statements fit well with what Descartes says about memory elsewhere, the sentence immediately following poses a problem: "However, the intellectual memory has universals rather than particulars as its objects, and so it cannot enable us to recall every single thing we have done." Apart from the fact that this statement conflicts with Descartes's belief that in the soul's survival of the body's death one can, through "intellectual memory which is certainly independent of the body," recognize those we knew in this life and who predeceased us (see Descartes to Huygens, 10 October 1642, AT 3:598; CSMK 3:216), it also creates difficulties for developing science, where the intellectual memory is called upon for more than recollecting universals. The statement quoted poses problems for what Descartes has elsewhere said about memory, where remembering is the cognition always accompanied by the cognition of *the same again*; the latter cognition need not be knowledge of a universal. Either Burman has misrepresented Descartes on this point, or Descartes is confused. It seems safe to opt for the former alternative.

there to be an intellectual memory is beyond question. According to at least some commentators, this much cannot be said about the intellectual imagination.

5. Imagination

One will not find much on intellectual imagination in studies on Descartes, and what there is usually consists in indirect statements which more often than not rule it out of existence.[37] But if Descartes does not allow a role for intellectual imagination, then he cannot generate science. Of this point some commentators seem vaguely aware, but by and large this is a neglected area whose disregard has often led to misinterpretation. Two recent articles bucking this trend of neglect are Dennis L. Sepper's "Descartes and the Eclipse of Imagination, 1618–1630" and "*Ingenium*, Memory Art, and the Unity of Imaginative Knowing in the Early Descartes".[38] Although they are concerned primarily with Descartes's pre-*Discourse* writings, they do at times extend into the later works. I shall therefore have occasion to draw on Sepper's work in following chapters. At this point, I shall merely indicate that my discussion of imagination is

[37] One such statement is in John J. Blom's *Descartes: His Moral Philosophy and Psychology* : "As indicated, the sensible realm, which, strictly speaking, is all we can 'imagine' . . . " (5). Another is in M. Glouberman, *Descartes: The Probable and the Certain* (Amsterdam, 1986): "[T]he imagination is internally linked by Descartes throughout the *corpus* with the senses" (292). We already found statements of this nature at various points in White's *Imagination*, 20–24. Georges Dicker contrasts "imagination" with "intellect" (68–69) hence assuming it to be corporeal only. And Dennis Des Chene writes only of "imagination or phantasia" which "is, after all, itself a 'genuine real body, extended and figured' . . . " (*Physiologia: Natural Philosophy in Late Aristotelian and Cartesian Thought* [Ithaca, 1996], 346; see the same restriction at work on page 388). Hiram Caton (in *The Origin of Subjectivity: An Essay on Descartes* [New Haven, 1973]) speaks of two kinds of imagination in Descartes, one of which he names "corporeal" while the other seems to come close to what I intend by "intellectual." Caton, however, confines it to limits (the "sensible-imaginable") beyond which I believe Descartes assigns it a role in both metaphysics and pure physics; Caton writes: "This property of 'symbol-manipulating' imagination is obscured by the stress on imagination as the corporeal mental counterpart to the extension of the world. But the utility of symbols to understanding is that although they are sensible-imaginable, i.e., themselves extended . . . " (66). Gaukroger, in his dozen references to "imagination" in *Descartes: An Intellectual Biography*, almost always identifies it as corporeal ("The imagination which, it must be remembered, is a corporeal organ . . . " [72]); on two occasions (pages 124, 393) he hints at more than corporeality, with the second of these the more explicit though remaining undeveloped beyond the statement that "Descartes has never treated the imagination as anything other than corporeal up to this point: now he suddenly ignores its corporeality. Why? Because conceiving of the imagination in terms of substantial union and conceiving of it in terms of a piece of animal physiology are two different things."

[38] See note 1 to this chapter.

one attempt at the task that Sepper, in the closing paragraph of the first of these articles, signals as needing to be undertaken (and which he in part executed in his *Descartes's Imagination*):

> Thus one might at the very least begin to recognize that imagination, intellect, and will have a complicated and changing relationship to one another in the philosophy of Descartes, and that ultimately none of them can be understood in complete abstraction from the others. From this perspective, we might look upon the early theory of imagination as Descartes' first attempt to conceive the nature of human being and to understand its powers and limits. When that theory broke down, he was already far advanced along a course that had no lesser ambition than to use . . . imagination to determine everything that the mind could know. . . . In this sense it is proper to think of imagination in the later philosophy as in eclipse: not gone but just hidden from view, ready to emerge at any moment from its occultation. What happened to imagination in this occultation? The answer ought now to become a focus of our attention.[39]

Descartes himself is at least in part responsible for this almost ubiquitous neglect because he never uses the phrase "intellectual imagination." But since he does use the phrase "corporeal imagination," and juxtaposes "corporeal" and "intellectual" in important discussions of memory, the qualification "corporeal" in "corporeal imagination" should alert us to the possibility of his also assigning a role to a noncorporeal imagination. As when I dealt with memory, let me begin with some of Descartes's statements about corporeal imagination.

In the *Passions* Descartes speaks of two kinds of "imaginations," but, in contrast to the occasions on which he speaks of two kinds of memory, he does not distinguish between a corporeal and a strictly noncorporeal imagination. This implies an additional distinction in his doctrine of imagination; in order to forestall confusion, we must first get it in clear focus.

The *Passions'* two kinds of imagination are those "formed by the soul"

---

[39] Sepper strikes the same sort of note in the opening of his second article: "[I]n writings preceding the *Regulae* Descartes conceived imagination as the chief faculty in the work of cognition. . . . In this light the *Regulae* will appear not simply as an early formulation of the principles of method, but as the tension-filled outcome of an attempt to think through the heuristic and cognitive competencies of imagination. . . . Although the inadequacies of this attempt ultimately led to the cognitive demotion of imagination, there are nevertheless reasons for thinking that the early framework, shaped by the primacy of imagination, was not so much rejected as transformed in Descartes' mature work." In an otherwise insightful article ("The Cartesian Imagination," *Philosophy and Phenomenological Research* 46, no. 4 [1986]: 631–42), F. M. Foti's main conclusions militate against this idea of "transformation." I draw upon her article, and take issue with her conclusions, in following chapters.

(these are introduced in article 20) and those "which are caused solely by the body" (article 21). The latter are "perceptions caused by the body" which "arise simply from the fact that the [animal] spirits, being agitated in various different ways and coming upon the traces of various impressions which have preceded them in the brain, make their way by chance through certain pores rather than others." Among such "imaginations" are "the illusions of our dreams and also the day-dreams we often have when we are awake and our mind wanders idly without applying itself to anything of its own accord." When the mind so "wanders idly," then "our will is not used in forming" what is imagined.[40] Such "imaginations" are to be explained in mechanistic terms. If there is any order among the ideas thus presented, it is the "order" of an association of ideas which depends mainly on the vicissitudes of past experience.[41] As the "aimlessness" of "idly wandering," such an association has nothing of the discipline exhibited by the succession of ideas which present themselves in the course of a scientific investigation, a succession determined by the possibility of necessary connections between or among these ideas. Because both will and order (hence reason) are absent, these are "imaginings which are caused solely by the body," differing from those "formed by the soul" in that the latter "depend chiefly on the volition which makes it aware of them." "Imaginings" "formed by the soul" depend on the will "chiefly" but not always entirely, for among this class of "imaginings" there are "pictures," and no "pictures" can be formed without the body.[42] But the will is in control here; it "aims" at something; mere "wandering" does not qualify; hence order is involved. In contrast to the idle wandering of dreams and daydreams where the notion of a successful accomplishment is irrelevant, one can be successful or fail, be right or wrong in the imagining which involves both will and order on the one hand and a "picture" on the other. I may will to imagine a Sphinx or a unicorn or a Chimera. If I only succeed in picturing to myself a lion with a serpent's tail, a horse with a man's head and chest, a goat with a one-horned head, then I have not imagined what I wanted to imagine even though what I then picture to myself may

40 Note the parallel with remembering. Whether corporeal or intellectual, memory requires an act of will and to that extent involves more than mere nature. The contrast Descartes is here drawing between the two kinds of imagination places one in the realm of mere nature and assigns to the other the presence of the nonnatural faculty of will. Only the latter, therefore, will turn out to have its use in the development of science.

41 In article 26 of the *Passions* Descartes returns to these "imaginings" and relates them to what is "fortuitous." Its heading states: "The imaginings which depend solely on the fortuitous movement of the spirits may be passions just as truly as the perceptions which depend on the nerves."

42 And to the extent that the body is involved, the explanation of this kind of imagining is a mechanistic one. See, for example, *Passions*, article 43.

in each case very well be something I would not have imagined except for an act of will. If I picture to myself a lion with a man's head, a horse with a single horn, a goat with a lion's head and a serpent's tail, I have been successful in what I wanted to imagine. Both will and order played a role in this picturing.

Both these two kinds of imagination involve the body. When they occur they must therefore be designated as instances of corporeal imagination. If there are acts of the mind which involve both will and order but no "picturing," acts which ought to be classified as neither remembering nor understanding, then there is noncorporeal imagination.

In the *Passions* Descartes says nothing explicitly of this third category, but certainly does not rule it out. In articles 91 and 92, for example, he writes of the emotions of joy and sadness which, under certain circumstances, can be "purely intellectual." If, when focusing on conduct, one finds Descartes speaking about body-based as well as purely intellectual joy, then one should at the least not be surprised that when focusing on thought he would speak about both corporeal and intellectual imagination. But we must return to writings whose chief concern is the development of knowledge rather than the conduct of life, if we are to find material which will allow us to settle the issue of the existence and role of an intellectual imagination. We must turn to works like the *Regulae*.

With variations in language Descartes states the following doctrine at several points in the *Regulae*: "[W]hile it is the intellect alone that is capable of knowledge, it can be helped or hindered by three other faculties, *viz.* imagination, sense-perception, and memory."[43] Rule 12 tells us how the intellect can be helped as well as hindered by the imagination. The imagination can help when thought concerns corporeal entities: "If . . . the intellect proposes to examine something which can be referred to the body, the idea of that thing must be formed as distinctly as possible in the imagination" (AT 10:416–17; CSM 1:43). The intellect then does not "act on its own" but turns "to the imagination in order to form new figures" (AT 10:416; CSM 1:42). Examples would be Descartes's use of diagrams in the *Geometry*, *Optics*, and *Meteorology*. That a diagram should be used at a particular point is there determined by the intellect, which also dictates the particular nature of the diagram. The intellect then leads and uses the

[43]   AT 10:398; CSM 1:32. See also AT 10:395–96, 410, 415–16, and the corresponding passages in CSM 1:30, 39, 42–43. Sometimes Descartes's verdict on the body's usefulness to the intellect seems less generous, as in the statement quoted by Burman: "The body is always a hindrance to the mind in its thinking . . . " (AT 5:150; CSMK 3:336). But the context makes clear that Descartes here speaks of the body's *accidental* interference: "when we prick ourselves with . . . some sharp instrument: the effect is such that we cannot think of anything else." Such statements carry no implication for the mind's *purposeful* use of the body, in which case such use can be either a help or a hindrance.

imagination. If the imagination were to lead the intellect, the situation would be a-normative, for that is the case in which "in a sense one ceases to make use of one's reason."[44]

This imagination Descartes qualifies as "corporeal." It hinders the understanding when thought concerns purely intellectual things, that is, entities which cannot be pictured. Thus we read in a letter to Mersenne written during the period when Descartes had begun to compose his metaphysical meditations: "The imagination, which is the part of the mind that most helps mathematics, is more of a hindrance than a help in metaphysical speculation" (AT 2:622; CSMK 3:141).

In some of the places where Descartes cautions us about the use of this hampering power of corporeal imagination, there are hints about noncorporeal imagination. In a passage in which he first speaks of corporeal memory and corporeal imagination, Descartes continues as follows:

> So we can conclude with certainty that when the intellect is concerned with matters in which there is nothing corporeal or similar to the corporeal, it cannot receive any help from those faculties; on the contrary, if it is not to be hampered by them, the senses must be kept back and the imagination must, as far as possible, be divested of every distinct impression (AT 10:416; CSM 1:43).

Because the senses always necessarily involve the body, they "must be kept back." If the imagination were as exclusively bound up with the corporeal as the senses are, then it too would have to be "kept back." But Descartes makes a distinction here: where the senses must be kept back, not so the imagination—"as far as possible" it must "be divested of every distinct impression." This would seem to allow the inference that "when the intellect is concerned with matters in which there is nothing corporeal," then the imagination can still help (in fact, the intellect may well be unable to do without it), but the imagination then has to be "divested" of whatever is corporeal. As this divesting proceeds, the imagination is not at the same time done away with. And if the divesting can be total, then what remains would be the noncorporeal or intellectual imagination. We shall see in chapters 4 and 5 that it is this totally divested imagination which plays its role in metaphysics and in the pure sciences; it there helps the intellect by presenting it with hypotheses, and so fills a role which is necessary for developing systematic knowledge but which the intellect by itself is unable to play.

Descartes uses the phrases "corporeal imagination" and "corporeal

---

[44] This is Descartes's by now familiar complaint about the "ancient geometricians" at AT 10:375; CSM 1:18.

fancy," and, as I suggested earlier, the qualification "corporeal" is hardly necessary unless there is an implied contrast. When he uses the qualifier,[45] he often makes it quite clear that he refers to a "faculty" which is not entirely on the side of the intellect but which depends on the body. For example, in the letter to Mersenne (July 1641, AT 3:392–93; CSMK 3:185–86), we read that this "faculty" cannot imagine purely intellectual things, which, he adds, "is not surprising, because our imagination is capable of representing only objects of sense-perception."[46] In a letter to Guillaume Gibieuf Descartes states that this imagination, like sense perception, belongs to the soul only as it is joined to the body. If we consider the soul as apart from the body, then neither sense nor corporeal imagination plays a role: "I do not see any difficulty in understanding on the one hand that the faculties of imagination and sensation belong to the soul, because they are species of thoughts, and on the other hand that they belong to the soul only in so far as it is joined to the body, because they are kinds of thoughts without which one can conceive the soul in all its purity" (AT 3:479; CSMK 3:203).

The "soul in all its purity" is soul without any bodily admixture, soul without sense perception, without corporeal memory, without corporeal imagination. Soul entirely pure is mind entirely out of nature. As the Second Meditation states in its tenth paragraph, once "I am beginning to have a rather better understanding of what I am," I also begin to understand what it is that is "foreign to me," namely, "corporeal things of which images are framed by thought, and which the senses investigate." I begin to realize that only whatever "cannot be pictured in the [corporeal] imagination" can be aspects which pertain to my real nature, to "my own self." I begin to understand that "my own self" is as little a part of physi-

---

45   Although Descartes uses the qualifier frequently, he does not use it as often as the CSM translation would make one believe. The translators have, at points, added the qualifier for the sake of clarity (always, as far as I have determined, with complete justification). See CSM 1:41 ff., a stretch of text where the translators supply the qualifier but in which there are as well important passages where Descartes does so himself, as at AT 10:415; CSM 1:42. Here Descartes writes about animals that we must "merely grant them a purely corporeal imagination [*sed phantasia tantum pure corporea admittatur*]." And across the page he writes about memory and imagination as follows: "But memory is no different from imagination—at least the memory which is corporeal and similar to the one which animals possess [*memoria vero illa, saltem quae corporae est similis recordationi brutorum*]." There then follows the passage about the "imagination . . . divested of every distinct impression [*omni impressione distincta exuendam*]"—a passage thus occurring in the paragraph in which there is the clear indication of the existence of noncorporeal memory.

46   In this letter, the French for "imagination" in the phrase "depicted in the imagination" is *fantaisie*, a term which—as the editors of this letter helpfully indicate in a footnote at this point—"Descartes frequently uses to denote the part of the brain in which the physiological processes associated with imagining take place."

cal nature as is God's.[47] If there could be a depiction of God or of the soul, then God or the soul would be the kind of being that at least could exist in nature. They would then be like some objects of mathematics. I could have the idea of a triangle even if no triangular objects had ever existed in nature. But it would still be possible for triangular objects to exist in nature, and all the proof I need for this is that I can depict them in the imagination. In contrast, God and the soul are so wholly other from anything that might exist in nature that I cannot depict them if I try. The "soul in all its purity" is, in words familiar from the *Discourse,*

> a substance whose whole essence or nature is simply to think, and which does not require any place, or depend on any material thing, in order to exist. Accordingly this 'I'—that is, the soul by what I am what I am—is entirely distinct from the body, and would not fail to be whatever it is, even if the body did not exist. (AT 6:33; CSM 1:127)

Both God and the human "soul in all its purity" are entirely distinct from body. Neither, therefore, possesses corporeal imagination—a point which, with respect to God, Descartes found it necessary to emphasize for Hobbes: "God does not possess any corporal imagination" (AT 7:181; CSM 2:127).[48] In contrast, in the Fourth Meditation Descartes states explicitly that with respect to God he does not rule out a different form of imagination—hence necessarily a noncorporeal form:

> Similarly, if I examine the faculties of memory and imagination, or any others, I discover that in my case each one of these faculties is weak and limited, while in the case of God it is immeasurable [facultatem recordandi vel imaginandi . . . in Deo immensam]. (AT 7:57; CSM 2:40)

Given the point in the *Meditations* at which this statement about God and the human "I" occurs, it would be unreasonable to deny the implication that both God and "I" possess noncorporeal imagination.

For Descartes there is no progress unless there are developments in science, and since he ties progress to utility, for all practical purposes this means that there is no progress unless there are developments in the applied sciences of mechanics, medicine, and morals. But no applied sci-

---

[47] See here as well Descartes's replies to Hobbes' fifth and seventh objections at AT 7:181–83; CSM 2:126–29.

[48] In the introduction to his *Descartes's Imagination,* Sepper takes this passage to limit imagination in God beyond what Descartes intended: "Ideas are like the forms of God's imaginings, if God had imaginings—which of course he doesn't!" (8). But this holds only for *phantasia,* not for the *facultatem imaginandi.*

ences can develop except on the purely "rational foundation" of meta-physics and pure physics. And no such rational foundation can be con-structed unless mind be taken as distinct and separate from nature. Hence the further reenforcement of my earlier statement: for Descartes, his dual-ism is a necessary condition for the possibility of science.

We are now in the better position of a less speculative mode to see some of the details pertaining to one of the poles of this dualism—details them-selves required for and hence not unlikely shaped by the desire for progress in (and through) science. The mind as separate from nature is characterized not just by freedom ("the action of the will") and by the powers of intuition and deduction ("the perception of the intellect"), but also by the powers of an intellectual memory and intellectual imagina-tion. That it possesses intellectual memory is clear enough from Descartes's explicit statements.That there is intellectual imagination is more difficult to establish from what Descartes in fact says about imagi-nation. All I have attempted in this section is to establish intellectual imagination as not just compatible with what Descartes wrote but implicit in some of his statements. The following three chapters will demonstrate that, although he did not use the phrase "intellectual imagination," Descartes constantly and consciously used the power which this phrase might have named. We must now turn to Descartes's practice as a philosopher and scientist to observe the uses he makes of all the powers of the mind, of intellect, sense perception, memory, and imagination. Because the existence of intellectual imagination may still be considered as problematic, and because of my claim that it is crucial for Descartes's developing science, I shall focus on it first.

3

A "Logic of Discovery"

1. THE "METHOD OF REASONING"

The phrase "logic of discovery" entered philosophical discourse relatively recently. Descartes had much to say about that to which the phrase for us refers, about the process necessary for making discoveries in the sciences, particularly (for Descartes) in metaphysics, mathematics, or pure physics, and the applied sciences—mechanics, medicine, and morals—based on them.

For some contemporary theorists it is at best problematic to say that there is a logic of discovery, that there is room for philosophical discussion of the area of reasoning which concerns the construction or leads to the selection of hypotheses, models, and experiments. Descartes's writings make it quite clear that he did believe there to be such an area of investigation. His description of the method is in fact a functional definition of reason; and all he wrote about method may be taken as discussion of the logic of discovery.[1] It is an account of how reason goes about its business in its pursuit of truth, aided in this quest by sensation, imagination, and memory (the latter two both corporeal and intellectual). It is these aids which allow the formation of hypotheses and their confirmation or falsification through the construction of diagrams, models, and experiments.

An extensive discussion of both reason and its aids would broaden the topic beyond my intentions. I will restrict myself as much as possible to reason's aids, and to their role in the activities of hypothesis formation and the construction of diagrams, models, and experiments. A further restriction is that I will give greatest attention to hypothesis formation, for it

---

[1] When some contemporary theorists identify methodology and logic of discovery, they usually take "methodology" in a far more restricted sense than did Descartes. Rather than referring to reasoning about anything whatsoever, it then tends to refer to limited aspects of scientific reasoning only. This is how it is used, for example, by Clark Glymour and Kevin Kelly in "Thoroughly Modern Meno" ("Methodology amounts to recommendations restricting procedures of inquiry"), in *Inference, Explanation, and Other Frustrations in the Philosophy of Science*, ed. J. Earnan (Berkeley, 1992), 14.

is here that the role of noncorporeal imagination comes most to the fore—
and it is this activity and form of imagination which have been most neglected by commentators and which nevertheless offer valuable insights
into Descartes's procedure as he develops his metaphysics and pure
physics. Method as the functional definition of reason will, then, enter
only to the extent that discussion of the aids to reason requires it.[2]

A good deal of what Descartes had to say about the logic of discovery
we find explicitly in his *Discourse on the Method* and implicitly in the
"Essays in this Method" appended to it. In the latter he "deduced many
specific results which illustrate the method of reasoning which I employ"
(AT 7:602; CSM 2:397); in the former he "discussed" the nature of this "deductive" "method of reasoning." About the relation between this implicit
and explicit presence Descartes writes to Mersenne:

> . . . I have not been able to understand your objection to the title; for I have
> not put *Treatise on the Method* but *Discourse on the Method*, in order to show that
> I do not intend to teach the method but only to discuss it. As can be seen from
> what I say, it is concerned more with practice than with theory. I call the fol-
> lowing treatises *Essays in this Method* because I claim that what they contain
> could never have been discovered without it, so that they show how much it
> is worth. I have also inserted a certain amount of metaphysics, physics and
> medicine in the opening *Discourse* in order to show that my method extends
> to topics of all kinds. (27 February 1637. AT 1:349; CSMK 3:53)

Descartes's discussion of a deductive method of reasoning is a treatment of that without which *no discoveries can be made in the sciences*. The
philosophy, physics, and medicine inserted in the *Discourse*, as well as the
essays on optics, meteorology, and geometry appended to it, are exercises
or "practice" in this method. But they are not "practice" in what already
existed in these disciplines (as one might, for example, instruct a beginner
in geometry to gain proficiency through exercise in Euclid's theorems),
for Descartes's "practice" resulted in new developments in these sciences.
In some cases the results were profoundly new. In philosophy, it began
the tradition in which the starting point and sure foundation is taken to lie
within the consciousness of the thinker, and in geometry it put the subdis-
cipline of analytic geometry on the map of the sciences.

Descartes believed that, had his method not been applied to these topics, there still would have been no science properly so called of any of

---

[2] I have provided an extensive discussion of method as the functional definition of reason in *The Imposition of Method: A Study of Descartes and Locke* (Oxford, 1980). Although the
following two parts of this chapter borrow from that discussion, I have kept overlap as
minimal as is consonant with providing the proper context for the discussion of reason's
aids. My borrowing is from *Imposition*'s chapter 1, section 3, and chapter three, section 4.

them. Without the method, "practice" in the *Discourse* and its essays would have been different from what it in fact is and could not have led to the particular results achieved: "what they contain *could never have been discovered without it.*"

If in some cases of its application Descartes's method led to new results, then that is one ground for taking the method seriously. But to prevent misunderstanding, a cautionary note is in order. It is one thing to say that, for example, what the *Geometry* and the *Meditations* contain could not have been discovered without the method. But it is another thing to say that the method is the one and only right method. Yet if one takes this method as the functional definition of reason, then it would make sense to hold that it is meant to be applied to any area where we can expect to find knowledge and develop science. Thus Descartes intends his method to be necessary if one wants to get valid results in any area where we can achieve systematic knowledge. However, Newton's physics differs from Descartes's physics, and a good case might be made for the statement that this is in part because Newton's method differed from Descartes's method. Locke's political theory differs from that of Aristotle, and, again, a similar statement may be made about their respective methods. This is not the place to reargue the point which I developed in *The Imposition of Method*, that one's methodological stance structures one's theory about the subject matter to which it is applied and even to an extent that subject matter itself. But if that argument is correct, then different methods applied to physical nature would result in different physics, and applied to politics would lead to development of different political theories (which, once enacted, produce different political states). To speak of method univocally is hardly legitimate, for some methods are reductionistic (and Descartes's is among these), while others tend toward holism; and there are nuances in between which allow for a vivid spectrum of methodologies often differing depending on the subject matter to which they are applied.

This having been said, the method being discussed in my study is the method Descartes takes to be necessary if one wants to make discoveries in the sciences, whatever their subject matter. The relevant point now is that for Descartes, therefore, there is room for philosophical discussion of how hypotheses are formed and rejected or validated, how diagrams, models, and experiments are constructed and used. In this chapter, I shall focus on parts of the description of this logic of scientific discovery; one of the features of each of the following two chapters is the illustration of Descartes's logic from his practice.

Before I turn to Descartes's description of his logic of discovery, there are two preliminary matters to be discussed. The *first* concerns the relation between Descartes's "early" and "mature" writings, an issue which is important because I have so far referred to Descartes's method, or

Descartes's logic of discovery, as if, from earliest to latest writings, there is *one* method and hence a *single* logic of discovery. The issue is not that of the difference between the two methods to which Descartes himself draws our attention, the method of exposition and the method of discovery—a difference which I will highlight later in this section as *the second* of the preliminary matters. Instead, it concerns the question whether there was any change in methodology from the *Early Writings* (whose internal evidence indicates they were composed during 1619–22) to the *Regulae* (generally assumed to have been written in 1628), the *Discourse* with its appended essays (published in 1637), and the *Meditations* (1641). In the preceding chapter there were several references to the *Regulae*, and I intend to continue to draw on that work in both this and the fifth chapter— a practice less than helpful unless this question about methodology allows for an answer which encourages or at the least permits such a use.

The *Early Writings* are too brief and too allusive to allow for anything like even the contours of a complete methodology. They offer, nevertheless, some intriguing statements which would seem to indicate methodological commitments of a kind which are apparently absent from the *Discourse* and *Meditations*. It would seem that a two-decade interval occasioned considerable change in doctrine. If that is so, it may become problematic to draw on the *Regulae* as I have done so far, as if there is no (substantial) change in doctrine from the *Regulae* to the *Discourse*. Composed at the midpoint of these two intervening decades, the *Regulae* may present a change in doctrine that was complete near the end of the first decade; on the other hand, the change might not yet have begun or might have been in mid-process. Hence the *Regulae* is possibly either an "early writing" or a transitional work as far as its methodology is concerned.

First, what do the *Early Writings* tell us about the young Descartes's methodological leanings?[3] Presumably because of its insubstantial nature, commentators have tended to neglect this text in their discussion of Cartesian methodology. The two important recent exceptions, Veronique Foti and Dennis Sepper,[4] relate these writings to Descartes's later work especially in terms of the changing role of imagination. Introduction of Foti's and Sepper's contributions pays double dividends. It helps me to

---

[3]   I refer to the *Early Writings* because it is the only material from this period extracts from which are easily accessible in translation presented in CSM (1:2–5; in AT these are in 10:213–19). Equally relevant, though not substantially different in doctrine on the matters of interest for my study, is the *Compendium Musicae*, the treatise on music written during 1618 (see AT 10:79–141). When, in a moment, we see Sepper make a claim more extreme than that of Foti for the cognitive power of imagination in these early texts, the legitimacy of this stronger claim lies in the *Compendium Musicae*. Since the difference involved is one of degree rather than of kind, it may be safely ignored in the sequel.

[4]   For Foti, see chapter 2, note 1, above.

work toward an answer to the question about methodological continuity or discontinuity, and it provides a platform of the most recent discussions about imagination from which to attempt to pass beyond them.

Both Foti and Sepper draw attention to the *Early Writings'* passage at AT 10:217; CSM 1:4:

> It may seem surprising to find weighty judgments in the writings of the poets rather than the philosophers. The reason is that the poets were driven to write by enthusiasm and the force of imagination. We have within us the sparks of knowledge [*semina scientiae*], as in a flint: philosophers extract them through reason, but poets force them out through the sharp blows of the imagination, so that they shine more brightly.

Foti comments that in the *Early Writings* "There is no indication, in this or other passages, of any tension between reason and imagination; rather they share a common task," that of "bringing to bloom the 'seeds of science' which lie dormant in the human mind."[5] Sepper goes a step beyond Foti, shifting the burden of the philosopher's task from reason to imagination: for "the young Descartes imagination was the most comprehensive power of the mind, virtually equivalent to mind itself," so that "imagination was not an incidental concern but rather the focus" of his "early" philosophy.[6] I need not belabor that Foti and Sepper are correct in holding that in the mature works it is reason, not imagination, which has the final word—a situation which is certainly different in the *Early Writings*.

How does the *Regulae* fit into this picture? My answer to this question is threefold. First, in the *Regulae* there is no priority of imagination over reason, or equivalence between the two, in determining truth. Second, imagination continues to play a crucial role in the development of science. Third, this role is not importantly different when we move from the *Regulae* to the *Discourse* and *Meditations*. This answer agrees with those of Foti and Sepper in that it does not locate the *Regulae*'s doctrine on the side of early thought; it differs from theirs in that, *to the extent that it concerns methodology*, I take the *Regulae* in most respects not to be a transition phase between early and mature doctrine. My answer, in short, is that the *Regulae* substantially expresses Descartes's mature methodological position. The parting of ways here with Foti and Sepper is in part motivated by the following considerations about their respective positions.

Foti contrasts the imagination of the *Early Writings* and that of the *Regulae*. In the latter, "it lacks spontaneity," since it is now "either bound

[5] Foti, 632.
[6] Sepper, "Imagination, Phantasms, and the Making of Hobbesian and Cartesian Science," in *Monist* 71 [1988]: 526.

to sense or controlled by the intellect"; the spontaneity and creativity formerly characteristic of imagination have now been allocated to the intellect.[7] However, the shift Foti here flags follows only if we take "imagination" to have a univocal sense. If we allow for the possibility of a corporeal and an intellectual imagination, there is still a shift, but it is different from the one Foti signals. Since we have seen that it is in the *Regulae* that Descartes begins to qualify "imagination" as corporeal in certain instances, it becomes at least problematic to take "imagination" univocally, as Foti here does. In addition to that which makes reason (rather than reason equally with imagination) the determiner of truth, what shift is there if we do not take "imagination" in a univocal sense? It is a shift involving a development of terminology indicating a bifurcation of "imagination" which makes it possible for Descartes to assign to corporeal imagination the role Foti assigns to imagination unqualified. The fact that corporeal imagination is both "bound to sense" and "controlled by the intellect" will then turn out to become crucially important rather than a negative feature, for it will allow the transition from pure science to physical reality, hence making thought *useful*. The negative feature of loss of spontaneity is not really a loss to imagination, for the mental function which now exhibits this spontaneity and creativity is the intellectual imagination. There is, then, a change in doctrine from the *Early Writings* to the *Regulae* which includes introduction of a dual meaning of "imagination," reflecting its two functions. This duality makes possible crucial moves which reason alone cannot perform: through intellectual imagination the move from imaginative assumption to rational intellectual certainty, and through corporeal imagination the move from rational intellectual certainty to imaged presence, hence physical possibility.[8]

Without the admission of a richer, dual function of imagination in the *Regulae*, Foti is forced into difficulties in her reading of later works. The progression from the *Early Writings* through the *Regulae* to the *Discourse* and *Meditations* becomes, for Foti, one in which there is an ever-decreasing legitimate role for the imagination. At times, she indicates uneasiness about this interpretation and allows that, given the nature of the *Meditations'* argument, it appears to involve a "paradox." The imagination plays a lesser role in the *Discourse* and *Meditations* because the "chief focus" is now on "imagination as the fabricator of dreams which threatens to subvert the certainty of knowledge." She adds that "In order to set reason apart from this 'mode of thought especially adapted to material things' and to defend the claims of reason against illusion," there is "the severance of reason from imagination.⁹" Foti ascribes all this negativity to imagination unqualified, where it should in fact be ascribed to only one form of imagination, namely, its corporeal expression (her quotation from the *Meditations* indicates as much, for it is about the "mode of thought especially adapted to material things"). And even in the *Discourse* and *Meditations* there is more than this negative note about corporeal imagination; for in both it remains unsevered from reason in order to allow development of certain knowledge about physical reality. In these works, there remains a crucial role for intellectual imagination as well—a role at which Foti hints when she says that in order to safeguard reason against imagination Descartes "must resort to a strategy (perfected in the *Meditationes*) which, paradoxically, gives imagination free rein so that it may be brought up against its limits." These limits are, presumably, encountered in the imagination's activity as "fabricator of dreams" and hence subverter of "the certainty of knowledge." The reference to "free rein" appears to reintroduce the imagination's creativity and spontaneity. As my next chapter will show, provided we do not read "imagination" univocally, this involves no "paradox" or retrogression in doctrine.¹⁰

Finally, I agree with Foti that in the *Regulae* it is "the imagination, not the intellect, which possesses" the "*ideae corporeae*"; "and since imagination is the power of summoning such ideas, it is imagination, with its obscure links to bodily nature, rather than the self-disclosed intellect which represents reality."¹¹ I agree, but only with the proviso that the imagination be here qualified as "corporeal." I then disagree with Foti's next sentence: "Representation is not, as yet, centered within the *cogito* of the subject." The contrast here drawn between the *Regulae* on the one hand and the *Discourse* and *Meditations* on the other is, I believe, nonexistent and finds its ground in allowing only a univocal reading of "imagination." The corporeal imagination's power, assigned to it in the *Regulae*, which enables it to form and possess ideas of a (potentially) corporeal world, is a power it retains after the appearance of the cogito in both the *Discourse*

⁹ Foti, 637.
¹⁰ In a footnote Foti comes close to ascribing this duality to "imagination" in the *Discourse* and *Meditations*: "It is noteworthy that, although a hidden and deceiving productive imagination would bring about a state of unfreedom, imagination (directed and productive) also allows one to formulate the fictive hypotheses which serve to shed doubt on truths so evident that reason cannot attend to them without spontaneous conviction. The bondage possibly worked by a concealed imagination can thus only be undone with the help of imagination" (638 n. 27). The matter of "fictive hypotheses" will receive considerable attention in my two following chapters; that of "bondage" will be part of the discussion in chapter 6.
¹¹ Foti, 635.

and *Meditations*. In the *Discourse*'s *Geometry*, for example, corporeal imagination plays exactly this role as articulated in the *Regulae*. And in neither
Discourse nor *Meditations* does "representation" become "centered within
the *cogito* of the subject" to the extent that this representation is of (possible) corporeal reality. For that, corporeal imagination remains crucial,
since the intellect as pure thought is incapable of it. So, "within the *cogito*
of the subject" there will be a "representation of reality," but it is of a reality concerning the realm of thought rather than that of matter.

In his first of three articles on Descartes and imagination,[12] Sepper
agrees with Foti that imagination plays an increasingly insignificant role
as Descartes's position develops. As in the case of Foti, I concur with
Sepper that this holds for the relationship between the *Early Writings*
and the *Regulae* but disagree that this is so for the latter in its relation to
the *Discourse* and *Meditations*.[13] And there remain pivotal roles for imagination in the *Regulae*, roles which it continues to play in Descartes's account of the development of science in the *Discourse* and in his practice
as a scientist both in the appendices to the *Discourse* and in the
Meditations.[14]

In his second article Sepper's most important point for now is that "we
must abandon the assumption that the method of the *Regulae* is virtually
that of the *Discourse*" and later works, one reason for this judgment being
that "the *Discourse* and the rest . . . operate with the intention of determining what is really existent, whereas the *Regulae* takes as a given the reality

---

[12]   These appeared in 1988, 1989, 1992; I shall deal with them in the order of their appearance. As Sepper's probing of the early Descartes's thinking gains depth, he becomes less
certain about the break in doctrine as far as it concerns imagination's function in Cartesian
method from *Regulae* to *Discourse*. At this point I will leave Sepper's *Descartes's Imagination*
in abeyance because it does not provide insight beyond that of his articles into the matter
here at issue.
[13]   Sepper, "Imagination, Phantasms," especially 536 ff. Although I disagree with
Sepper's view about the kind of downgrading that occurred with respect to imagination, I
agree that certain aspects of earlier doctrines involving imagination were abandoned after
the *Regulae*, among them the *Regulae*'s psychophysiological picture in which the *phantasia*
receives an imprint of sense objects from the external sense organs as wax receives im-
prints from a seal—an imprint of which the cognitive power could then achieve intellectual awareness.
[14]   My position and that of Sepper are in fact closer than some of his statements would
seem to indicate, for he too allows that there remain "essential" roles for imagination in
both Descartes's metaphysics and geometry. The place to draw attention to the specifics on
which there is agreement rather than disagreement will be in the following two chapters.
In the meantime, it is of interest to observe that Sepper's awareness of the fact that one of
these "essential" roles involves a nonimaging and the other an imaging imagination (see
"Imagination, Phantasms, 536 and n. 38) would seem to indicate that he is on the way toward the distinction between intellectual and corporeal imagination. We shall see that in
the last of these articles he actually uses the phrase "intellectual imagination" and distin-
guishes it from "corporeal imagination."

of the images and leaves to the physicist the question whether there is a real basis for them."[15] But this change in Descartes's doctrine is not of a methodological nature, at least not in the sense in which Descartes uses "method." This change concerns the status of the image of corporeal imagination. It raises the question: Is there an extramental reality (at least in some ways) exactly corresponding to an image I have? In the *Regulae*, given its physiology in which the wax-and-seal simile is to be taken in a near-literal sense, this question does not arise. Once Descartes abandons this physiological dogma, the question of correspondence of image and object becomes important; then sensation and experimentation come to play their crucial role. However, sensation enters the scene only once the scientific doctrine is already (at least partially) in place as a contribution to pure science. And this scientific doctrine could have come into being only through methodic procedure. Has Sepper provided good evidence that this methodic procedure differs from the *Regulae* to the *Discourse*? For an answer we need to consider his third article.

In it, hesitantly, Sepper comes to see the *Regulae* as a "halfway house" later abandoned.[16] Various statements reveal that he is not fully committed to this position: "[T]he early framework, shaped by the primacy of imagination, was not so much rejected as transformed in Descartes' mature work"; and "It almost seems that the *Regulae* has in fact achieved the perspective of the later Descartes. . . . There is much to be said for this, but I prefer to see the *Regulae* as a halfway house."[17] What, according to Sepper, is it in the *Regulae* which makes it seem an expression of mature Cartesian thought, and what is it which prevents it from being that for him? Answering these questions requires that we relate Sepper's views on the doctrine of the *Early Writings* to the *Regulae* and the *Discourse*.

In the *Early Writings* Sepper finds two kinds of imagination at work, which he labels "lower" or "corporeal imagination" and "higher" or "intellectual" or "spiritual imagination."[18] The poetic imagination which strikes forth truth as sparks from flint he identifies as an instance of intellectual imagination. It appears that Sepper conceives of it as I do, that is, as imageless imagination, for there is another passage from the

---

[15] *"Descartes and the Eclipse of Imagination,"* 386–87. Sepper elucidates this comment by adding that "the realm in which the *Regulae* operates corresponds to that of the so-called objective reality of ideas in the third meditation, where . . . our ideas seem to refer to something external but nevertheless can be considered without any immediate intention of determining whether they have an external existence."

[16] *"Ingenium,"* 153, 154.

[17] Ibid., 142, 154.

[18] Ibid., 143–45.

Early Writings to which he connects these two forms of imagination, a passage which then leads him to a discussion of the methodology of the *Regulae*:

> The things which are perceivable by the senses are helpful in enabling us to conceive of Olympian matters. The wind signifies spirit; movement with the passage of time signifies life; light signifies knowledge; heat signifies love; and instantaneous activity signifies creation. (AT 10:218, CSM 1:5)

This passage is an illustration given in the preamble to the statement which juxtaposes poets and philosophers, imagination and reason:

> Just as the imagination employs figures in order to conceive of bodies, so, in order to frame ideas of spiritual things, the intellect makes use of certain bodies which are perceived through the senses, such as wind and light. By this means we may philosophize in a more exalted way, and develop the knowledge to raise our minds to lofty heights. (AT 10:217; CSM 1:4)

Sepper identifies intellectual imagination with the intellect which, through making use of things perceived through the senses (such as wind, movement, light, heat), conceives of higher things (such as spirit, life, knowledge, love). Whereas the lower things are picturable, these higher things are not. Hence, although he does not say so explicitly, it would seem that Sepper is here contrasting an imaging to a nonimaging imagination.[19] This is important for connections which may be made at this point with the *Regulae*. Since (adopting words Sepper uses at this point) "intellectual imagination is constituted to use corporeal things to conceive things of the spirit," and since science in the *Regulae* depends on knowing the "order" or "measure" (that is, certain intellectual relationships) which holds within, between, and among things corporeally imaginable, intellectual imagination may well turn out to play a crucial role in the *Regulae*'s prescriptions for developing science. Although there are hints that Sepper will be following this path,[20] in the end he balks at it and takes a different direction. I discern three reasons for this refusal. The first is that in his reading of the *Regulae* he does not exploit his in-

---

[19] This introduces intellectual imagination on tenuous grounds. Why should it be intellectual *imagination*—rather than just the intellect—which conceives notions like "spirit," "life," "knowledge," "love"? Stronger grounds are intimated a page earlier in Sepper's text when he writes about the imagination's prominent role "in the physical and mathematical writings of the early 1620s," where it "visualizes," "conceives," and "postulates." The difference between the first and last of these activities could have been explicated to give clear grounds for Descartes's nonunivocal use of "imagination."
[20] As in *"Ingenium,"* 145: "[I]ntellectual imagination is . . . fundamental to all disciplinary knowing."

sight expressed in the terminology of "corporeal" and "intellectual" imagination. Second, he fails to clarify the distinction between "intellectual imagination" and "intellect." This failure probably causes him not to exploit his insight concerning the nonunivocal notion of "imagination" and, third, keeps him from taking seriously Descartes's statements in the *Regulae* concerning the strict dichotomy of *res extensa* and *res cogitans*. Sepper recognizes this dichotomy as crucial to Descartes's mature thought,[21] so that his assertion of its absence in the *Regulae* reduces the latter to a transitional work for him.

Because Descartes's mature doctrine involves this strict dichotomy, the intellect is necessarily dependent on other functions for it to achieve useful knowledge. For example, it needs intellectual imagination to advance hypotheses, and corporeal imagination to determine whether scientific doctrines developed through the use of hypotheses are about a possibly existing world. Descartes clearly introduces this dichotomy in the *Regulae*, and Sepper's dismissal of it rests on implausible grounds.[22] Restoration of this dichotomy to the *Regulae*, coupled with Sepper's recognition that, in this work, Descartes holds that the intellect needs to be paired with other human abilities if we are to develop "a comprehensive and universal method for knowing," would remove the first four words from his sentence "It almost seems that the *Regulae* has in fact achieved the perspective of the later Descartes."[23]

There is one further ground for my belief that the *Regulae* has achieved this later perspective. It concerns its date of composition. Descartes (as Sepper notes)[24] continued to work on the *Regulae* until 1629, which was the year in which he began writing *The World*. In the latter work, the imagination functions much as in the former. Passages which indicate as much Descartes incorporated in the *Discourse*'s part 5 (e.g., AT 6:42; CSM 1:132) with the rest of that work's theory. In addition, a strong case has been made that Descartes wrote parts of the *Regulae*'s rule 4 while he was pre-

---

[21] "In . . . the mature philosophy of Descartes . . . the *res extensa* is radically distinguished from the *res cogitans* . . . " (*"Ingenium,"* 157).

[22] Sepper's introduction of the dichotomy, and its ejection from the *Regulae*, occurs in *"Ingenium,"* 154–55: "True, Descartes makes a sharp distinction between the knowing power and the body, but the analogy he uses ('this power through which we properly know things is no less distinct from the whole body than the blood is from the bone, or the hand from the eye') suggests that this is something less than the full-blown real distinction between *res cogitans* and *res extensa.*" Why should it—or how *could* it—suggest "something less," given Descartes's words that the intellect of the *Regulae* is "distinct from the whole body"? When Sepper relates this statement to "a very similar locution in the sixth set of replies to objections against the *Meditations*," he is now bound to deny that this similarity does "establish that the *Regulae* passage belongs to the later conceptual framework" (see 161 n. 31).

[23] *"Ingenium,"* 154.

[24] Ibid., 157 n. 1. For further similarities which Sepper registers (but finds puzzling) between the *Regulae* and *The World*, see page 153 of this article.

occupied with the argument of his *Meditations*.[25] Descartes would hardly have incorporated, or added to, earlier doctrine at a later ("mature") date if he had given up on (substantial parts of) that earlier doctrine.

The upshot is that there exists at the very least sufficient continuity between the doctrine of the *Regulae* and that of the *Discourse*, and between this doctrine and its implementation in the metaphysics of the *Meditations* and the pure physics of the essays appended to the *Discourse*, for me to have drawn on the *Regulae* as I did in my second chapter. Moreover, my continued use of the *Regulae* in the following sections of this chapter, as well as in chapter 5, will be found to be sufficiently illuminating to establish its validity. In my belief that, in addition to differences, there is this strong continuity, I am hardly alone.[26] That it is a continuity in which two forms of imagination occupy important positions will be clearer from the

[25] See Frederick Van De Pitte's "The Dating of Rule IV-B in Descartes' *Regulae ad directionem ingenii*," *Journal of the History of Philosophy* 29 no. 3 (1991): 375–95. David Rapport Lachterman's *The Ethics of Geometry: A Genealogy of Modernity* (New York, 1989), 174 and esp. 230–31 n. 120 provides support for Van De Pitte's dating and introduces several additional grounds for it. In "Whatever Should We Do with Cartesian Method?—Reclaiming Descartes for the History of Science" (in Voss, 195–223), John Schuster writes that rule IV-B probably "predates the surrounding text of the *Regulae*" (214); but this dissenting voice provides no grounds for its opinion.

[26] To mention just one recent commentator, Evert van Leeuwen writes that "In many respects the *Discourse on Method* contains the outline of modern philosophy. Only in the last seventy years has it become clear that the Cartesian method has an even richer source in the *Regulae*." (See van Leeuwen's "Method, Discourse, and the Act of Knowing" in Voss, 224. See as well pages 227, 228, 240 n. 17). In the same collection there is Daniel Garber's dissenting voice: "Descartes . . . gave up his famous method sometime in the late 1630s or early 1640s, and so I do not want to identify the question of Descartes's scientific procedure with that of his method" ("Descartes and Experiment in the *Discourse* and *Essays*," 288–89). For "a full defense of this view" Garber refers us to his *Descartes' Metaphysical Physics* (Chicago, 1992), chap. 2. But this "full defense" is far from convincing. In it, Descartes's *Discourse* is pronounced to be "a work that reflects a philosophical conception of scientific inquiry that had ceased to fit his actual practice for at least five or six years" (49). Furthermore, when, in the *Meditations*, Descartes "became a system-builder, it is not surprising that the method, central to his earlier thought, would become obsolete," for "to make use of the method, we must first set a specific question for ourselves" (50). Finally, when, in the 1647 preface to the *Principles of Philosophy*, Descartes recommends practicing the method on questions simpler than those of the *Principles*, this is to be taken as an indication that the method is now given "roughly the status of the provisional morality" (48). None of these are convincing arguments. Descartes was too astute and coherent a thinker to advocate a practice which he had abandoned years before. Moreover, the *Meditations* most certainly set a very specific question—as the reading in my first chapter, to be reinforced by that of the closing chapter, indicates well enough. And, last, with the method as a functional definition of reason, its practice in matters simpler than those of the *Principles* would be a necessary requirement for those who want to understand and then continue the *Principles'* sort of work: in order "to discover truths that one does not know," it is necessary that one "conduct his reason well"—and only exercise in simpler problems produces the right mental "habitudes" for such work (a point Descartes consistently maintains from the early *Regulae* to the late preface to the *Principles*). Apart from this issue, there is considerable agreement between Garber and my earlier stated (and here in part reiter-

next sections of this chapter, as well as from the following two chapters. Before we turn to them, there is, however, the *second* of the two preliminaries, that concerning Descartes's mention of two methods.

These two methods are the method of exposition and the method of discovery. It is the latter which is necessary for the very possibility of science. The method of discovery has two aspects.

First, there is what Descartes variously identifies as "analysis," "reduction," "resolution," or "division"; this is the deriving and isolating from one another of "simple entities" which are knowable per se and thus understood intuitively or nondiscursively. Knowledge of these isolated simple entities is not, for Descartes, "scientific" knowledge but only knowledge of the necessary foundations or "first principles" of science (see, e.g., AT 7:140; CSM 2:100). "Science," for Descartes, is systematic knowledge developed through a process he calls "synthesis," "composition," or "combination." It is the second aspect of the Cartesian method necessary for the extension of knowledge, for the development of science.

Descartes uses the terms "analysis" and "synthesis" in his discussions of method. But since the term "method" itself is not univocal for him, this makes for a difference in connotation of "analytic" and "synthetic" depending on the particular meaning of "method."

To convey the results of one's thinking to others one can, says Descartes, use either the analytic or the synthetic method. When he speaks this way (as in the Second Set of Objections and Replies, AT 7:155–56; CSM 2:110–11), Descartes considers both as *methods of exposition*. He himself uses the former as the method of exposition in the *Meditations*. It involves, first, resolution or analysis to "simples" or truths known per se and, second, (re)composition or synthesis to intelligible complexity. He explicitly tells us that he is using this method when, in the dedication of the *Meditations*, he relates that he

> was strongly pressed to undertake this task [of writing these meditations] by several people who knew that I had developed a method for resolving certain difficulties in the sciences [*excoluisse Methodum ad quaslibet difficultates in scientiis resolvendas*]—not a new method (for nothing is older than the truth), but one which they had seen me use with some success in other areas; and I therefore thought it my duty to make some attempt to apply it to the matter in hand. (AT 7:3; CSM 2:4)

Of the synthetic method of exposition Descartes gives an illustration in the appendix to his Second Set of Objections and Replies (AT 7:160–70; CSM 2:113–20), where he presents the *Meditations'* arguments "arranged

---

ated) position; compare, for example, Garber's "Descartes and Experiment," 301–5, with my *Imposition of Method*, chap. 3, section 4.

in geometrical fashion." As in traditional geometry, the starting points for the arguments consist of definitions, postulates, and axioms; and as in traditional geometry, it is not shown how one obtains these starting points. Since the synthetic method does not show how the starting points are obtained, that is, since the synthetic method of exposition omits the process of resolution to "simples" or truths known per se, it is not really suitable for philosophic or scientific exposition. This is clear enough when one recognizes that there is no cogito statement in these "arguments . . . arranged in geometrical fashion"; hence one has not made one's way to an "Archimedean point" which can serve as fully understood starting point, as lasting foundation, for composition.

In contrast to the synthetic method of exposition, the analytic method of exposition includes both analysis and synthesis. It is therefore the proper one to use in philosophy and the sciences, and this not just in their exposition but also in their development, for it is this analytic method which is, in addition, the method of discovery. This is because it incorporates the two fundamental aspects of reason's procedure: analysis (resolving complex items to their simpler or simplest clear and distinct constituents) and synthesis (combining the results of analysis into intelligible complex wholes). Since the analytic method is the method of discovery, it will be the one of interest to us. And since I am especially concerned with the *development* of—as distinct from reaching the foundations for—science, my main focus in this chapter will be on that aspect of the analytic method variously called deduction, composition, or synthesis. More specifically, it will be on deduction and the role of reason's aids (particularly imagination) in making discoveries in the sciences.

2. Deduction and Imagination

Deduction consists in a "train of reasoning," and "in all reasoning it is only by means of comparison that we attain exact knowledge of the truth." For we must "think of all knowledge whatever—save knowledge obtained through simple and pure intuition of a single, solitary thing—as resulting from a comparison between two or more things" (AT 10:439–40; CSM 1:57). The question is: Assuming that one knows one of the "two or more things" to be compared with another, how does one obtain the relevant other thing(s)? This is the question in the logic of discovery which Descartes took as crucially important: "In fact the business of human reason consists almost entirely in preparing for this operation" of "comparing" "two or more things." He adds that "when the operation is straightforward and simple" (as it is when one recognizes that there is an immediate logical implication between thought and existence, or between thinking and entertaining ideas), then "we have no need of a technique to help us intuit the truth which the comparison yields; all we need is the light of nature" (ibid.). Deductive thought is not that of recognizing immediate logical relations. It therefore requires "a technique," an aid to "the light of nature." This help comes from memory, imagination, and sense.

Except for a comment near the end of this section, I shall not deal with sensation in the following pages because it comes to play this role of helper only once the foundations for medicine, mechanics, and morals have been provided in metaphysics and geometry. I shall focus on the role of the imagination in these foundational sciences and shall have opportunity in passing to indicate the role of memory. Since I will be dealing with the role of imagination in the *foundational* sciences, the imagination in question is in the first place the intellectual imagination. I say, "in the first place" because, even in the foundational science of geometry, corporeal imagination plays an important role in that it provides the link between that foundation and the applied sciences. In brief, the relations between the various sciences and reason with its various aids—for the moment disregarding the role of memory because we know that Descartes takes it not to be a "source" of knowledge—may be put as follows. In metaphysics (as in, e.g., the first five of the *Meditations*), reason and intellectual imagination give the foundation for geometry or pure physics. In the *Geometry* reason and intellectual imagination develop pure physics, and corporeal imagination then enters to determine which parts of the theory developed are potentially about the world in which we live—that is, corporeal imagination provides the link between pure and applied science in that it determines the extent to which geometry can be foundational for mechanics, medicine, and morals. Finally, in the applied sciences, reason uses all its aids to achieve the power-giving knowledge which is to allow for mastery over nature.

I shall not attempt to demonstrate any of these relationships in this section; such discussions will form parts of various sections of the next two chapters. Neither shall I argue for the statement that the imagination used in deduction at this stage is intellectual imagination. I intend to make the latter statement convincing beginning with the last part of this chapter and, more so, in the following chapter when I deal with the "practice" rather than the "discussion" of developing science. My reference to imagination in this section will, however, provide an occasion for comments on the role of doubt in making discoveries; these comments are relevant both because doubt plays a role in making discoveries and because commentators sometimes identify Descartes's method as "the method of doubt," thus perhaps leaving the impression that for Descartes doubt is of greater importance than imagination.

Imagination helps reason in proposing judgments as "things" to be compared with whatever is already known; some of these judgments allow for the extension of the "train of reasoning." These judgments have to be presented in a certain order; if they were to be introduced prematurely (even if true and eventually relevant to the science in question), "that would interrupt the flow and even destroy the force of my arguments" (as Descartes writes to Mersenne, 24 December 1640, AT 3:267; CSMK 3:164). Thus questions about right order and proper use of imagination are questions about how to discover and develop truth. The prohibition against interrupting the flow of arguments points to the presence of memory: one cannot know this flow unless at least some of it is kept before the mind. Thus at the same time as the mind is extending the train of reasoning, it must cast itself backward for the sake of right order.

If we consider some of the details which Descartes offers with respect to "analysis" as the method of discovery, this will allow for more to be said about imagination and, incidentally, about memory and doubt. We find most of these details in the *Regulae* and the *Discourse*. In the latter we met the four precepts (AT 6:18–19; CSM 1:120) which, if we make "a strong and unswerving resolution never to fail to observe them," are quite "sufficient" as methodological principles for the discovery of truth. The third of these deals with composition or deduction, and (as we saw in the first chapter) in it Descartes makes an implicit reference to imagination when he states that one must direct one's thinking "in an orderly manner, by beginning with the simplest and most easily known objects in order to ascend little by little, step by step, to knowledge of the most complex, *and by supposing some order even among objects that have no natural order of precedence [et supposant mesme de l'ordre entre ceux qui ne se precedent point naturellement les uns les autres]*." This supposing of an order involves the formation of hypotheses, and that is the work of the imagination. As we read in the *Regulae*, when there is not "any apparent order," "what we shall do is to invent an order [*ordo . . . fingimus*], so as to test every conjecture [*omnia praejudicia*] we can make" about the matter before us (AT 10:404: CSM 1:35). Thus the assumed order is an "invented" or imaginary order, and the "things" that "follow" once the order is "supposed" are "conjectures," *judgments* which it would be *pre*-mature to incorporate as parts of the scientific system as soon as the imagination offers them, thus *prae-judicia*, pre-judgments.

In the *Regulae* Descartes refers to these conjectures as "enumerations."[27] Hence it is through the imagination that we generate our enumerations. Since what is enumerated must be prima facie relevant to the particular problem at hand—a fact which again brings in the necessity of memory—the use of imagination does not lead us to make our "way to the truth of things as others do by way of aimless and blind inquiries, with the aid of luck

---

27   Chapter 5 will show that Descartes uses the same terminology, for the same practice, in the *Geometry*.

rather than skill" (AT 10:403; CSM 1:35); it prevents us from "wasting our time by making random and unmethodical [*casu et sine arte*] guesses" (AT 10:405; CSM 1:36). Required is a rational, methodical use of the imagination.

In the ninth and tenth rules of the *Regulae* Descartes pays special attention to the relation between reason and imagination. The opening paragraph of rule 9 states:

> We have given an account of the two operations of our intellect, intuition and deduction, on which we must, as we said, exclusively rely in our acquisition of knowledge. In this and in the following Rule we shall proceed to explain how we can make our employment of intuition and deduction more skilful and at the same time how to cultivate two special mental faculties, *viz.* perspicacity in the distinct intuition of things and discernment in the methodical deduction [*artificiose deducendo*] of one thing from another.

Rule 9 then deals with "perspicacity" which, as is stated also in rule 11, constitutes a further discussion of intuition. Rule 10 deals with "discernment." Its references to "play," "invention," and "imaginary order" indicate that Descartes is here dealing with the use of imagination. Since (as we just saw) "discernment" is called one of "two special mental faculties," and since a discussion of "discernment" is a discussion of the proper uses of imagination, imagination must be taken to be subsumed under the "two special mental faculties" which help in the pursuit of knowledge by making "our employment of intuition and deduction more skilful." How it is thus subsumed is indicated in rule 10. But in rule 11 Descartes writes that rule 10 deals "only with enumeration." Hence the justification for my earlier statement that the function of the imagination is to provide enumerations.

The examples given in rule 10 make clear that it is concerned with the enumeration which, in rule 7, Descartes calls the kind of "enumeration, or induction" which "consists in a thorough investigation [*perquisitio*] of all the points relating to the problem at hand" (AT 10:388; CSM 1:25). That in generating enumerations the imagination must be disciplined Descartes states many times in this tenth rule. It obtains its discipline especially from "number-games and any games involving arithmetic, and the like," for "it is surprising how much all these activities exercise our minds, provided of course we discover them for ourselves and not from others" (AT 10:404; CSM 1:35). Thus in general the relation between reason and imagination can be put as follows: Imagination is necessary to generate deductions, it can fulfill its role only if it is disciplined, and it is disciplined by the mathematical sciences which themselves are structured by method. Imagination is necessary for deduction to progress, for it alone is capable of presenting reason with methodically generated inductive enumerations. Since the method of discovery is applied in the search for "causes" of experienced "effects," what the imagination presents to reason are *possible* "causes" of experienced "effects."

Although the crucial role of intellectual imagination in the development of the mathematical sciences will be central to my fifth chapter, it is relevant here to anticipate that discussion in order to make clearer the use of mathematics as an area in which to discipline imagination. In the mathematical sciences we meet the imagination's successes when we meet well-developed complete theories. For it is in such theories that reason has been able to authorize some of the imagination's hypotheses as the correct next step to be taken in the argument. Reason has then validated these hypotheses as truths. Hence, through practice in rationally established mathematical theory, imagination meets its successful self. Which is to say that, to an extent, the imagination's discipline through practice in mathematics is the imagination's self-discipline.

We now possess the general answer to the question raised earlier: Given that the mind has before it one of the "things" to be compared, how does it obtain the other "thing" which is relevant? The general answer is that for any "effect" the imagination will enumerate a (if possible exhaustive) number of alternative "causes," with each of these as simple as the context allows. These "causes" are presented as hypotheses, conjectures, *praejudicia*. The cause which can withstand the test of doubt is the cause that can be seen (i.e., intuited) to have a necessary connection with the effect. Thus the role of doubt is to help determine whether a proposed cause or hypothesis must be accepted or rejected. If it can withstand the test of doubt, then the hypothesis in question becomes a true and relevant proposition, and another link has been forged in the deductive chain.

If we reformulate the question stated in the first sentence of the preceding paragraph to read: (*a*) What, precisely, is the next step to be taken in the argument, and (*b*) how do we know that this is the right next step to take? it will be seen that the general answer provided gives us criteria for answering the second part of the question. However, more needs to be said about both the first and second parts.

The imagination allows the understanding to assume as "causes" those for which it does not yet have proof. These conjectures are not presented without justification; much more than mere chance is involved. Enumeration of the relevant hypotheses is determined by the contents of the ideas of these hypotheses; and which of these ideas are possibly relevant is at least in part determined by the "effect" to be explained. Thus each inductive enumeration requires suitable preparation. This preparation includes acquiring thorough familiarity with the details of the argument as far as it has been developed, and keeping the currently most relevant of these details before the mind as it constructs hypotheses. That is, required are careful attention to all details, and awareness of at least the most immediately relevant of them through memory. Hence Descartes's statement about analysis: It "contains nothing to compel belief in an . . . inattentive reader; for if he fails to attend even to the smallest point, he will not see the necessity of the conclusion" (AT 7:155–6; CSM 2:110).

Once a complete enumeration of possible "causes" has been made, the role of the imagination is over. What remains to be done is elimination of those conjectures which are false. In this process of elimination the deduction is "discovered." Again, the means for elimination is provided by the methodological principle of doubt: It involves examining the relationship between what is already known or remembered as known, and the various hypotheses proposed as relevant. Can a conjectured "cause" be intuited to have a necessary relation to the relevant item or items of knowledge which we already possess? If it cannot withstand this test, can it be seen to be necessarily related to some still only partially intelligible item which is thus only partially incorporated in that body of knowledge? If the answer to both questions is negative, then we have successfully doubted such a "cause" or explanation to be the true one, and such doubt requires us to reject it as false.

In the *Regulae* Descartes states that

> if our method properly explains how we should use our mental intuition to
> avoid falling into . . . error and how we should go about finding the deduc-
> tive inferences [*deductiones inveniendae sint*] that will help us attain this all-
> embracing knowledge, then I do not see that anything more is needed to
> make it complete. (AT 10:732; CSM 1:16)

The use of "finding" or "discovering" in "how we should go about finding the deductive inferences" involves one more point of importance to be noticed about the imagination. Descartes uses a form of the same word in the passage from the Second Set of Objections and Replies in which he comments on analysis as the method of discovery: "Analysis shows the true way by means of which the thing in question was discovered methodically and as it were *a priori* [*Analysis veram viam ostendit per quam res methodice et tanquam a priori inventa est*]" (AT 7:155; CSM 2:110).[28]

---

[28] CSM provides an unhelpful and misleading footnote at this point: "Descartes' use of the term *a priori* here seems to correspond neither with the modern, post-Leibnizian sense (where *a priori* truths are those which are known independently of experience). . . . " As we have already seen, and as will be clearer as we go on, Descartes's use is very much the modern use. At this point, the old translation of Haldane and Ross does greater justice to Descartes than does CSM. Haldane and Ross interpret *tanquam a priori* by means of the phrase "as it were effect from cause." This free translation is justifiable in view of what Descartes says elsewhere about the method of discovery, especially in view of *Principles* 1:24: "This is the way to acquire the most perfect scientific knowledge, that is, knowledge of effects through their causes."

Invenire does not mean "discover" in our modern sense of "invent." Given the philosophical tradition in which this word plays an important role,[29] as well as the context in which Descartes uses it, its meaning is best given in the translation from the *Regulae*: "go about finding"—"finding" as in "coming upon," that is, "discovering" something already in existence. Further, the use of *tanquam a priori* in the Second Set of Replies seems to indicate that Descartes is using "a priori" in a tentative sense, to indicate provisionality. Finally, since in its usual sense *invenire* is an achievement verb, it must be understood as doing duty here for itself and for some activity verb, such as "seeking," "looking for," "following." For it is such a verb which would naturally receive the adverbial modifications *methodice* and *tanquam a priori*. Thus *methodice* pertains not to a mode of discovery but to a mode of proceeding in making the discovery possible; and *a priori* qualifies a description of the method and not of the results or achievements attained by following it. Hence a properly clear translation of the sentence would be: "Analysis shows the true way through which a thing has been sought-and-discovered methodically and, as it were, a priori." In the light of the qualifications just introduced, its meaning would be: analysis shows us the true way which, if followed methodically and, as it were, a priori, leads the seeker to the discovery of a thing. "Following methodically" would include the controlled use of imagination to give an inductive enumeration of all the relevant (i.e., *possibly* necessary) "causes." To this work of the imagination there attaches an *"as it were, a priori"* element: *Which* of the several "causes" it proposes will turn out to be the correct one is to be settled through doubt and intuition. Whichever of the "causes" can withstand the test of doubt will be intuited as the correct one(s). In metaphysics there will be only one such "cause" for a particular "effect." In geometry or pure physics there may be several, perhaps an indefinite number of "causes" (for there are several, perhaps an indefinite number, of possible worlds). If we want to develop a geometry or physics about the world in which we live, we have to discover which of the several possible "causes" is the actual one; the applicability of pure theory to the actual world is to be in part determined through the corporeal imagination. Narrowing down applicability to the specific bodies and events existing and occurring in this world through development of mechanics, medicine, and morals requires experimentation, that is, the use of imagination and sensation combined. Thus (leaving aside for now the role of corporeal imagination), doubt and experimentation have simi-

---

[29]   See, e.g., Boethius's comments in the first book of the second *Commentaries* on the *Isagoge* of Porphyry, in Richard McKeon's *Selections from Medieval philosophers* (New York, 1929), 1:74.

lar and complementary functions: whereas doubt eliminates those hypotheses that cannot be intuited to have a necessary connection with the knowledge already developed, experimentation eliminates those hypotheses that do have such a connection but that do not allow for sensuous verification in the world in which we find ourselves.[30]

It will by now be clear that it is precisely through the imagination that there can be developments in science, for it is the imagination which introduces *new* things to fit with what is already known. It is here that we find the major distinction between traditional syllogistic deduction and the deduction of the Cartesian method of analysis. "Syllogisms" are of use at best in the "exercise [of] the minds of the young"; and the cause of progress in science is hardly served by "those chains with which the dialecticians suppose they regulate human reason," for "the syllogistic forms are of no help in grasping the truth of things" (AT 10:363, 365, and 439–40; CSM 1:11, 12, and 57). In contrast, Cartesian analysis allows both the attainment of the foundation for philosophy and science and—not the least through the work of imagination—the construction of the edifice of philosophy and science upon it.

3. DEDUCTION, DOUBT, AND EXPERIMENTATION

In developing science, doubt and experimentation play similar and complementary roles. More now needs to be said about this similarity, and an important difference has to be brought into focus as well.

The role assigned to doubt in the context of composition, and its relation to that of the imagination, may be further clarified as follows. In part 4 of the *Discourse* Descartes restates the first of the methodological principles articulated in part 1, when he writes that "I thought it necessary to . . . reject as if absolutely false everything in which I could imagine [*imaginer*] the least doubt." (AT 6:31; CSM 1:126–27) In part 2, the first principle sets limits to this doubt through the criterion of clarity and distinctness: "include nothing more in my judgements than what presented itself to my mind so clearly and so distinctly that I had no occasion to doubt it" (AT 6:18; CSM 1:120). With respect to all judgments I introduce as I attempt to extend my train of reasoning, I can, prima facie, imagine some ground of

---

[30] Descartes's logic of discovery has many points of contact with contemporary discussions. He could quite easily have accepted (and then expanded upon) a statement like that of Glymour and Kelly: "Suppose we think of inquiry as posing discovery problems, a question or questions, and a class of possible worlds or circumstances that determine various answers to the question. Depending on which world or circumstance is ours, different answers will be true" (12).

doubt. In this activity imagination and doubt work in tandem; it is imaginative doubt applied to judgments which imagination has itself brought into the mind. The very fact that I can imagine some ground for doubting these judgments reveals their prima facie hypothetical nature. In sum, the role of doubt is to work with the imagination to show that judgments proposed by the imagination as new links for the deductive chain are in fact hypotheses. If such a new item (though appearing in the form of a judgment) is given by reason itself rather than by the imagination—as, for example, in the statements that "Something cannot arise from nothing" and "There must be at least as much reality in the efficient and total cause as in the effect of that cause"—then the item is not hypothetical, no good grounds for doubting it can be imagined,[31] hence if it is doubted it can immediately withstand this test. That is because these statements were not introduced by the imagination; there was no "comparison" and there were no steps which led to their "construction." Instead, they are items known per se and as such immediately "manifest by the natural light" (AT 7:40; CSM 2:28).

From the first precept of the method it is clear that doubt is part of the method, that doubt is therefore "methodological" and must be used whenever we develop science. Thus the use of doubt may be called "systematic." Since the method is to apply to everything, therefore the phrase "universal doubt" is apt—Descartes himself uses it in *The Search for Truth* (AT 10:515; CSM 2:409). It should, however, be clear that a distinction must be made when we consider the application of the latter phrase. Under normal conditions, it is used properly in a statement if the user means to say that doubt can be applied to any belief or any item of knowledge. It is employed improperly if that statement is meant to imply that none of the items to which doubt is applied are able to withstand the test. Thus doubt can be applied to any belief, to any item of knowledge, but in the course of this universal application some of these items will show themselves impervious to it. The class of items which is impervious to doubt are the foundational items of science: in philosophy, concepts like *thought, existence,* and principles like *There must be as much reality in the cause as in the effect;* in mathematics, concepts like *unity* and *equality.* That is, impervious (under normal conditions) are items known per se, items to which analysis leads but beyond which it cannot go, items which are the starting points for synthesis.[32] Once synthesis proceeds, doubt becomes at

---

31   As I shall demonstrate in my final chapter, this statement holds only after metaphysical doubt has been dispelled.

32   To say that they are impervious to doubt is not to say that they cannot become vulnerable to doubt under some abnormal condition. In my first chapter, I presented a reading of the *Meditations* which assumes that that which reason gives to itself, namely, items known

least prima facie effectual, for all next steps in the development of science—apart from those which consist in reason's introduction of items known per se—are steps in which the imagination guides, and none of these can be accepted to begin with as the correct move to make. Here, the role of doubt is, first, to reveal that with respect to every single one of these moves certain questions must be asked, and, second, to show that under specific conditions some of these moves are the right ones. These are the moves where doubting leads to intuitive awareness of necessary rather than contingent connections between what is already known and what is proposed for extension of this knowledge, the moves in which that which initially has hypothetical status gains the characteristic of certainty.

The imagination intended in the preceding paragraphs is intellectual rather than corporeal. This distinction becomes operative here because of a difference in roles to be filled. In their respective realms, corporeal imagination and sense or experimentation both set limits to the combined activity of intellectual imagination and doubt in the development of science. These limits concern the possible and the actual. In geometry or pure physics, corporeal imagination determines which developments are about a possible world; in an applied science like mechanics, sensation or experimentation determines which developments are about the world in which we actually find ourselves. Thus whereas doubt and intellectual imagination are part of the general method for developing science, corporeal imagination and sense or experimentation are not, or at least not in the intrinsic way in which we must say this of doubt and intellectual imagination. In the development of science, doubt, intellectual imagination, corporeal imagination, and experimentation are instruments which allow for the next step(s) to be taken. But corporeal imagination and experimentation have more limited roles in this process than do doubt and intellectual imagination. This is because, first, neither corporeal imagination nor sensation ought to play a role in developing the metaphysical foundations for science. And, second, even when corporeal imagination and sensation play their roles as restriction instruments determining possibility and actuality, they do so only after intellectual imagination and doubt.

The next two chapters will tell more about the absence of corporeal imagination and sensation in the development of metaphysics, and about the presence at a certain stage (namely, following the lead of intellectual imagination) of corporeal imagination in geometry. In order not to transgress into the realms of these chapters, but at the same time illustrate the point of the preceding paragraph, let me turn to the area of applied science and to

---

per se, are submitted to metaphysical doubt—a form of doubt which, for a time, we do not know is efficacious. In my final chapter this reading will be further developed.

the role of sensation or experimentation in it. After this illustration I will return to discuss the role of imagination in the final section of this chapter.

In applied science, Descartes does not assign to sense or experimentation a fundamental role in the construction of scientific systems, or certainly not when "construction" means "initiation" or "creation." Instead, experimentation tells something about scientific systems once they have been constructed or, more practically, as they are being constructed. In the latter case, that of scientists' reflection on a step already taken in the construction of a system, experimentation plays a crucial role. For it tells scientists which of the possible "causes" are actual "causes," and thus it determines the direction which scientists take as they forge new links to the deductive chain. However, the starting point for the deductive chain is known intuitively, and each successive link (unless it consists in adding an item known per se) is initially provided by imagination followed by the application of doubt and, if the item given by the imagination can withstand the test of doubt, by subsequent intuition. In this total process of forging link to link, sense or experimentation plays a strictly limited role. Only the question: Which link is to be added, *this* or *that*? is answered by experimentation. And the question is asked only under certain circumstances, namely, when one wants to develop an applied science, and it is answered—in fact can only be asked—after imagination and doubt have played their role.

The question whether a body of knowledge is or is not about the material universe is external to that body of knowledge. In that sense experimentation is not part of the procedure which produced the body of knowledge. Which is not to detract from the fact that in applied sciences it does play its role in answering questions which lead to adding one link rather than another, and in that sense experimentation helps to determine the body of knowledge. In view of Descartes's repeated emphasis on the need to develop *useful* science, this role of experimentation is of crucial practical importance.

The role I have sketched for sense or experimentation in the two preceding paragraphs is one supported by various texts. Let me introduce just two of these. The first is from the *Discourse*, part 6:

> I also noticed, regarding observations,[33] that the further we advance in our knowledge, the more necessary they become. . . . First I tried to discover in general the principles or first causes of everything that exists or can exist in the world. . . . Next I examined the first and most ordinary effects deducible from these causes. In this way, it seems to me, I discovered the heavens, the

[33] At this point CSM offers the following footnote: "Fr. *experiences*, a term which Descartes often uses when talking of scientific observations, and which sometimes comes close to meaning 'experiments' in the modern sense (its root being derived from Lat. *experior*, 'to test')."

stars, and the earth; and, on the earth, water, air, fire, minerals, and other such things. . . . Then, when I sought to descend to more particular things, I encountered such a variety that I did not think the human mind could possibly distinguish the forms or species of bodies that are on the earth from an infinity of others that might be there if it had been God's will to put them there. Consequently I thought the only way of making these bodies useful to us was to progress to the causes by way of the effects and to make use of many special observations. . . . I have now reached a point where I think I can see quite clearly what line we should follow in making most of the observations which serve this purpose; but I see also that they are of such a kind and so numerous that neither my dexterity nor my income (were it even a thousand times greater than it is) could suffice for all of them. And so the advances I make in the knowledge of nature will depend henceforth on the opportunities I get to make more or fewer of these observations. (AT 6:63–65; CSM 1:143–44)

The second is from a letter to Mersenne (11 October 1638, AT 2:380; CSMK 3:124) in which Descartes gives "comments on Galileo's book," *Discourse and Mathematical Demonstrations concerning Two New Sciences*:

I find he philosophizes much more ably than is usual, in that, so far as he can, he . . . tries to use mathematical methods in the investigation of physical questions. On that score, I am completely at one with him, for I hold that there is no other way to discover truth. But he continually digresses, and he does not take time to explain matters fully. This, in my view, is a mistake: it shows that he has not investigated matters in an orderly way, and has merely sought explanations for some particular effects, without going into the primary causes of nature; hence his building lacks a foundation.

To the extent that one "has not investigated matters in an orderly way," one is working unmethodically and hence cannot then develop a thoroughly systematic account. This is why, according to Descartes, Galileo "continually digresses" and does not "explain"—or demonstrate—"matters fully." Only in the context of demonstration is it meaningful to look for an answer to the question whether the "causes" introduced as explanation of "particular effects" are indeed the explanation. Applied physics is therefore as "deductive" for Descartes as is any of the theoretical sciences.

The relation between deduction and experimentation may now be put as follows. A hypothesis introduced by intellectual imagination in an applied science loses its hypothetical status only after it has withstood two tests. The first is that of doubt, and if the hypothesis can withstand that test, it will be intuited as a possible next link in the chain. It is still a *possi-*

ble next link because deduction alone cannot provide actual causes for particular effects. The second test is therefore observation or experimentation to see whether these particular effects are indeed explained by a cause already intuited as possibly the right one. Only after this second process is the proposed hypothesis or cause rejected as irrelevant or accepted as the right one. In the latter case the proposed cause loses its hypothetical status and another link has been forged in the body of knowledge which is about the world in which we live.

This twofold testing can be put in the language from *The Principles* 3:4. (i) The "aim" is "to deduce an account of effects from their causes." This is the deductive part of the demonstration; it involves intellectual imagination and doubt but does not involve sense. (ii) After that task has been carried to a certain stage, it will become necessary (for the sake of practical use) "to deduce . . . causes from their effects. The intention is [then] simply to direct our mind to a consideration of some effects rather than others from among the countless effects which we take to be producible from the selfsame causes." This is the empirical part which tells something about the demonstration; it tells us whether the knowledge deduced is knowledge about the particular and contingent entities which constitute the world in which we live.[34]

It is clear that Descartes's position on this point differs from that of contemporary science. Contemporary scientists often use experimentation as a means to verify the correctness of results obtained. But for Descartes experimentation is not a tool which provides evidence for the correctness or incorrectness of science as a whole or parts thereof. Instead, it provides evidence for the correctness or incorrectness of a judgment made about a scientific statement or a body of such statements, namely, a judgment as to whether it is an account of the world in which we live.

4. Forms of "Imagining"

Although Descartes does not employ the phrase "intellectual imagination" to indicate the presence of nonimaging or noncorporeal imagination, I have used it. The statement that such a use is justified I base on the material covered in this chapter; it demonstrates that, quite deliberately, Descartes assigns a crucial role to intellectual imagination. Recapitulation of its salient aspects (as in the following paragraph) will allow for further substantiation even before we proceed to considering imagination at work in Descartes's practice.

Intellectual imagination occupies a prominent place in the precepts of

---

[34]   See also Descartes to Morin, 13 July 1638, AT 2:197–99; CSMK 3:106–7.

the method articulated in the *Discourse*, where, to further the argument, we must *suppose* some order, a supposing which involves formation of hypotheses. This notion is first stated in the *Regulae* where, when order is not apparent, we *invent* an order; the order which follows is a *supposed* order, and the judgments which are the content of this order are *conjectures*, and so the order is an *imaginary order*, an order consisting of the kind of *praejudicia* which makes deduction possible. We will be on the path of all-embracing knowledge once we know how we should go about *inventing the deductive inferences*, that is, once we know how to discover things *methodically and as it were a priori*. We must become proficient at the controlled use of imagination to provide an inductive enumeration of all possibly relevant next steps to be taken in the argument. Once we have these various options before the mind, we imaginatively doubt in order to eliminate those hypotheses which do not further the argument: we *reject as absolutely false everything in which I could imagine the least doubt*. In the development of applied science, imagination and sense combined allow for each next step to be taken in the argument: imagination in proposing the step, imaginative doubt and sensuous experimentation in confirming or disconfirming the correctness of the step proposed. As will be firmly established in my fifth chapter, the same must be said for pure science, with the exception that the role played by sense is there assumed by corporeal imagination.

The italicized phrases reveal that intellectual imagination is assigned a crucial role. All of these phrases are Descartes's own: *suppose (supposant) order; invent (fingamus) order; invent (invenire) deductive inferences; imagine (imaginer) the least doubt*. All of these point to instances of imageless imagining.

A brief detour will help to establish that Descartes was well aware of this role of imageless imagining. This detour is by way of some of our own century's work on the concept of imagination which closely aligns "imagining" with "inventing," "supposing," and "pretending" (a word which—as we shall see in the next chapter—in some contexts is a legitimate translation for Descartes's use of *fingamus*). The work I have in mind is, for example, some of Gilbert Ryle's.

In *The Concept of Mind*,[35] Ryle writes about "the concept of imagining or make-believe" (256); the heading of one of the sections of his chapter on "Imagination" is "Pretending" (258). In this section he argues that "Assuming, supposing, entertaining, toying with ideas and considering suggestions are all ways of pretending to adopt schemes or theories" and that the user of these schemes or theories is said to be "wielding them . . . in a hypothetical, not a categorical frame of mind," a frame of mind he

[35] London, 1949.

"advertises" "by using such special signals as the words 'if', 'suppose', 'granting', 'say' and so on" (263). In his posthumously published "Thought and Imagination,"[36] many of the same terms reappear in his characterization of imagination and imagining. At the same time, Ryle there distances himself from a position which his earlier characterization in *The Concept of Mind* helped to reinforce. Where he had at first written about "the concept of imagining or make-believe," his later position repudiates this identification to the extent that it involves limitation: he distances himself from it by explaining "why we are so apt to limit imagination to make-believers" (61) and by arguing for the importance of imagination in making discoveries. On the latter, he writes that "a man's imaginativeness shows itself in any of those moments of his thinking in which he innovates, when he invents, discovers, explores, essays, experiments . . . " (ibid.). Connecting this wider sense of imagination with that of his earlier limitation, Ryle comments that "imaginativeness is not *more* of a necessity for make-believe than it is for advancing knowledge . . . " (63).

The reason for this detour was to show that a thinker other than Descartes refers to imagining by means of words like "assume," "suppose," "invent," and "discover." For Ryle as for Descartes, there is no supposing or inventing without imagining. In his earlier position, Ryle even used words like "imagining" and "make-believe" as synonyms. His later rejection of that restriction in fact brings him closer to Descartes's use: for both of them, assuming, supposing, inventing, discovering, and pretending are forms of imaginative thinking.[37] It hardly needs to be said that the comparison between the two ought not to be pressed beyond this point. In addition to its dismissal of mental facilities as mental faculties, Ryle's *The Concept of Mind* is explicitly anti-Cartesian in its antidualism.

The point of comparison is this. If, in addition to "imagine," Descartes regularly uses words like "suppose," "assume," "invent," "discover," "pretend," in a context which makes it clear that there is, or can be, no imaging, then there is no reason to conclude that Descartes was not aware of the fact that he was having recourse to imageless imagining. To hold otherwise would be uncharitable—a lack of charity possibly grounded in

[36]   In *On Thinking*, ed. Konstantin Kolenda (Oxford, 1979), 51–64.

[37]   Where Descartes speaks of the faculty of thought and the faculty of imagination, Ryle of course denies the legitimacy of faculty talk. This metaphysical difference should not hide the fact of their closeness at this point. In "Thought and Imagination" we read, "[I]magining is . . . innovating, inventing, exploring . . . creative . . . thinking" (63). And in the eighth paragraph of the Second Meditation the question "[W]hat is a thing that thinks?" is answered with "A thing that doubts, understands, affirms, denies . . . imagines. . . . "

the mistaken belief that for Descartes all thinking necessarily involves having images. But that belief violates Descartes's text.[38]

What the comparison does not allow as a conclusion is that the instances of supposing, assuming, etc., are in the case of both Descartes and Ryle instances of intellectual imagination. Had Descartes used it, that phrase would function precisely because of his dualistic position: intellectual as opposed to corporeal imagination. Since Ryle rejects Cartesian dualistic positions, to say that Ryle's employment of terms like "suppose" and "assume" is just like Descartes's would illegitimately restrict Ryle's use.

In this chapter, my discussion of intellectual imagination has remained relatively abstract. I am now in the position to become more concrete by showing this intellectual imagination at work in Descartes's practice.

---

[38] It might be objected that both Descartes and Ryle were wrong in taking activities like supposing and pretending to be instances of imagining. This is, in fact, Alan White's position (see *The Language of Imagination*, chaps. 16 and 17). I find White's analysis less than convincing.

4

Practice in Metaphysics

In this as well as in the sixth chapter, parts of the first chapter's journey through the Meditations will be given greater depth. I will focus on important features which still require attention in order to make Descartes's arguments and intentions clearer. Among these features are the crucial role assigned to intellectual imagination (which forms a part of the discussion in this chapter) and (in the sixth chapter) the role to be played by human freedom in its relation to Descartes's Archimedean point.

1. DISMISSAL OF CORPOREAL IMAGINATION

In the *Discourse* Descartes led his readers into both his theory about and practice of making discoveries in science. Discussion of the theory in fact introduced his practice, illustrated in the disciplines of metaphysics, physics, medicine, optics, meteorology, and geometry. I have followed Descartes in first discussing aspects of his "logic of discovery" and am now about to show this logic employed. I paid attention especially to intellectual imagination and made references to corporeal imagination, intellectual and corporeal memory, and sense where appropriate. And I shall continue this emphasis for the reasons already articulated, namely, that since Descartes does not use the phrase "intellectual imagination," it is incumbent on me to demonstrate that he nevertheless quite consciously draws on the mental power it names, that until recently commentators have either denied its existence or almost totally ignored it in their discussions, and that it occupies a crucial place in Descartes's practice.

In my illustration of this practice I shall draw from two areas, those of metaphysics, and of geometry or pure physics. This chapter will consider the first of these, the next chapter the second. When I deal with metaphysics there will naturally arise the opportunity to expand the picture beyond that of the role of intellectual imagination, through saying more first about intellectual memory, next about corporeal imagination and sense. And when I focus on geometry, the picture will obtain even greater relief through further comments about corporeal imagination and sensation.

As I progress through these two chapters there will be references to applied science. These will, however, remain brief, for there is too much excellent material in recent work on Descartes's procedures in applied science (including the role of sensation or experimentation) for me to have to cover again much of that ground.[1] My task is to supply what must be seen as the still predominantly missing parts of the background to these existing studies.

The fact that this chapter deals only with metaphysics provides one reason for its emphasis on intellectual imagination. Apart from doubt, in the first three Meditations intellectual imagination is the only power of the mind which is assigned a positive role, and this in contrast to corporeal imagination which is there decisively dismissed. It is intellectual imagination which is instrumental in leading us to our first metaphysical certainty. Once that has been reached and its immediate implications drawn out, there is a positive role for both reason and intellectual memory in Meditations 4 and 5. And although, in Meditation 6, corporeal imagination and sense are reintroduced and assigned their places, this is primarily to prepare the possibility for their positive roles in the nonmetaphysical sciences.

To keep the picture clear as well as give some greater scope to my argument in this chapter, let me return for a moment to a passage on imagination which Descartes wrote in his mid-twenties,[2] in which he contrasted imagination and reason and contrasted poets to philosophers in a manner more favorable to the former than to the latter: Philosophers extract innate sparks of knowledge through reason, poets strike them out through the sharp blows of imagination, with the result that their sparks shine more brilliantly.

Now sparks, however bright, may arrest attention for a moment, but as the fiery particles cool they quickly lose their brilliance. They are uncon-

---

[1] For examples, see Daniel Garber's *Descartes' Metaphysical Physics* as well as several of the contributions to John Cottingham's *The Cambridge Companion to Descartes* and Stephen Voss's *Essays on the Philosophy and Science of René Descartes*. For Cartesian science in its broader intellectual context, see Dennis Des Chene's *Physiologia*.

[2] That at AT 10:217; CSM 1:4; quoted in chapter three, section 1, above.

nected moments of light, one not necessarily leading the eye to another. For the Descartes of the *Regulae, Discourse,* and *Meditations,* the truth of poetic imagination has remained just that: transitory brilliance which reason cannot place in a coherent system to serve as guide for life. His admiration for the poet's imagination is that of the thinker who has not yet developed rules to discipline the imagination into a source for reason to draw on in seeking and finding scientific truth. Such a disciplined imagination generates the steady glow of possibility without which there is no subsequent flame of a rational scheme with the supposed potential to brighten humankind's path through applications of scientific truth. It is the mature Descartes's conviction that only the steady flame of scientific, not the evanescent spark of poetic, truth allows for the possibility of human progress. Poetry, says a forty-year-old Descartes, "has quite ravishing delicacy and sweetness," but is to be placed among the subjects which "it is good to have examined . . . in order to know their true value and guard against being deceived by them" (AT 6:5–6; CSM 1:113). Indeed, the sparks of poetic truth "shine more brightly" than the glow of imaginative scientific possibility. But Descartes believes that only this glow has the potential to become the steady light of science by which all sparks pale and which dispels the darkness to which poetry brings but fleeting relief.

Nevertheless, disciplined intellectual imagination retains its affinity with that of poets. Thus one subsidiary item to be revealed in this chapter is that, if intellectual imagination's path to truth is through fiction, then in some sense fiction plays its role in all of Descartes's work. Then poetry and philosophy, art and science have one common root in the indispensable role of intellectual imagination. It is a point not without irony. For much of Western philosophy and science is widely acknowledged to be Descartes's legacy. This legacy includes the troublesome divide between poetry and philosophy, arts and sciences. The irony is that Descartes's work points to these two sides having a common root in imagination.[3]

This conclusion about intellectual imagination implies that it plays a more extensive role than does its corporeal counterpart. That this holds for Descartes's thought is one of the points of the preceding chapter which will now be established more firmly beginning with this chapter. We will

---

[3]   The mature Descartes, if not fully conscious of this fact, at least goes beyond the link between imagination and science to that between poetry and minds which are "strong" and "refined." His last mention of poetry and imagination occurs less than a year before his death, in the correspondence with Elizabeth (AT 5:281; CSMK 3:367). It links mind (imagination) and body (animal spirits) in a passage which lauds poetry as the product of "a mind which is stronger and more refined than usual" and finds itself under extreme pressure—such as the mind of Socrates while in prison awaiting death, and the mind of Elizabeth while sick and in anguish over Cromwell's beheading of her uncle, the deposed King Charles I.

see Descartes at great pains in the *Meditations* to restrain, even dismiss, corporeal imagination, while at the same time intellectual imagination is the one mental power on whose activity depends the possibility of the *Meditations'* argument. This, however, is only part of the story, for under specific circumstances the products of intellectual imagination are themselves judged by means of corporeal imagination. In the first instance, intellectual imagination plays its crucial role as source of hypotheses. In the second—to be further developed in my next chapter—some of the abstract thought of which intellectual imagination is at least in part the source is shown by corporeal imagination to bear the promise of concrete possibility. First, then, to the *Meditations* and their dismissal of corporeal imagination.

Although intellectual imagination plays a dominant role in the first three of the Meditations, the voluminous and ever-growing literature on them contains scant mention of it.[4] It is not as if, in these three Meditations, Descartes does not refer to imagination. But when he does, he makes it very clear that at this stage in the argument recourse to imagination is illegitimate and, if nevertheless persisted in, will not keep us on the track which leads to the required foundation for all systematic knowledge. This dismissal of imagination may be one reason why commentators have paid little attention to the role of intellectual imagination. But if that is so, this neglect is ill founded, for the imagination whose use Descartes here prohibits is the corporeal one.

Corporeal imagination exits the stage in the seventh paragraph of the Second Meditation:

> What else am I? I will use my imagination [*Imaginabor*]. . . . I know that I exist; the question is, what is this 'I' that I know? If the 'I' is understood strictly as we have been taking it, then it is quite certain that knowledge of it does not depend on those things of whose existence I am as yet unaware; so it cannot depend on any of the things which I invent in my imagination [*quae imaginatione effingo*].

The "things which I invent in my imagination" (says Descartes in this paragraph) are: that I am "that structure of limbs which is called the hu-

---

4   This in contrast to work done on the corporeal imagination. For a valuable example of the latter, one might do well to start with J. J. MacIntosh, "Perception and Imagination in Descartes, Boyle and Hooke," *Canadian Journal of Philosophy* 13 no. 3 (1983): 327–52. My judgment about the paucity of work on intellectual imagination stands in spite of recent extensive work on imagination by Dennis Sepper who, even in Descartes's later works such as the *Meditations*, tends to connect imagination and image. In any case, Sepper's interesting work—including that in *Descartes's Imagination*—has more to do with Descartes's early rather than later thought.

man body," or "some thin vapour which permeates the limbs—a wind, fire, air, breath, or whatever I depict in my imagination; for these are things which I have supposed to be nothing." It is that supposition which, near the end of the First Meditation, is elevated to the guiding principle of the argument: "I . . . admit that there is not one of my former beliefs about which a doubt may not properly be raised. . . . So in future I must with-hold my assent from these former beliefs just as carefully as I would from obvious falsehoods, if I want to discover any certainty." And the begin-ning of the Second Meditation enumerates some of the important beliefs about whose truth we must now learn to live in suspension by balancing them with their opposites: hence, "there is absolutely nothing in the world, no sky, no earth, no minds, no bodies." There are "no bodies," so it is no use to try and answer the question "What else am I?" through enu-merating bodily things. And although I know that I am "a thinking thing," there are "no minds," at least not to the extent that their function-ing necessarily involves a corporeal aspect—as does the corporeal imagi-nation which, for Descartes, involves shapes or pictures in the brain traced there by the mind's activity. Therefore the answer to the question "What else am I?"

> cannot depend on any of the things which I invent in my imagination . . .
> for imagining is simply contemplating the shape or image of a corporeal
> thing [and] all such images and, in general, everything relating to the na-
> ture of body, could be mere dreams and chimeras. . . . I thus realize that
> none of the things that the imagination enables me to grasp is at all relevant
> to this knowledge of myself which I possess, and that the mind must there-
> fore be most carefully diverted from such things. . . . [5]

So the corporeal imagination is shooed off the metaphysical stage, not to be allowed its comeback until the Sixth Meditation where, at first men-tion, Descartes stresses once more that it is not part of the "I" which we know to exist in the Second Meditation: "I find in myself faculties for cer-tain special modes of thinking, namely imagination and sensory percep-

---

[5] In the French version of the *Meditations*, "such things" is replaced by *"cette façon de con-ceuoir."* The fact that it says *façon* rather than *méthode* is important. Descartes uses *méthode* to refer to his general method of procedure. This method has among its "helps" sensation and corporeal imagination. But use of these helps cannot be legitimized until the general method has itself been validated—and *that* takes place in the first three of the Meditations through the validation of reason. Hence, at this stage, if *façons* are allowed to play a role, they do so illegitimately. Thus Descartes's technical use of terms here supports my inter-pretation. (For the technical uses of *méthode* and *façon*, see Schouls, *Imposition of Method*, 63–75.)

tion. Now I can clearly and distinctly understand myself as a whole without these faculties . . . " (AT 7:78; CSM 2:54).

But none of this entails anything about a noncorporeal imagination. Quite the contrary, it allows the possibility of the existence of the noncorporeal imagination precisely because it is noncorporeal. Let me now demonstrate that a noncorporeal imagination exists at the very time when corporeal imagination is ruled not to exist, in fact, is the cause of this presumed nonexistence as of the presumed nonexistence of "world," "sky," "earth," "minds," "bodies"—but also of the presumed existence of "God" as an evil deceiver. It is best to begin with the latter.

2. Intellectual Imagination and the Deceiving God

A statement from the *Discourse* is helpful for leading us into our discussion of intellectual imagination in the argument of the first three Meditations:

> Thus I conclude that it is at least as certain as any geometrical proof that God, who is the perfect being, is or exists.
>
> But many are convinced that there is some difficulty in knowing God, and even in knowing what their soul is. The reason for this is that they never raise their minds above things which can be perceived by the senses: they are so used to thinking of things only by imagining them (a way of thinking specially suited to material things) that whatever is unimaginable seems to them unintelligible. This is sufficiently obvious from the fact that even the scholastic philosophers take it as a maxim that there is nothing in the intellect which has not previously been in the senses; and yet it is certain that the ideas of God and of the soul have never been in the senses.(AT 6:36–37; CSM 1:129)

In this passage "imagining" is closely linked with "the senses" as both are modes of thinking which require the body; it implies that the idea of God cannot be grasped through the corporeal imagination. We can, nevertheless, conceive or think of God. We may extrapolate and say that the malicious demon cannot be thought through the corporeal imagination either, for this demon has all and only the characteristics of God except that supreme goodness is replaced with "the utmost power and cunning" (*summe potentem et callidum*) which makes him "malicious" in that he is always deceiving us.[6] However, the deceiving God is not *known* to exist but

---

6 That it is God and not some interloping minor devil we must here think of is clear enough from statements to be introduced later; in the meantime, these sentences from

is *supposed* or *imagined* to exist. His existence is a hypothesis. Descartes explicitly labeled it as a hypothesis, and it is important to note what he said about it. In response to a question from Buitendijck (1643, AT 4:64; CSMK 3:229–230), he wrote:

> Once the true God is clearly known . . . it is not possible for the human mind to attribute anything false to him, as I have explained in my *Meditations*. . . . But the case is not the same with . . . God, if he is known only in a confused way. To attribute . . . something false as a hypothesis can be either good or bad, depending on whether the purpose of framing such a hypothesis is good or bad. For what is thus imagined and attributed hypothetically is not thereby affirmed by the will as true, but is merely proposed for examination to the intellect. . . . Thus, take the case of someone who imagines a deceiving god—even the true God, but not yet clearly enough known to himself or to the others for whom he frames his hypothesis. . . .

In the opening Meditations, either God is clearly known to Descartes and he frames his hypothesis for others, or God is not yet clearly enough known to himself. Whatever the case, it is not reason which provides the hypothesis, but imagination.

Why cannot reason be its source? Ignoring the fact that this would violate Descartes's causal principle, suppose we did take reason to be its origin. This would be going against the grain of the First Meditation's argument where it has just been decided that no credence may be given to any of reason's utterances. In other words, circularity would erupt where no one has ever surmised its lurking. Second, if we were to disdain circularity by placing our faith in reason, we would, though prematurely, reintroduce the faculty which—apart from the metaphysical doubt of the *Meditations*—Descartes has always held to be infallible. In words from the *Principles of Philosophy*, reason "cannot incline to falsehood," "can never encompass any object which is not true in so far as it is indeed encompassed by this faculty."[7] Now the hypothesis about the deceiving God shares with any hypothesis the characteristic that we do not yet know it to be true and that it may be false; moreover, the hypothesis will turn out to be false because contradictory.[8] Contradictory statements can be imag-

---

Principles 1:5 will help to establish that point: "[W]e have been told that there is an omnipotent God who created us. Now we do not know whether he may have wished to make us beings of the sort who are always deceived even in those matters which seem to us supremely evident."

[7]   These are phrases from *Principles* 1:43 (AT 8A:21; CSM 1:207) and I, 30 (AT 8A:16, CSM 1:203) respectively.

[8]   Descartes's comment about this hypothesis in his conversation with Burman is that "what the author says here is contradictory, since malice is incompatible with supreme

ined and remembered but not understood. We can understand that a statement is contradictory, but we cannot understand the contradictory statement. We are in error if we assert the truth of a contradictory statement, and, strictly speaking, the understanding cannot err.[9] No contradiction or, in general, no falsehood is clear and distinct qua falsehood; and the understanding or reason can grasp only what is clear and distinct. Whether there is in fact anything which is clear and distinct is a crucial question for the opening Meditations.

If, in the first three Meditations, it is not the understanding which is at work in the "supposing" of the existence of the deceiving God, then it must be either intellectual memory or intellectual imagination. It must be "intellectual" in either case if only because anything corporeal is there stipulated to be nonexistent. But it cannot be memory, for (i) Descartes consistently holds memory to be incapable of originating anything, and (ii) to the extent that memory serves as a repository of received items, it itself needs validation (hence the second paragraph of the Second Meditation brusquely dismisses it: "I will believe that my memory tells me lies. . . . ").[10] Since the hypothesis about the deceiving God shares with

---

power." (AT 5:147; CSMK 3:333). See also AT 5:150–51: "*et si fas est dicere malignum. . . .*" "*Addito illa restrictio ibi ideo, quia auctor contradictoria loquitur. . . .*" This passage is not in CSMK, but is in John Cottingham's *Descartes' Conversation with Burman* ([Oxford, 1976], 9) where it is rendered as "and, if it is permissible to say so, malicious?" "The restriction is added here because the author is saying something contradictory. . . . "

9   That Descartes restricts understanding to what is true is clear from how he solves the problem of error in the Fourth Meditation, and it is reinforced through his rebuttal of Gassendi's attack on that position. Gassendi asserted that we can "understand . . . obscurely" and that "error arises . . . from the fact that the perception of the intellect is faulty. . . . " Hence he held that will and intellect "extend" equally: Both "extend" to the clear and distinct as well as to the obscure, and to anything in between. So he demanded, "[W]ill you please tell us if the will can extend to anything that escapes the intellect?" (AT 7:315; CSM 2:219). Descartes's reply nicely illustrates the distinction we just met:

> You here ask me to say briefly whether the will can extend to anything that escapes the intellect. The answer is that this occurs whenever we happen to go wrong. Thus when you judge that the mind is a kind of rarefied body, you can understand that the mind is itself, i.e. a thinking thing, and that a rarefied body is an extended thing; but the proposition that it is one and the same thing that thinks and is extended is one which you certainly do not understand.

To understand that mind is a certain sort of body would be to understand a falsehood, namely, the contradiction that thought is a kind of extension. This the understanding cannot do. Hence Descartes ends this part of the reply with the reassertion of the position of the Fourth Meditation: "Again, we never understand anything in a bad fashion; when we are said to 'understand in a bad fashion', all that happens is that we judge that our understanding is more extensive than it in fact is" (AT 7:376–77; CSM 2:259).

10   Although Descartes does not present it in the *Meditations*, an argument about memory parallel to that about sense perception can easily be developed. Any specific "memory" claim may be false. To check any of these claims, we must compare it with other memory claims and / or with our sense experience. Since any particular sense experience has been

any hypothesis the characteristic that we do not yet know it to be true and that it may be false, therefore the understanding itself is incapable of proposing it.

This, then, is the situation. Reason is incapable of proposing the hypothesis of the deceiving God's existence because it cannot be the source of any hypotheses.[11] Corporeal imagination cannot be its source because (i) the demon is as noncorporeal as is "the true God" and therefore cannot be corporeally imagined,[12] and (ii) since the hypothesis rules corporeality to be nonexistent, no use can be made of a corporeal imagination during the time the hypothesis is in force. Memory cannot be its origin because strictly speaking it cannot be the origin of anything. Hence the only power that can account for this hypothesis is intellectual imagination.

In the Second Set of Objections and Replies Descartes comments on the argument as it stands at the end of the Third Meditation:

> Since God is the supreme being, he must also be supremely good and true, and it would therefore be a contradiction that anything should be created by him which positively tends towards falsehood. . . . Hence you see that once we have become aware that God exists [*postquam Deum existere cognitum* est] it is necessary for us to imagine [*fingamus*] that he is a deceiver if we wish to cast doubt on what we clearly and distinctly perceive. And since it is impossible to imagine that he is a deceiver, whatever we clearly and

---

shown to be untrustworthy, therefore any memory belief or set of such beliefs based on past sense experiences (coherent though that set may be) is untrustworthy. Thus there is the possibility that we may have a set of coherent "memory" claims which are nonveridical: the malignant demon may have given us a set of coherent "memories" of a nonexistent past. In fact, if he has "employed all his energies in order to deceive me," so that there is no sky, air, earth, colors, shapes, sounds, and "all external things are merely the delusion of dreams which he has devised to ensnare my judgment" (to use words from the final paragraph of the First Meditation), then the conclusion just stated is implicit, for many of the "memory" claims which make up the set of one's coherent "memory" claims are about "external things." To check any particular "memory" claim for its verdicality against a set of such claims is therefore as useless as checking a particular sense-based judgment against those based on other "sensations" I may now appear to be having.

[11]   As we saw in my third chapter, hypotheses are prejudgements, preconceptions, and as such cannot be the work of reason. Descartes's language throughout the *Meditations* remains careful in this context. So we read in paragraph 4 of the Third Meditation: "And whenever my preconceived [*praeconcepta*] belief in the supreme power of God comes to mind, I cannot but admit that it would be easy for him, if he so desired, to bring it about that I go wrong even in those matters which I think I see utterly clearly with my mind's eye."

[12]   See here again Descartes's reply at AT 7:181; CSM 2:127: "Here my critic wants the term 'idea' to be taken to refer simply to the images of material things which are depicted in the corporeal imagination; and if th.is is granted, it is easy for him to prove that there can be no proper idea of an angel or of God."

distinctly perceive must be completely accepted as true and certain. (AT 7:144; CSM 2:103)

This is at the end of the Third Meditation, where reason has weathered the whirlwind of metaphysical doubt and is to be accepted as absolutely trustworthy. Hence when reason cognizes God as existing, it must cognize him as nondeceptive. As long as we do that, it is at the same time "impossible to imagine that he is a deceiver." But at the beginning of the *Meditations*, with reason itself requiring validation, before we know "whether there is a God, and, if there is, whether he can be a deceiver," "it seems that I can never be quite certain about anything else" (as the fourth paragraph of the Third Meditation has it). I can then "never be quite certain," that is, I have no trustworthy cognitions, because of the regime of a supposition or a precognition, of a hypothesis which is the product of intellectual imagination.

Descartes's extremely careful use of language throughout the first three Meditations fully supports the conclusion of the preceding sentence. The deceiving God is introduced in the First Meditation's ninth paragraph with the sentence "How do I know [*scio*] that he has not brought it about that there is no earth . . . ?" Since I do not *know*, I am free to bring in the hypothesis—which Descartes does in this Meditation's final paragraph: "I will suppose [*supponam*] therefore . . . some malicious demon of the utmost power and cunning. . . . " The Second Meditation finds its point of departure here. Its first two paragraphs state that "Anything which admits of the slightest doubt"—as the French version has it: "*en quoy je pourray imaginer le moindre doute*"—"I will set aside" and "I will suppose [*suppono*] then . . . that nothing is certain." The "Archimedean point" is reached while this supposition is in force, and it remains in force immediately after: "But what shall I now say that I am, when I am supposing [*suppono*] that there is some supremely powerful and . . . malicious deceiver . . . ?" says its sixth paragraph. In the fourth paragraph of the third Meditation this is, again, made the point of departure: "And whenever my preconceived belief [*praeconcepta*] in the supreme power of God comes to mind, I cannot but admit that it would be easy for him, if he so desired, to bring it about that I go wrong even in those matters which I think I see utterly clearly with my mind's eye."

The very fact of the imagination's keeping this hypothesis before the understanding is what allows for progress in establishing the sought-for "stable and lasting" foundation for the sciences. It forces reason to self-consciousness and to the consciousness that it must pass beyond the self if further knowledge is to be possible. Hence the continuation of this paragraph:

And since I have no cause to think that there is a deceiving God, and I do not yet even know for sure whether there is a God at all, any reason for doubt which depends simply on this supposition is a very slight and, so to speak, metaphysical one. But in order to remove even this slight reason for doubt, as soon as the opportunity arises I must examine whether there is a God, and, if there is, whether he can be a deceiver. For if I do not know this, it seems that I can never be quite certain about anything else.

Once, in the Third Meditation, the understanding attends to the idea of God with which the imagination constantly confronts it, Descartes's language begins to change. He "carefully concentrates on," "diligently attends [*attendo*] to" this idea (AT 7:45; CSM 2:31); and "If one concentrates carefully [*diligenter attendenti*]," then it becomes "quite evident by the natural light [*sit lumine naturali manifestum*]" (AT 7:47; CSM 2:32) that God exists and cannot be a deceiver. Says its penultimate paragraph:

> The whole force of the argument lies in this: I recognize [*agnoscam*] that it would be impossible for me to exist with the kind of nature I have—that is, having within me the idea of God—were it not the case that God really existed. By 'God' I mean the very being the idea of whom is within me, that is, the possessor of all the perfections which I cannot grasp, but can somehow reach in my thought, who is subject to no defects whatsoever. It is clear enough from all this that he cannot be a deceiver, since it is manifest by the natural light [*lumine naturali manifestum est*] that all fraud and deception depend on some defect.

Descartes needs the imagination to introduce hypotheses. Without hypotheses there is no way of establishing the metaphysical foundation for science, let alone developing the sciences to be erected on this foundation. At this metaphysical foundation the imagination in question is intellectual, not corporeal. With the trustworthiness of reason, of sense, and of memory in question, there remains no way of proceeding except by intellectual imagination. Where there is no certainty, that to which by definition there never attached certainty to begin with—namely, intellectual imagination—may be used without fear of circular argumentation.[13]

The use of imagination in this metaphysical argument is not essentially

---

[13] More needs to be said about this part of the argument than I can here state. There is no imaginative activity without an exercise of freedom, and since Descartes questions not only the existence of reason but also the existence of freedom in the first three Meditations, we do not know whether we are in fact imagining when we think we are imagining or, in general, whether we are in fact active (rather than passive) when we experience ourselves to be active. I develop this part of Descartes's argument in my final chapter.

different from its employment in any other situation where there is an attempt to develop knowledge. The problem Descartes here sets himself is to find a firm foundation for the sciences. The traditional "grounds" for certainty in science are reason and sensuous experience. Can either of these be trusted without a shadow of doubt, so that an absolutely certain foundation can be established? Rational arguments from illusion and delusion cast some doubt on sense, which is therefore disqualified. But we must go beyond reason to cast doubt on reason. Thus intellectual imagination enters, forced to do so by the knowledge we already have which, in this case, is knowledge that we do not yet know but do want to discover whether absolute or metaphysical certainty is achievable. Hypotheses, if they are legitimate, must come in a context of genuine doubt. They must at least prima facie answer a genuine question. And that is what this hypothesis does. Reread part of what I quoted from Descartes's letter to Buitendijck, and at the end add a few phrases which I earlier omitted:

> [T]ake the case of someone who imagines a deceiving god—even the true God, but not yet clearly enough known to himself or to the others for whom he frames his hypothesis. Let us suppose that he does not misuse this fiction for the evil purpose of persuading others to believe something false of the Godhead, but uses it only to enlighten the intellect. . . .

Descartes certainly believed that the hypothesis about the malicious God "enlightened the intellect." It led to his "Archimedean point," from which he showed the metaphysical trustworthiness of reason. That placed him in the position from which he could then explain the problem of error and give a rule which, if scrupulously followed, would make error a thing of the past. And it put him in the position to argue for the conditions under which we can trust the senses and memory. What more can one ask of a hypothesis at this stage of one's metaphysics if it allows one "to demolish everything completely" and then places one in the position from which to "start again right from the foundations" without ever having to go wrong?

In the preceding chapter we met the statement from the Second Set of Replies (AT 7:155–56; CSM 2:110–11) that "Analysis shows the true way by means of which the thing in question was discovered methodically and as it were *a priori*. . . . " Of the fact that in the "*tanquam a priori inventa est*," the "inventing" is the work of the intellectual imagination, the first three of the Meditations offer the best of all possible illustrations, because their "a priori" "invention" of the "deceiving God" rules out the use of any other faculty and so forces our attention on its indispensable central role. Without the use of intellectual imagination, there would have been no cogito-experience, no proof of God's existence, no validation of reason—

that is, no foundations for systematic knowledge could have been put in place.[14]

There are other passages in the *Meditations* in which intellectual imagination plays its role. Some of them introduce aspects that have so far insufficiently come to the fore. I shall introduce two of these.

1. Paragraph 11 of the First Meditation contains the statement:

> I think it will be a good plan to turn my will in completely the opposite direction and deceive myself, by *pretending* for a time that these former opinions are utterly *false and imaginary* [*falsas imaginariasque esse fingam*]. I shall do this until the weight of preconceived opinion is counter-balanced and the distorting influence of habit no longer prevents my judgement from perceiving things correctly.

Here, like Ryle in *The Concept of Mind*,[15] Descartes uses "pretend" as equivalent to "imagine": what is pretended *is* imaginary, what is imagined *is* pretense. The pretending in question is performed by intellectual imagination: Descartes pretends or imagines it to be false that senses and reason can be trusted paths toward truth. That under conditions of metaphysical doubt whatever is pretended or imagined must also be rejected as false gives us one indication of the crucial role intellectual imagination here plays in the *de*compositive part of Descartes's methodic procedure. Its use is to help free the mind from all encumbrances which would prevent it from achieving truth, so that the truth achieved may be experienced as incontrovertible. In this use of intellectual imagination Descartes instituted what Peter Gay has described as an aspect integral to the intellectual style of the eighteenth-century Enlightenment: the notion of "balance"[16] to free the mind from prejudice.

[14]   There were moments in Dennis Sepper's earlier work which might have pointed in the direction of the conclusion I here draw, moments such as when he wrote: "The metaphysician (of the *Meditations*) not only reaches metaphysics by exercising imaginative doubt ..." ("Descartes and the Eclipse of Imagination," 401). When he comes to discuss the *Meditations* in *Descartes's Imagination*, Sepper takes a different line. All that functions there as imagination is "corporeal imagination" which "must be disarmed by the cognitive power of doubt" (265). The difference Sepper then draws between imagination and intellect reinforces for him the point that there is no role for intellectual imagination in the *Meditations*: "The difference between imagination and intellect was therefore not so much between two powers as between two locations (or one location and the absence of location); the knowing force was at work in both, but in one case with phantasia, in the other case without" (269). My point is that "in the other case" a distinction needs to be made between hypothesis-generating intellectual imagination and truth-discerning intellect, and that it is the first of these which leads the second to the truth of the cogito.
[15]   See chapter 3, section 4, above.
[16]   See Peter Gay, *The Enlightenment: An Interpretation*, vol. 1: *The Rise of Modern Paganism* (London, 1966), xiii, 160. Gay's misascription of originality to the eighteenth century on this matter illustrates the fact that Descartes is the source of attitudes which are still often ascribed to thinkers and movements flourishing a century (or more) after his death.

2. In the third paragraph of the Second Meditation Descartes states his first certainty: "*I am, I exist*, is necessarily true whenever it is put forward by me or conceived in my mind." The fourth through seventh paragraphs then recapitulate the argument in order to return us to this certainty which, because of this recapitulation, should now be grasped with greater conviction and assurance. This review is announced in the fourth paragraph:

> But I do not yet have a sufficient understanding of what this 'I' is, that now necessarily exists. . . . I will therefore go back and meditate on what I origi-nally believed myself to be, before I embarked on this present train of thought. I will then subtract anything capable of being weakened, even minimally, by the arguments now introduced, so that what is left at the end may be exactly and only what is certain and unshakeable.

Meditating on what I originally believed myself to be is possible be-cause the intellectual imagination is able to confront the mind with be-liefs which, in the argument of the First Meditation, have been shown to be possibly false. The outcome is the reestablishment of the conclusions that, for all I now know, I have no body and therefore can trust neither sense perception (paragraph 6) nor corporeal imagination (paragraph 7), but I nevertheless do know that I am "a thing that thinks." In this reca-pitulation the functions of the two kinds of imagination are indicated in a single sentence in paragraph 7. The words which I have added in square brackets help place this point in greater relief.

> What else am I? I will use my [intellectual] imagination. I am not that struc-ture of limbs which is called a human body. I am not even some thin vapour which permeates the limbs—a wind, fire, air, breath or whatever I depict in my [corporeal] imagination; for these are things which [through the use of intellectual imagination] I have supposed to be nothing.

My introduction of "intellectual" in the first line is perhaps problem-atic, but it makes more sense to read the passage this way than it would had I entered the word "corporeal" at that point. For would not the use of corporeal imagination in an argument which totally disqualifies corporeal imagination raise the specter of circularity? What is not problematic is us-ing the word "corporeal" in the last of the quoted sentences; Descartes himself explicitly identifies it as such in the rest of this paragraph. Neither is the phrase "through the use of intellectual imagination" problematic, because intellectual imagination is the only faculty available for introduc-ing suppositions. It is this activity of supposing which rules out of exis-tence whatever can be depicted in the corporeal imagination. Since that includes both body and therefore corporeal imagination itself, we are forced to recognize that whatever "comes from" senses or corporeal imagination cannot be trusted and that all we have as platform from which to continue the argument is that I am "a thing that thinks." It is therefore acts of intellectual imagination which now return us to the Archimedean point, just as its activity led us there in the first place.

At this point I draw the conclusion that, for Descartes, truth is reached through fiction.[17] In the first three of the Meditations this is the fiction of the deceiving God. Here, then, is a philosopher who joins poets in their dependence on imagination. Perhaps going beyond what Descartes might have been willing to acknowledge, it is now clear why one might say that in Descartes's use of imagination we see the common root of literature and philosophy, of humanities and sciences.

Now if we were to stress Descartes's rationalism to the extent that we allow no source for truth except reason (in this way disregarding the roles Descartes assigns to imagination as well as to sensation), then the idea of this common root would not fit as part of the position of the progenitor of modern philosophy and of a good deal of modern science. But as much recent scholarship has established, it would be wrong so to stress the role of reason in the Cartesian system. Moreover, is not the relation between imagination and reason as it finds expression in tentativeness and certainty, hypothesis and theory, fiction and fact a relation found in all thinking which progresses from the unknown to the known, in all mental activity open to questions and driven by wonder? Does not this relationship characterize (for example) Plato's *Theaetetus* as much as Descartes's *Meditations*? Which is not to say that, in the *Meditations*, there is not something very special about Descartes's use of fiction that sets him apart from his predecessors and successors. In the attempt to doubt whether one doubts, or in the attempt to imagine that one might not be imagining when one believes oneself to be imagining, Descartes meant to

[17] This conclusion overlaps with Dalia Judovitz's in "Derrida and Descartes: Economizing Thought" (in *Derrida and Deconstruction*, ed. Hugh J. Silverman [New York and London, 1989]). Judovitz writes that her study "will address one of the major paradoxes of Cartesian philosophy as a discourse that attains certitude through the use of fiction, in order to posit truth as an entity beyond fiction" (41–42). Her use of "certitude" introduces the cogito, and her use of "fiction" points to the imagination: "[T]he truth of the *cogito*'s existence is here established through the exercise of an impossible fiction, through a rhetoric of negation whose truth is based on the totalizing character of fiction . . . " (47) by means of "the fiction of the evil genius" (51). This, she believes, is the first time in the history of philosophy that truth is achieved through fiction: the *Meditations*' " 'historicity' is constituted by . . . philosophy's use of the ruses of literature, feint, and the fiction of the evil genius through which Cartesian discourse founds its veracity as a metaphysical discourse" (57). As my text will make clear, I disagree with some of the aspects of Judovitz's argument.

extend this fiction to absolutely everything, itself included. That, however, is part of the story for my concluding chapter.

3. METAPHYSICS AND INTELLECTUAL MEMORY

We might now be tempted to say that, except for intellectual imagination, in the First Meditation all the aids to reason are rejected as hin-
drances on the path to truth as long as there is the specter of metaphysical
doubt. Suppose that, for the moment, we accept this statement as correct.[18]
It is certainly correct to add that, by the end of the Third Meditation,
Descartes is convinced that he has dismissed this specter once and for
all:[19] Reason is established as absolutely trustworthy, and since intellectual imagination played a dominant role in this process, its efficacy is itself
established through the successful outcome of this part of the enterprise.

It is not until Meditation 6 that, as its heading states, Descartes turns to
"The existence of material things" and so to the existence of the human body.
It is therefore not until this final Meditation that Descartes considers the re-
instatement of corporeal memory, corporeal imagination, and sensation as
aids to reason. In the meantime there has been a good deal of argument in
Meditations 4 and 5. These arguments are of a compositive kind, and arguments of this nature require the aids of both intellectual imagination and intellectual memory. Is there anything in the first three Meditations which
points to the legitimacy of the latter's use in Meditations 4 and 5? I believe it
can be shown that there is, but before I attempt to answer this question, we
must be clear on what the now relevant function of intellectual memory is.

In chapter 2, section 3, we saw that it is intellectual memory which allows for the knowledge that a certain trace-dependent experience is to be
classified as one of remembering. It is intellectual memory which tells me
that the picture of an object or an event now before my mind's eye—the
tree outside my window, the winning goal in the 1998 World Cup soccer
final—is a memory image rather than one constructed by the imagination.
We there also saw that intellectual memory is required for remembering
purely intellectual things, i.e. for remembering that of which there cannot
be corporeal traces. It is the latter manifestation of intellectual memory
that is now our concern. Its function may be described as being (i) the

---

18   In my final chapter it will be argued that no faculty or experience is going to be im-
mune from metaphysical doubt. The exclusion of intellectual imagination is therefore only
for the sake of the argument at this point.
19   Recall Descartes's statement to Bourdin about the *Meditations*: "arguments by means of
which I became the first philosopher ever to overturn the doubt of the sceptics" (CSM
2:375–76; AT 7:550–51).

repository of knowledge we possess but to which we are not at the moment paying attention, and (ii) the presenter to reason of whatever of this repository of knowledge reason requires in order to make its next move (which may consist in adding steps to an argument in process, or in drawing the conclusion of a lengthy argument which is complete except for that conclusion). Scientific knowledge—as distinct from knowledge of its foundations—may then be called intellectual insight into the materials organized in and through memory.[20]

In the First Meditation (paragraph 5), Descartes uses memory in the second of these roles in the course of the argument which destroys the trustworthiness of sense perception. How do I know "that I am here in my dressing-gown sitting by the fire" rather than "in fact . . . lying undressed in bed"? "Indeed! As if I did not remember other occasions when I have been tricked by exactly similar thoughts while asleep! As I think about this more carefully, I see plainly that there are never any sure signs by means of which being awake can be distinguished from being asleep."

Strictly speaking, Descartes draws more from this argument than he is at this point entitled to do. This is clear from the Sixth Meditation's final paragraph when he dismisses "the principal reason" for doubt of the senses, "namely my inability to distinguish between being asleep and being awake." The difference between the two states is that "dreams are never linked by memory with all the other actions of life as waking experiences are." How do we know about these links? What is it that gives us the criterion of coherence and allows us to apply it in order to identify experiences as memory experiences? The answer given there is that reason plays this role. "If, while I am awake, anyone were suddenly to appear to me and then disappear immediately . . . it would not be unreasonable for me to judge that he was a ghost." Now the dismissal of the senses in the First Meditation occurs before imagination has introduced the deceiving God, hence before the trustworthiness of reason is called into question. But this means that the criterion of coherence can be applied as well here as it will eventually be applied at the end of the Sixth Meditation. Since memory can still function here as it will again at the end of Meditation 6, Descartes's conclusion about the senses is premature. Premature, but not false even in the short run. For it is only four paragraphs later that the deceiving God is introduced, and once that move has been made, reason has become untrustworthy; and this entails that coherence can no longer

---

[20] This definition fits Descartes's statement in rule 11 of the *Regulae*: "[I]f we look on deduction as a completed process . . . it no longer signifies a movement but rather the completion of a movement." And when the deduction "is complex and involved," then "the intellect cannot simultaneously grasp it as a whole, and its certainty in a sense depends on memory, which must retain the judgements we have made on the individual parts . . . if we are to derive a single conclusion from them taken as a whole" (AT 10:408; CSM 1:37).

serve as a criterion of veridicality. Then it follows that all comparison of my present state with any others is useless, for both reason's concept and experience of coherence themselves may be instances of the deceiver's trickery. And the experiences among which we judge this coherence to pertain may be illusory: The deceiver is quite capable of giving us a coherent set of "memories" of a nonexistent past.[21] Hence, with metaphysical doubt in full possession of the field, the Second Meditation's second paragraph can legitimately open with the sentences "I will suppose then, that everything I see is spurious. I will believe that my memory tells me lies, and that none of the things it reports ever happened."

The implication is clear. As long as there is metaphysical doubt, we cannot have recourse to memory. That we cannot have recourse to corporeal memory is not in question at all, for its very name indicates its possible nonexistence as soon as doubt about corporeality has gained its foothold. But the intellect then still exists. We are still imagining, doubting, thinking. But (intellectually) remembering? I believe Descartes would deny the latter. As long as the deceiving God is on the metaphysical stage, no veracity attaches to what we used to accept as recalled knowledge.[22] All we may acknowledge as trustworthy is a specific *momentary* experience of certainty: "*I am, I exist,* is necessarily true *whenever* [or, *each time*] it is put forward by me or conceived in my mind."

Knowledge of the cogito is knowledge of a self-evident, contextless item, an item known per se rather than *per aliud*. The incontrovertible truth attaching to its conception therefore in no way depends on a coherence test, for no coherence test can be applied unless there is a context. Hence knowledge of the cogito does not involve context-implicating memory knowledge.

As soon as reason comes to be disqualified, then, for all I know, "my memory tells me lies." As soon as reason is validated, memory can again function, because the coherence test is assumed to be validated in the validation of reason. It is a test of coherence among ideas. The coherence is that given to the understanding by a memory which holds before it chains of ideas linked by necessary connections. Memory then presents both

[21] This is the doctrine we met before as one to which Bertrand Russell gave some prominence in our century in his *Analysis of Mind* (159) and *Human Knowledge: Its Scope and Limits* (189).

[22] There is one statement which may seem to cast doubt on this conclusion at the same time as it confirms the role of memory as an aid to reason. It is the last sentence of the Second Meditation: "But since the habit of holding on to old opinions cannot be set aside so quickly, I should like to stop here and meditate for some time on this new knowledge I have gained, so as to fix it more deeply in my memory." This statement, however, comes at the end of the argument which begins in the tenth paragraph, an argument designed to break the trust in the aids to reason. The outcome is that *if* there are bodies, then they "are not strictly perceived by the senses or the faculty of imagination but by the intellect alone." In other words, the argument is one which temporarily sets aside metaphysical doubt. In that circumstance, there is no prohibition against introducing memory.

these ideas and their links as a necessarily cohering set. This test can be applied to sets of ideas and sets of judgments only, not to that to which these ideas and judgments refer if their reference possibly pertains to corporeality. That is, it is only intellectual memory which is validated prior to Meditation 6. It is validated implicitly through the validation of reason in Meditation 3, an implicit validation which is corroborated through the successful use of deductive reason in Meditations 4 and 5. Since the arguments in Meditations 4 and 5 are about noncorporeal matters only, there is no problem with employing only intellectual memory here. Questions about correspondence of that which coheres in the intellect with that given as extramental reality through the senses are not yet relevant.

Reason restricted to the aids of intellectual imagination and intellectual memory can give us the foundations for and contents of pure science. It can tell us all we need to know about how to "avoid error" by "remembering to withhold judgement on any occasion when the truth of the matter is not clear" (as the Fourth Meditation's penultimate paragraph has it). It can tell us of "[t]he essence of material things" and (as my next chapter will demonstrate) can deal with their possible configurations and relationships. It can present a compositive or deductive (in addition to the Third Meditation's intuitive) argument for the existence of God (as in Meditation 5). But apart from the existence of God, reason thus restricted cannot tell us anything about the existence, particular configurations, and relationships of specific objects in our world and hence cannot provide the *useful* knowledge which is Descartes's chief interest.

4. METAPHYSICS AND REASON'S CORPOREAL AIDS

Useful knowledge is about our bodies, about objects in the world in which we live, and about the relations between and among these. Its development results in the sciences of medicine, mechanics, and morals. For these sciences, reason must employ all its aids. Those dismissed before must therefore be reintroduced and their legitimate functions reestablished. How, after their initial rejection, do these aids fare in the metaphysical argument? Since my interest is in the development rather than in the storing of knowledge, I shall limit the discussion to corporeal imagination and sensation. Even then, the discussion will remain of a preliminary nature as far as the validation of their use is concerned, for some of the important questions about their validation are best taken up in my final chapter.

Concerning both corporeal imagination and sense, what is rejected in the early Meditations is not that they are "modes of thinking" (AT 7:29, 34–35; CSM 2:19, 24) but that they are modes of thinking which, because they are taken to be body-based, necessarily implicate the existence of a human body. In addition, sense is taken to implicate corporeal things external to the human body because sensation always includes a feeling of compulsion.[23] In order to be able to make the right use of reason's corporeal aids, we must be able to distinguish clearly between and among understanding or intellect, corporeal imagination, and sense. Their distinguishing marks come to the fore in the last part of the Second Meditation (while the metaphysical doubt about both *res extensa* and *res cogitans* is temporarily suspended) and in the Sixth Meditation (with the doubt about reason fully overcome).

Corporeal imagination is distinguished from the intellect because it is more limited than the intellect and because (except in the cases indicated in the preceding footnote) it is active rather than passive. I will now highlight these two distinctions.

We have seen that intellectual imagination has a wider scope than the understanding, that we can imagine what we cannot understand. In contrast, the understanding has a wider scope than the corporeal imagination, for things may be intelligible which are not imageable. My knowledge of the nature of a piece of wax, for example, does not derive from "what I picture in my imagination . . . for I can grasp that the wax is capable of countless changes . . . yet I am unable to run through this immeasurable number of changes in my imagination" (AT 7:31; CSM 2:20–21). Or to take the example from the second paragraph of Meditation 6:

When I imagine a triangle, for example, I do not merely understand that it is a figure bounded by three lines, but at the same time I also see the three lines with my mind's eye as if they were present before me; and this is what I call imagining. But if I want to think of a chiliagon, although I do understand that it is a figure consisting of a thousand sides just as well as I understand the triangle to be a three-sided figure, I do not in the same way imagine the thousand sides or see them as present before me. . . . For it dif-

---

[23] In dreaming, and sometimes even in daydreaming, there is something like this feeling of compulsion also in corporeal imagination, for the "I" "imagines many things even involuntarily" (AT 7:28; CSM 2:19). During the course of such experiences, this feeling makes us believe that the experiences originate from bodies external to us. On this phenomenon depends part of the argument for the rejection of the existence of the external world in the First Meditation. But when we account for these experiences once we look back on them, their explanation does not involve aspects external to the human body. "We need [corporeal] imagination in order to dream, but to be aware that we are dreaming we need only the intellect" (AT 7:359; CSM 2:248). The intellect then explains dreaming in terms of brain traces: "[T]he illusions of our dreams and also the day-dreams we often have when we are awake and our mind wanders idly without applying itself to anything on its own accord . . . arise simply from the fact that the [animal] spirits, being agitated in various different ways and coming upon the traces of various impressions which have preceded them in the brain, make their way by chance through certain pores rather than others" (*The Passions of the Soul*, article 21).

fers in no way from a representation I should form if I were thinking of a myriagon, or any figure with very many sides. Moreover, such a representation is useless for recognizing the properties which distinguish a chiliagon from other polygons.

To depend on corporeal imagination can be worse than useless, it can in fact hinder the understanding from progressing in science as, for example, the "ancient geometers" were stopped in their tracks when they limited geometry to the corporeally imaginable.[24] On the other hand, corporeal imagination has its uses when we deal with physical objects: in developing applied science the fact that we can picture things may give us clues about how to proceed, what models to construct, what experiments to perform.

In its synopsis Descartes writes that "in the Sixth Meditation, the intellect is distinguished from the imagination; the criteria for this distinction are explained" (AT 7:15; CSM 2:11). One of these criteria is that corporeal imagination is necessarily tied up with the body. As the first paragraph of Meditation 6 has it, "[W]hen I give more attentive consideration to what [corporeal] imagination is, it seems to be nothing else but an application of the cognitive faculty to a body which is immediately present to it, and which therefore exists." The possibility of corporeally imagining therefore depends on the actuality of a body with which the mind is intimately connected; this body is not to be mediately (as by way of the senses) but "immediately" present. As we read in this Meditation's third paragraph,

> [I]f there does exist some body to which the mind is so joined that it can apply itself to contemplate it . . . then it may possibly be this very body that enables me to imagine corporeal things. So the difference between this mode of thinking and pure understanding may be simply this: when the mind understands, it in some way turns towards itself and inspects one of the ideas which are within it; but when it imagines, it turns towards the body and looks at something in the body. . . .

The Fifth Set of Objections and Replies states a conclusion to be drawn from these passages: Because "in understanding the mind employs only it-

---

[24]   As we saw from rule 4 of the *Regulae* (AT 10:374–75; CSM 1:17–18). This is not to say that corporeal imagination can never be of help even in mathematics. In contrast to its role in metaphysics, its role in mathematics is under certain circumstances crucially important, so much so that Descartes can say that although it "is more of a hindrance than a help in metaphysical speculation," the corporeal imagination "is the part of the mind that most helps mathematicians" (AT 2:622; CSMK 3:141). Nevertheless, it is *only* a *help* even in geometry and (as my next chapter will demonstrate) becomes a hindrance as soon as it there usurps the authorizing role of reason. For discussion of a specific accomplishment in which Descartes was able to surpass the ancients in geometry through limiting the role of corporeal imagination, see my *Imposition of Method*, chap. 3, section 3.

self, while in imagination it contemplates a corporeal form," therefore "the powers of understanding and imagining do not differ merely in degree but are two quite different kinds of operations" (AT 7:385; CSM 2:264).

This discussion clarifies what was obscure in the earlier comparison between understanding and corporeal imagination. There it might have been concluded that because we can understand the nature of both a pentagon and a chiliagon but can imagine only the former, the distinction between the two functions is one of degree in potency. That difference in degree exists, but it is not the important one. The important difference is the independence from body of the first, and the dependence on body of the second.[25] It is the absence or presence of body which makes the distinction one of kind rather than merely of degree.

The second distinction in kind between understanding and corporeal imagination is that freedom is absent in the first and present in the second. As the Sixth Meditation's second paragraph states, "I can . . . imagine a pentagon, by applying my mind's eye to its five sides and the area contained within them. And in doing this I notice quite clearly that imagination requires a peculiar effort of the mind which is not required for understanding; this additional effort of mind clearly shows the difference between imagination and pure understanding." In the case of both intellectual and corporeal imagination, it is their characteristic freedom which makes progress in science possible.[26] In the mind's eye, I can construct and thus "see" possibilities which are constructible as models and experiments even though their objective counterparts do not yet exist. In the realm of applied science, corporeal imagination is, therefore, a bridge for novelty and hence for the possibility of progress.

Whatever the use we must make of corporeal imagination and the abuses we must avoid, we have no metaphysical warrant for either unless we know that the body exists. The existence of body is also required if the other of reason's corporeal aids, that of sense, is to be legitimized as a proper tool in the development of science. All that need now be said about the role sense is to play is that it is the only way in which we can get beyond the person as a being of soul and body to the extrapersonal reality which we take to be the physical world in which we live, the only way in which we can pass from pure science about possible worlds to applied sci-

---

[25] The "corporeal imagination is located . . . in the brain"; it is "a genuine part of the body, and is large enough to allow different parts of it to take on many different figures and, generally, to retain them for some time; in which case it is to be identified with what we call [corporeal] 'memory' " (AT 10:414; CSM 1:41–42).

[26] See also *The Passions of the Soul*, article 20. "When the soul applies itself to imagine something non-existent—as in thinking about an enchanted palace or a chimera—the perceptions it has of these things depend chiefly on the volition which makes it aware of them. That is why we usually regard these perceptions as actions rather than passions."

ence of the actually existing world. It is, in short, as necessary for the development of *useful* knowledge as are reason and imagination.

This is not because sensuous experimentation can be used as a means to verify the correctness of results obtained through imagination judged by reason. As we saw,[27] once reason has been shown to be infallible, the results it obtains or authorizes stand in no need of verification. We do, however, require corroboration of judgments about these results. Here we saw sensation to be crucial in that it provides evidence for the correctness or incorrectness of the judgment: it is *useful* knowledge because it is an account of the world in which we live.

The ideas of sense are "the ideas which I take to be derived from things outside of me" because "these ideas do not depend on my will" (AT 7:38; CSM 2:26). Or as the Sixth Meditation rephrases this articulation from the Third, "[T]here is in me a passive faculty of sensory perception, that is, a faculty for receiving and recognizing the ideas of sensible objects" (AT 7:79; CSM 2:55). Once it has been shown that I am indeed passive when I believe myself to be passive, so that I can trust these ideas to have originated from a source external to the self, I need reason only to show me which of these ideas are ideas of sense rather than involuntary ideas of the corporeal imagination. That is, the argument in the concluding paragraph of the *Meditations*, which identifies some of the corporeal imagination's ideas as being of dreams through showing their lack of coherence with the rest of our experience, at the same time identifies ideas of sense as being of external reality through their coherence with the vast majority of our ideas.

Most of corporeal and all of noncorporeal imagination differ from both understanding and sense in that the former are active and the latter passive, so that the former involve freedom and the latter do not. It is the former, therefore, which continue to lead in the process of making discoveries. We have seen in this chapter that it is the noncorporeal imagination which leads in the process of developing metaphysics. We are now ready to examine how imagination continues in this leading role in mathematics or pure physics and how, as well as where, the other aids to reason enter to perform their function in the development of science. Once these various aspects of Descartes's position are clear, it will be time to return to the *Meditations* to examine in greater depth how reason and its various aids are given the metaphysical justification which, for Descartes, is to warrant our trust that they can in fact fill these functions in ways which make the results the kind of science which is "stable and likely to last."

---

[27] In chapter 3, section 3.

5

Practice in Geometry or Pure Physics

1. WHY GEOMETRY?

From his letter to Mersenne,[1] we already know how Descartes saw the relationship between the *Discourse* and the three treatises appended to it: The content of these treatises (and thus of the *Geometry* as one of them) "could never have been discovered" without the *Discourse*; the *Discourse* made possible the generation of these treatises—a generation which, in turn, makes one understand the value of the *Discourse*. In a letter to Jacques Dinet[2] Descartes writes about these treatises that they "illustrate the method of reasoning which I employ." To achieve the scientific results presented in these essays, Descartes's method dictates that specific use be made of the aids to reason. It is these aids which will again occupy center stage as I discuss the kind of reasoning which leads to the discoveries presented in these sciences.

Descartes's statement to Mersenne is particularly important, for it reveals his belief that without the application of the method the particular content of these treatises would not be what it in fact is. Thus Descartes's method dictates not just a particular approach to the subject matter but, at least to an extent, the nature of the subject matter to which it is applied. This is Descartes's ground for the statement that what these treatises contain could never have been discovered without the method. In the *Geometry*, the method's application turned the discipline of geometry into a coherent, rational discourse; as well, it put a new discipline on the map, that of analytic geometry. In the creation of analytic geometry, intellectual imagination played a crucial role.

This invention of analytic geometry might by itself be good grounds for now turning to a discussion of geometry rather than to one of the applied sciences (which, in any case, will not be totally neglected in this chapter, for

---

[1] 27 February 1637, AT 1:349; CSMK 3:53.
[2] Appended to the Seventh Set of Objections and Replies. The relevant passage is at AT 7:602; CSM 2:397.

I will devote most of its final section to them). But there are two additional reasons for taking geometry as the discipline to be discussed to begin with.

The *first* of these is that in the *Geometry* we meet not just a species of Cartesian mathematics but Descartes's (pure) physics. In the appendix to the Fifth Set of Objections and Replies (AT 9A:212–13; CSM 2:274–75) Descartes refers to those of his critics who "think they clearly see that mathematical extension, which I lay down as the fundamental principle of my physics, is nothing other than my thought, and hence that it does not and cannot have any subsistence outside my mind, being merely an abstraction which I form from physical bodies." These critics then conclude that the whole of Descartes's physics "must be imaginary and fictitious, as indeed the whole of pure mathematics is." This they contrast with "real physics" which deals "with the things created by God" and therefore "requires the kind of matter that is real, solid and not imaginary." Descartes professes himself to be quite pleased with the connections these critics make, as they "here link my physics with pure mathematics, which I desire above all that it should resemble."[3]

In another passage, this time from the letter which Descartes used as the preface to the French edition of the *Principles of Philosophy*, we meet the well-known simile in which he likens philosophy to a tree. In this comparison he does not mention mathematics: "The roots are metaphysics, the trunk is physics, and the branches emerging from the trunk are all the other sciences" of which the "three principal ones" are "medicine, mechanics and morals" (AT 9B:14; CSM 1:186). The physics in question concerns "the true principles of material things," that is, "the general composition of the entire universe" (ibid.). In part 2 of the *Principles*, the location of mathematics (particularly of geometry) in the tree of philosophy is unambiguously revealed: "The only principles which I accept, or require, in physics are those of geometry and pure mathematics; these principles explain all natural phenomena, and enable us to provide quite certain demonstrations regarding them," states Principle 64. In the explanation of this principle Descartes adds: "I recognize no matter in corpo-

---

3   Descartes's critics are here in fact objecting to what (in chapter 1, section 2) I have called Descartes's use of the "ancient assumption" of the rational universe whose essence is accessible to rational human beings. A different way of putting this is along the lines followed by Jonathan Bennett when he argues that "Descartes had a subjectivist theory about the nature of necessity—not perceptions of necessity but the thing itself," such that "if the objective concept does not keep in step with the subjective one . . . it will be direly subversive." This "theory of modality" is rooted in a God whose will is to be taken as voluntaristic: "Given that all modal truths are at bottom truths about what we can conceive, and given that God made us how we are (this being a truism for Descartes), it follows that God gives modal truths their status as truths." "Descartes's Theory of Modality," *Philosophical Review* 103, no. 4 (1994): 647–49.

real things apart from that which geometers call quantity, and take as the object of their demonstrations, i.e. that to which every kind of division, shape and motion is applicable. Moreover, my consideration of such matters involves absolutely nothing apart from these divisions, shapes and motions."[4]

Hence, in dealing next with geometry, I am (as in the preceding chapter) again following Descartes's own order: beginning with metaphysics I now advance to geometry, whose study includes the principles of the pure physics which explains "all natural phenomena." These two chapters then provide the sort of discussion which is often absent from but ought to form the foundation for the various existing studies on Descartes's applied physics, that in which he deals with the particular natural phenomena which are the objects and relations of the world in which we live. In between metaphysics and the treatment of particular objects we must first deal with the intelligibility of objects. This we can do because, for Descartes, there is no distinction between the realm of the ontological and that of the intelligible—though only in the sense that whatever has physical being must be intelligible, not in the sense that whatever is intelligible must for us have ontic status.[5]

The intelligibility in question is mathematical intelligibility. It makes physical objects fundamentally homogeneous quantitative entities, which allows for their natures to be expressed in the ratios of algebra. The restriction that whatever is intelligible does not necessarily have ontic status for us we will come to see as crucially important.

To say that mathematical thought, even in the form of pure physics, is free from ontological commitment does not imply that geometry has no proper object of knowledge. My discussion of the nature of Descartes's method in the second part of my third chapter is as relevant to the present discussion as it is to a treatment of any of Descartes's mature thought. Thus also here *invenere* retains the meaning not of "inventing" that which in no way exists but of "discovering" something already in existence. In

---

[4] The identity of the subject matter of geometry and pure physics is also stated earlier in part 2 of the *Principles*, i.e., in principles 11 and 12, where we read that "[T]he extension constituting the nature of a body is exactly the same as that constituting the nature of space," so that "there is no more difference between them than there is between the nature of a genus or species and the nature of an individual"—which is to say that "the difference between space and corporeal substance lies in our way of conceiving them." Descartes does insist on an important difference between geometry and physics in that the latter includes motion. For complications and problems this entails, see Emily R. Grosholz's valuable discussion in her *Cartesian Method and the Problem of Reduction* (Oxford, 1991), chaps. 3 and 4.

[5] This is not a restriction on, but a different description of, what Barber has called the shift from the *Weak Model* to the *Strong Model* in early modern epistemology. See chapter 1, note 9, above, and Barber and Gracia, 4–5.

some cases these discoveries will be of rationally graspable mathematical concepts which can be used as formulae guiding sensible constructions. In others, they will be of rationally graspable concepts which do not allow for constructions in three-dimensional space. In both the first and second of these cases we transcend the bounds of Euclidean geometry, but in different ways. In the first case we do not transcend the realm of Euclidean space, but, as will become clear, classical geometry will be transformed and incorporated into a true *science* which can deal with the world in which we find ourselves. It is for the sake of this first case that Descartes requires the use of corporeal imagination and of diagrams in his geometry: they are necessary to determine the extent to which the objects of analytical geometry concern the domain of our physical world.[6] In the second case we transcend the bounds of classical geometry, for here we enter a scientific realm for whose objects, given our sensuous experience, there are no ontic counterparts.

The *second* of the additional reasons for now selecting geometry as the discipline for my main focus is this. The tree simile indicates that geometry forms a natural link between a discussion of metaphysics and a discussion of applied science in terms of the aids to reason which are involved in the various stages of science. In metaphysics it was intellectual imagination which propelled the argument. In geometry or pure physics both intellectual and corporeal imagination will be seen to function as reason's aids. Finally, in the applied sciences these two will necessarily be joined by sense.

Now it is not as if sense does not enter at all in Descartes's geometry. Diagrams play an important role, and these can, of course, be seen. Their *construction*, however, is to be accounted for through the intellectual and corporeal imaginations; and their being seen by the body's eye (as distinct from the mind's eye) in principle adds nothing to either their construction or the illustration of the problem they are to elucidate or to help demonstrate. In this respect, therefore, sense in principle plays no role in geometry.

In all three of them—metaphysics, geometry, and applied science—

---

[6]   That mathematical thought is free from ontological commitment is reflected in the French ending of the Fifth Meditation: "And now it is possible for me to achieve full and certain knowledge . . . also concerning things which belong to corporeal nature in so far as it can serve as the object of geometrical demonstrations *which have no concern with whether that object exists*." And that this necessitates a role for the senses is clear from the Sixth Meditation: It is only once it has been shown through metaphysical argument "that corporeal things exist" and are accessible to me through "my sensory grasp" that it can be stated that there are objects in the world which "possess all the properties which I clearly and distinctly understand, that is, all those which, viewed in general terms, are comprised within the subject-matter of pure mathematics" (AT 7:80; CSM 2:55). This aspect, and the role of corporeal imagination in its context, will be given further consideration in the third section of this chapter.

memory plays its role, intellectual memory in metaphysics from the Fourth Meditation on, joined by corporeal memory in the other sciences. But we know that memory is a repository of knowledge rather than a path toward new knowledge, and that Descartes consistently maintains that the role of memory is to be curtailed as much as possible; hence I shall continue referring to it infrequently.

2. GEOMETRY AND INTELLECTUAL IMAGINATION

Classical geometry becomes the novel discipline of *analytic* geometry when Descartes brings a new mode of algebraic thinking to a traditional way of geometrical thinking. Algebra was not unknown in the "unsophisticated and innocent age" in which "the founders of philosophy would admit no one to the pursuit of wisdom who was unversed in mathematics" (AT 10:375–76; CSM 1:18). But Descartes's algebra differs from that of the ancients if only because the latter dealt with numbers as things, as ontic entities which could be physically individuated and counted. Because Descartes frees algebraic thought from any ontological commitment, it no longer implicates a perceptual physical world. For the ancients, perceptual objects, whether given through the senses or accessible through the corporeal imagination, were taken to be individuated; they were distinguished from other entities through their own physical properties. As abstract concepts, the objects of Descartes's analytic geometry, having no necessary relation to physical existence, have their nature determined not through properties taken to be exclusively their own but through the conceptual relations of the intellectual context in which they function. Although all of these objects are imaginable, many of them are not imageable. Even of those that can be imaged it must be said that they differ from the objects of classical geometry. For traditional geometricians, the senses apprehended lines and figures as particular existences with particular proportions; for Descartes, they are conceived as presentations of general items, so that the visualized images or sensed objects retain their generality. In Descartes's geometry, in other words, lines and figures no longer are traditional geometrical objects in their own right.[7]

[7.] In Lachterman's words, "[T]hey symbolize or explicate the terms in a sequence of ratios among any magnitude whatever." See *The Ethics of Geometry*, 167–69. Four decades earlier, L. J. Beck sketched a similar position in *The Method of Descartes: A Study of the Regulae* (Oxford, 1952), 227. See also Hiram Caton, *The Origin of Subjectivity*, 176: "Although the lines Descartes uses to represent equations are for the [corporeal] imagination identical with any other line, to the understanding they are by no means the same. . . . Cartesian space is symbolic because its figures are generated and conceived by computational meth-

There are various aspects of the *Geometry* in terms of which we can discuss the role of intellectual imagination. One of these is Descartes's use of symbols. A second is the use of hypotheses in the technique of "assuming the problem to be already solved" by *(a)* supposing an unknown but potentially knowable quantity, or by *(b)* supposing something unknown which cannot possibly come to be known. Each of these aspects helps to give the *Geometry* its distinctively new character as compared with earlier, particularly Greek, treatises on the subject.

First. Descartes would have applauded Alfred North Whitehead's statement that "by relieving the brain of all unnecessary work, a good notation sets it free to concentrate on more advanced problems and, in effect, increases the mental power of the race."[8] In the *Regulae*—which, in rules 16 through 21, is partially parallel to the *Geometry*—the heading of rule 16 states:

> As for things which do not require the immediate attention of the mind, however necessary they may be for the conclusion, it is better to represent them by very concise symbols rather than by complete figures. It will thus be impossible for our memory to go wrong, and our mind will not be distracted by having to retain these while it is taken up with deducing other matters.

In the body of this rule, Descartes contrasts his procedure with that then still current: "[A]rithmeticians usually represent individual magnitudes by means of several units or by some number, whereas . . . we are abstracting just as much from numbers as . . . from geometrical figures . . . or from any matter whatever" (AT 10:455–56; CSM 1:67). As he writes near the beginning of the *Geometry*, "[O]ften one has no need so to trace these lines on paper, and it suffices to designate them by certain letters,

---

ods that are independent of 'existence' or the world." Here one finds a striking similarity between Descartes's position and that of Kant. See the *Critique of Pure Reason*, A713–14 / B741–42. This similarity was brought home to me through reading and discussing with him Willem R. de Jong's "How Is Metaphysics as a Science Possible? Kant on the Distinction between Philosophical and Mathematical Method," *Review of Metaphysics* 48 (1995): 235–74. There are many points of both difference and similarity between Descartes and Kant which this article evokes.

[8]   See Philip J. Davis and Reuben Hersh, *The Mathematical Experience* (Boston, 1981), 124. Rule 16 presents various of Descartes's statements of which Whitehead's is an echo: "[F]or the sake of convenience, we shall employ the letters *a, b, c*, etc. to express magnitudes. . . . With this device we shall not just be economizing with words but, and this is the important point, we shall also be displaying the terms of the problem in such a pure and naked light that, while nothing useful will be omitted, nothing superfluous will be included—nothing, that is, which might needlessly occupy our mental powers when our mind is having to take in many things at once" (AT 10:455; CSM 1:67). Another statement along these lines follows in the text.

one for each" (AT 6:371; O 178).[9] The resulting abstract entities then become symbols such as a, b, and c for the parameters, x, y, and z for the unknown quantities,[10] as well as their relevant squares, cubes, etc. represented by a^2, x^3, etc.[11] These symbols, in turn, come to function in relations—the kind of relations called "equations." As Michael S. Mahoney has pointed out, the shift in attitude is strikingly indicated by "the change in name of the discipline": "What in the sixteenth century still bears the name *'algebra, sive ars rei et census'* (algebra, or the art of things and counting), in the seventeenth century is called *'algebra, seu doctrina aequationum* (algebra, which is the doctrine of equations).' "[12] It is these relations which now become the thinker's objects. They are objects radically free from any physical interpretation, objects which give entry into a mathematical world in which "geometry" and "algebra" become interchangeable modes of thinking.

In these equations, the symbols are mathematically interpreted so that they allow for the kinds of manipulation familiar from arithmetic, namely, addition, subtraction, multiplication, division, and extraction of roots. Descartes introduces "these arithmetical terms into geometry, in order to make [himself] more intelligible" (AT 6:370; O 177). Not only does he make *himself* more intelligible by the use of symbols; the increase in intelligibility reflects the fact that their use has allowed the *discipline* to achieve a greater degree of systematicity, which is to say that it is more of a science. Consider the simple example introduced in rule 16, that of finding the length of the hypotenuse (AC) in a right-angled triangle the length of whose other two sides (AB and BC) are 9 and 12 units. We could make this a matter of the senses and through measurement obtain the result; but this would give no more than a specific result in a particular situation, hence would not be science. Or we could take the square of 9, add it to the square of 12, find the square root of their sum (225) and come up with the correct answer (15) now arithmetically determined. In this case, we have given names to the lines (AB, BC, and AC), have abstracted from these names by replacing them with numbers, and used these numbers in the

[9]   All translations from the *Geometry* are quoted from Paul J. Olscamp's *René Descartes: Discourse on Method, Optics, Geometry, and Meteorology* (New York, 1965) (hereafter, O).

[10]   In rule 16, Descartes's use is to "employ the letters a, b, c, etc. to express magnitudes already known, and A, B, C, etc. for ones that are unknown" (AT 10:455; CSM 1:67). In the *Geometry* the capital letters are replaced by x, y, z, etc.

[11]   Such symbolism was introduced before Descartes in François Viète's *Introduction to the Analytic Art* (1591). Descartes claimed that he had not read this work until after he had published his *Geometry*. On both Viète and Descartes's difference from Viète, see Michael S. Mahoney's "The Beginnings of Algebraic Thought in the Seventeenth Century" in Gaukroger, *Descartes: Philosophy, Mathematics and Physics*, 143–44.

[12]   Mahoney, 146.

arithmetical manipulations of multiplication, addition, and root extraction. But we are still dealing with specific numbers (hence with a specific triangle), and the number from which we extracted the root (225) does not reveal that it is composed of two magnitudes in a specific relation. But if we abstract from lines, names, *and numbers* (so that $AB = 9 = a$, $BC = 12 = b$, and $AC = ? = c$), the solution can be written as $c = \sqrt{a^2 + b^2}$ This is not only a truly general statement; it is also one which keeps the various elements distinct. Hence Descartes writes

> We insist on these distinctions, seeking as we do a knowledge of things that is evident and distinct. The arithmeticians, however, make no such distinctions: they are quite content if the sum they are seeking comes to light [*si occurrat illis summa quaesita*], even though they have no idea how it depends on the data; yet that, quite simply, is what knowledge strictly speaking [*scientia proprie*] consists in. (AT 10:458; CSM 1:69).

For this manipulation of symbols in equations we depend on imagination. The imagination in question is intellectual rather than corporeal, for the symbols arose in the first place through abstraction from "matter," "geometrical figures," and "numbers."[13] And it is imagination rather than reason, for the equations in which these symbols function contain unknown quantities, namely, some of these symbols themselves, such as x, y^2, z^3 (or, in the above example, c).[14]

The fact that these symbols are entirely abstract allows for their use as magnitudes in general in all sorts of proportions. Thus they no longer signify perceptible relations between, say, a square and a cube whose sides are of equal length. More than that, their abstract nature allows for ratios between or among entities which are not perceptible or imageable, entities like a^4, a^5, or, in general, a^n. The ratios among these entities depend entirely on the rules of algebra; hence both these entities and their relations are free from the constraints of sense or corporeal imagination. And as we shall see in a moment, some of these entities are free even from the con-

---

[13] This process of abstraction appears as parallel to a process which we met in the fifth section of my second chapter, that of "divesting" the imagination "of every distinct impression."

[14] I believe Schuster to be wrong when he argues that Descartes abandons the *Regulae* precisely at the point where he realizes that "imaginative representation" (i.e., use of *corporeal* imagination) "or geometrical presentation at all" cannot "ground" "mathematical truths" and therefore moves to "a more abstract-relational view of the grounds of mathematical truth." I believe the latter view is already that of the *Regulae* and that the example I have just used illustrates precisely this point. See "Whatever Should We Do with Cartesian Method?"

straint of intelligibility: Descartes allows for a nonintuitive element in the postulation of negative roots.[15]

This use of symbols in analytic geometry places Descartes in a situation far removed from that of the ancient geometers. For them diagrams, that is, imageable or sensible data, were the loci in which discoveries are made. For Descartes, geometrical discoveries are made in the first place in the abstract realm of algebra.[16] This priority of the abstract has as a consequence that when some of these discoveries allow for their representation on paper, then what is conveyed through these diagrams is itself universal. Thus a Cartesian geometrical diagram never conveys relations which hold only in the pictured instance. The fact that its construction was governed by an algebraic equation insures that it is never one of a kind.

The objects of analytic geometry are symbols and the equations in which they function. These objects are relational and in this respect quite unlike the objects of sense or of corporeal imagination. In contrast to the latter, these objects have no properties peculiar to themselves which would allow their individuation. I now want to turn to more limited aspects of these objects.

Second. Intellectual imagination plays its role in geometry through the use of hypotheses in the technique of "assuming the problem to be already solved" by (1) supposing an unknown but possibly knowable quantity, or by (2) supposing something unknown which cannot come to be known.

1. *Supposing that which can become an item of knowledge.* As in the *Meditations*, so in the *Geometry* we meet the terms which Descartes employs as indicators for the presence of intellectual imagination, as in "[I]f we wish to solve some problem, we should first of all consider [*considerer*]

---

[15] I here use "nonintuitive" rather than "counterintuitive." The latter is the term used by Stephen Gaukroger in "The Nature of Abstract Reasoning: Philosophical Aspects of Descartes' Work in Algebra," in Cottingham, *Cambridge Companion to Descartes*, 98. Descartes's concept of "negative roots" may be counterintuitive in terms of Aristotelian logic, but I am not sure whether that would in this instance be a strong enough ground for Descartes to want to apply that term to the situation.

[16] When Emily Grosholz writes that, for Descartes, *(a)* "algebraic expressions and manipulations had to be referred back to the geometric diagram, in order to avoid mistakes which arise in the manipulation of empty symbols," and that *(b)* "the geometric diagram is then the source of discovery," this *(a)* restricts the limits of analytic geometry in a way which Descartes resisted (there is more to analytic geometry than what can be referred to geometric diagrams), and *(b)* that "discovery" is then only about the relation between the possible and the actual, not about the possible (that is, the geometrical) as such. See her "Descartes' Unification of Algebra and Geometry"; the first quotation (in which Grosholz quotes T. LeNoir) is from page 168; the second is from page 160.

it solved" (AT 6:372; O 179) and "I assume [*suppose*] the problem to be already solved" (AT 6:382 and 414; O 186 and 207). The supposition, in these cases, is the assumption of a hypothesis in the form of an equation or a set of equations, in which we work with symbols some of whose values we know and some of whose values we do not know, and in which the unknown values are to be determined through comparison or relation with the symbols whose values are known. The act of assuming the problem to be already solved occurs in introducing the symbols for which we do not yet have values, and the actual solving of the problem (if it can be solved) occurs in relating these symbols to those for which we do have values.

These assumptions may introduce not just symbols representing unknown quantities but, as well, symbols which indicate whether such quantities are positive or negative. The assumption usually involves more than a single supposition. There is a single supposition only in those cases where we can imagine no more than a single possible solution to a problem. In most cases, various solutions are imaginatively possible, and each of these possibilities must be enumerated as one of the suppositions. When he introduces these, Descartes in some instances uses a form of the word "imagine," and sometimes of "suppose," but both cases are clearly of the same kind.

In the following passages the intellectual imagination's presence is indicated through the use of some form of *supposer*. In solving geometrical problems by means of equations, "we must find as many such equations as we assume [*suppose*] there to be unknown lines" (AT 6:372; O 179). "[T]he equation by which we look for the quantity x or y or another such quantity—assuming [*en supposant*] [the lines] *PA* and *PC* are known . . . " (AT 6:417; O 211). "[T]he signs + and − can be assumed [*suppose*] to be however we wish . . . " (AT 6:422; O 214). "[T]he invention of assuming [*l'invention de supposer*] two equations of the same form, in order to compare separately all the terms of the one with those of the other, and so to get several equations from one . . . can be used in an infinity of . . . problems" (AT 6:423; O 214). "[I]n each equation there can be as many different roots (that is, values of the unknown quantity) as the unknown quantity has dimensions. For example, if we assume [*suppose*] x equal to 2 . . . " (AT 6:444; O 229). "And if, without knowing the value of the roots of an equation, we wish to increase or diminish it by some known quantity, it is only necessary to assume [*supposer*], in the place of the unknown quantity [x], another which is greater or lesser than this unknown quantity by the given number . . . " (For example, if we want to increase x by 3, then x comes to be substituted by y, where $y − 3 = x$) (AT 6:447; O 231).

These various uses of *supposer* mark the presence of intellectual imagination, for each of these examples introduces an unknown but hypothetically posited quantity symbolically represented, or involves experimental manipulation of the positive or negative value of this quantity. In each of the cases there is the expectation that (through the relationships holding in the equation of which the unknown quantity is a part) the unknown quantity will have its symbolic representation replaced with a specific and known quantity. These instances of symbolic representation are analogous to what happens when hypotheses are verified in the physical sciences: both symbol and hypothesis disappear qua symbol and hypothesis, in that both become a known part of the relevant system.

2. *Supposing that which cannot become an item of knowledge.* There are other cases of the use of *supposer* or of *imaginer* where, in a crucial respect, the outcome is different. Here, intellectual imagination supposes unknown quantities some of which cannot come to be known. This allows us the clearest possible indication of the presence of intellectual imagination in the *Geometry*. The cases in question are some of those in which Descartes introduces roots. One of these is at AT 6:453–4; O 236:

> For the rest [note that] the true roots, as well as the negative ones, are not always real, but sometimes only imaginary [*imaginaires*]; that is, while we can always conceive [*imaginer*] as many roots for each equation as I have stated, still there is sometimes no quantity corresponding to those we conceive [*qu'on imagine*]. Thus, although we can conceive [*qu'on imagine*] three roots in the equation
>
> $$x^3 - 6x^2 + 13x - 10 = 0$$
>
> there is nevertheless only one real root, 2, and no matter how we may augment, diminish, or multiply the other two, in the way just explained, they will still be imaginary [*qu'imaginaires*].

The concept of roots which are "sometimes only imaginary" so that "there is sometimes no quantity to those we conceive [*qu'on imagine*]" corroborates two points made in this chapter. First, it illustrates that Descartes frees mathematical science from its Greek understanding in which the objects of mathematical thought were always identifiable quantities. Second, it illustrates the presence of intellectual imagination: the imaginary roots for which there is "no quantity" are entities of a purely abstract nature, nonrepresentable, nonintuitable objects arising out of purely structural considerations.[17]

[17]   My interpretation at this point follows that of Mahoney. He writes: "[T]he intuitive aspects of geometry diminish. According to Descartes, every equation $x^n + a_1x^{n-1} + \ldots + a^n = 0$ is a complex relation that consists of the simpler relations $x - a = 0, x - b = 0, \ldots, x - s = 0$. Each quantity $a, b, c, \ldots, s$ is a root of the original equation, that is, each may be substituted for x without disturbing the equality. From experience, however, Descartes knows that quite often not all roots of a given equation can be found numerically or geometrically.

The passage quoted from AT 6:453–54: O 236 contains the conclusion of a line of argument which started a few pages earlier in Descartes's text. If we backtrack to these earlier pages, this will further confirm the role of intellectual imagination. At At 6:444–45; O 229–30 we read

> I must say something in general about the nature of equations—that is, about sums composed of many terms, partly known and partly unknown, some of which are equal to others, or rather, all of which taken together are equal to nothing, for it is often best to consider them in this way.
>
> Understand, then, that in each equation there can be as many different roots (that is, values of the unknown quantity), as the unknown quantity has dimensions. For example, if we assume [*suppose*] x equal to 2, or else $x - 2$ equal to zero; and again $x = 3$, or else $x - 3 = 0$, then by multiplying these equations, $x - 2 = 0$ and $x - 3 = 0$, by each other, we will have $x^2 - 5x + 6 = 0$, or else $x^2 = 5x - 6$, which is an equation in which x has the value 2, and simultaneously has the value 3. And if again we make $x - 4 = 0$, and multiply this by $x^2 - 5x + 6 = 0$, we will have $x^3 - 9x^2 + 26x - 24 = 0$, which is another equation in which x, having three dimensions, also has three values, which are 2, 3, and 4.
>
> But it often happens that some of these roots are negative, or less than nothing.

If some of these negative roots are nonintuitable but still part of the discipline, they must be imaginable. We then have the power of imagining them, but not corporeally so. The fact that we cannot corporeally imagine them is reflected in Descartes's statement that these roots cannot function as entities which allow for geometric construction: "we know . . . that the four roots of the equation . . . are imaginary; and that the problem for which we discovered this equation is plane by nature, but that it cannot in any way be constructed, because the given quantities cannot be added" (AT 6:461; O 241).

At the end of the *Geometry* Descartes makes it quite clear why his new geometry cannot be restricted to what may be corporeally imagined or

---

For example, if one tries to factor the equation $x^3 - 1 = 0$ into the form $(x - a)(x - b)(x - c) = 0$ one finds $a = 1$, of course, but no values at first for b and c. Nevertheless such values must exist or at least be imagined in order for the structural analysis of the equation to retain its generality. Hence Descartes summons his 'imaginary' roots into existence. He does not say much more about these roots, but it suffices for our purpose that they exist at all. For, for the first time there appear new, purely abstract, non-intuitive objects in mathematics, which arise out of structural considerations" (146).

constructed with ruler and compass. In its final paragraph he comments on the fact that he has provided a way of solving all plane and solid problems in geometry,[18] and then adds that "we have only to follow the same method in order to construct all problems to an infinite degree of complexity. For in the matter of mathematical progressions, once we have the first two or three terms, it is not difficult to find the others." The degree of generality in the phrase "construct *all* problems to an *infinite* degree of complexity" implies that the equations of analytic geometry must be considered independently of the possibility of their being corporeally represented in the pictures of imagination or the diagrams of geometry. For we can find the roots for an equation of the nth degree, where n may stand for any number whatsoever. With respect to geometrical problems which are *one, two,* or n degrees more complex than those of solid geometry, visualization or spatial construction is impossible. Three-dimensional space determines the limits of human ability corporeally to imagine and sensibly to construct. Descartes refuses to accept these limits as boundaries for his geometry. Nevertheless, when he writes about those elements of his geometry which are "not real" in that they have "no quantity," hence can be neither pictured nor constructed, he writes about their being "imagined." The conclusion that this is nonimaging, noncorporeal imagination is inescapable.

Intellectual imagination is, then, crucial to Descartes's geometry in three ways. It makes it possible for the understanding to work with hypotheses in the assumption of solutions through the use of symbols whose values are unknown. It allows these symbols a power beyond what is imageable or constructible on paper, and thus allows geometry to pass the boundaries of Euclidean space. And in the concept of "negative roots" it allows some of these symbols to be beyond our power of imaging and understanding.[19] The question next to be considered concerns the symbols

[18]   It is in terms of the *generality* which characterizes his system that Descartes dismisses the charge of being a follower (or even a copier) of François Viète (1540–1603). To Mersenne, Descartes writes "[I]f you compare what I wrote . . . concerning the number of roots in each equation with what Viète has written on this topic . . . you will see that I determine this question for all equations in general. He, by contrast, gives merely some particular examples. . . . Thus I began where he left off" (end December, 1637, AT 1:479; CSMK 3:78). In any case, Descartes denied ever having read Viète. On this point, see Rodis-Lewis, 110 and 243–44 n. 38.

[19]   In his *The Origin of Subjectivity: An Essay on Descartes* Hiram Caton comes close to articulating the distinctive functions of corporeal and intellectual imagination which are central to my account. He writes: "[T]here are two meanings of imagination . . . : it means the picture or ikon of something corporeal, and notation or symbolism. Notation, though visible and imaginable, is like pure intellect in that it stands in no direct relation to the world. This property of 'symbol-manipulating' imagination is obscured by the stress on imagination as the corporeal mental counterpart to the extension of the world" (173).

which *are* imageable. These are the ones with a potential purchase on the physical world. At this point, the corporeal imagination legitimately, in fact necessarily, enters the scene.

3. GEOMETRY AND CORPOREAL IMAGINATION

There is no dearth of diagrams in Descartes's *Geometry*. Diagrams can be pictured in the corporeal imagination and physically constructed on paper with ruler and compass or with the more complex tracing machines Descartes introduces in book 2 (e.g., AT 6:391 and 408–10; O 192 and 204–5). It was through his insistence that in geometry the intellect must not be hindered by sense or corporeal imagination that Descartes was able to create in effect a new geometrical object which was treated in a new geometrical discipline. But is the presence of these diagrams an indication that, although he in part overcame an earlier mode of mathematical thinking, Descartes was not himself very clear about what he was doing and, confusedly, regularly fell back into the earlier mode? Answering this question in the affirmative would be a serious misreading of Descartes's intentions. Of the various reasons why this is so, I shall state three.

The first of these is a matter of *motive*. The reason Descartes published his *Discourse* and the appended *Essays* in the first place was for the sake of *utility*. In this context, what he writes in part 6 of the *Discourse* bears repeating:

> I have never made much of the products of my own mind; and so long as the only fruits I gathered from the method I use were my own satisfaction regarding certain difficulties in the speculative sciences . . . I did not think I was obliged to write anything about it. . . . But as soon as I had acquired some general notions in physics and had noticed . . . where they could lead and how much they differ from the principles used up to now, I believed that I could not keep them secret without sinning gravely against the law which obliges us to do all in our power to secure the general welfare of mankind. For they opened my eyes to the possibility of gaining knowledge which would be very useful in life, and of discovering a practical philosophy . . . and thus make ourselves, as it were, the lords and masters of nature. (CSM 1:142; AT 6:61–62)

The abstract thinking required for pure science is, for Descartes, never to be an end in itself; the time devoted to it, though necessary, should remain minimal. It is necessary to devote sufficient time to the metaphysical and abstract physical foundations of the practical sciences, but it must be remembered that this thinking has instrumental value only, that it serves to lay the foundations for mastery. Hence, in a letter to Princess Elizabeth of Bohemia (28 June 1643, AT 3:690–95; CSMK 3:226–29), Descartes restates and augments the sentiment expressed in the sixth part of the *Discourse*: "[N]ever . . . spend more than a few hours a day in the thoughts which occupy the imagination and a few hours a year on those which occupy the intellect alone"; although it is true that it is "the study of mathematics which exercises mainly the imagination in the consideration of shapes and motions [and that it] accustoms us to form very distinct notions of body," it is just as true that what we really want to know is what affects the human being (the particular "union of the soul and the body"), and that "is known only obscurely by the intellect alone or even by the intellect aided by the imagination, but is known very clearly by the senses."

This restatement contains some barely restrained impatience with those of his correspondents who (like Elizabeth) wanted to have him continue spending much of his time on pure thought alone: "[I]t would be very harmful to occupy one's intellect frequently in meditating upon . . . the knowledge of God and of our soul . . . since this would impede it from devoting itself to the functions of the imagination and the senses." More than six years had elapsed since the publication of the *Discourse*, but the obligation remained the same: move from abstract thought to useful, practical knowledge as soon as this is legitimate, that is, as soon as abstract thought is sufficiently advanced to serve as proper foundation. The passage from the purely abstract to the fully concrete is, in the first place, by means of the corporeal imagination. Hence, in the *Geometry*, imaging has its place. It is, in fact, necessary that imaging be brought into play as soon as there is a sufficient foundation in analytic geometry to allow for its proper use. This necessity is one of duty: we can only understand and manipulate what affects beings composed of soul and body once we understand extension, and "nothing falls within the scope of the imagination without being in some way extended"— as Descartes writes to Henry More (5 February 1649, AT 5:270; CSMK 3:362). The imaged presentation of the relationships expressed in analytic geometry is the imaging of properties that potentially belong to the physical world.

I shall explicate the importance of this nexus of intellect and extension when I discuss the third reason which makes the *Geometry*'s diagrams necessary. But before I do so, I must state the second reason.

It concerns the relationship of Descartes's geometry to that which already existed and had its roots deep in ancient Greek thought. We must remember that the *Geometry* plays a complex instrumental role. It is one of the sciences which Descartes uses in order to demonstrate the utility of his method. One illustration of his geometry's utility is that it serves as foundation for applied science, while another is in terms of solving geometrical problems whose (complete) solutions eluded both the ancient geometricians and those of his own day. As Emily Grosholz has put it with respect to the latter role, "Descartes began where he should have begun, demonstrating the power of his method within the canon of Greek geometrical problems"; he had to start here because, as a successor to that of the Greeks, analytic geometry had to be "justified in part by [its] ability to reproduce or account for results already attained in the predecessor field."[20] Descartes's statement to Mersenne shortly after the publication of the *Discourse* is quite revealing on this point:

> In the *Optics* and *Meteorology* I merely tried to show that my method [*ma méthode*] is better than the usual one; in my *Geometry*, however, I claim I have demonstrated this. Right at the beginning I solve a problem which according to the testimony of Pappus none of the ancients managed to solve; and it can be said that none of the moderns has been able to solve it either. ... (End of December 1637, AT 1:478; CSMK 3:77–78)

Since all of these problems were set in Euclidean space, their solutions allowed for diagrammatic representation. In the presentation of his solutions Descartes therefore naturally and legitimately introduced the relevant diagrams.

Descartes's work on these problems accomplished more than providing their solutions. (1) Providing their solutions was at the same time a practical justification or authorization of his method. This justification was not of a method limited to solving *particular* problems but included the demonstration of its *generality*. (2) Therefore another reason for dealing with existing problems, their diagrams, and their partial solutions if there were any, was to show that they can all be solved by *a single procedure*; and since this procedure is *ma méthode*, which is itself a functional definition of reason, these various problems and their solutions are now part of a rational scheme. Thus, in the process of justifying his method Descartes believed he had not just created the science of analytic geometry, but for the first time in history made a true science of classical geometry.[21] Use of the method resulted in dispelling the "superficiality" of the "proofs which are discovered more through chance than method and which have more to do with our eyes and imagination" (*Regulae*, rule 4). Methodic procedure caused these proofs to be "squared with the standards of reason" (*ajustées au niveau de la raison* [AT 6:14; CSM 1:117]. (3) In this process Descartes relativized the diagrams which illustrate these proofs in the sense that their Euclidean nature now no longer delimits the extent of these proofs; being

---

20   "Descartes' Unification of Algebra and Geometry," 161.
21   Stephen Gaukroger comes close to articulating this position when he writes that many of the solutions advanced by Greek mathematicians "were more often than not the result of ingenious one-off solutions of problems rather than being due to the application of some general procedure. It is precisely such a general procedure that Descartes develops and puts to use in the *Geometry*" ("The Nature of Abstract Reasoning," 92).

perfectly general, the proofs hold for any number of lines, for x^4, x^5, and x^n no less than for x, x^2, and x^3.

This introduces the third reason which makes these diagrams necessary. Diagrams introduce a double relativization in Descartes's *Geometry*: a relativization *of* diagrams and a relativization *through* diagrams. First, relativization of diagrams allows geometrical insight to extend beyond the confines of Euclidean space; thus Descartes passes beyond classical geometry. Second, diagrams in turn serve to indicate the extent to which Descartes's analytic geometry is potentially relevant to the physical world in which we live, and so they relativize the new geometry. Diagrams reveal that not all of this analytic geometry can serve as the link between metaphysics on the one hand and medicine, mechanics, and morals on the other. For the world in which we find ourselves, diagrams help to determine the nature and extent of the possible linkage between pure and applied science. In other words, Descartes's geometry needs diagrams—requires corporeal imagination—as a necessary complement. This is because pure geometrical thought reveals a realm some of which is possible in our world and some of which transcends such possibility. Pure geometry by itself does not identify the possible, or the possibly actual, configurations of our physical world.[22]

The matter of priority is, however, crucial. It is reason and intellectual imagination, not corporeal imagination or sensation and hence not diagrams, which determine the contents of geometry. Ideas of the intellect are logically prior to the images of corporeal imagination.[23] Thus, again, there is not only nothing wrong with using corporeal imagination, and even sense, in geometry—at a certain stage their role becomes necessary. They must, however, play their proper role, and that precludes their tem-

[22]   This mutual "relativizing" or "limiting" has been discussed by various recent commentators. See, e.g., David Lachterman's *The Ethics of Geometry*, 173–74 and 196. On the latter page he writes that "The range of intelligibility, then, does not coincide with the domains either of perceptual accessibility or of algebraic tractability." Only that which can be constructed in a continuous manner according to an algebraic formula is accepted as potentially descriptive of the physical world; that which cannot be so constructed will not receive this acceptance.

[23]   In this connection, Amélie Oksenberg Rorty writes about the discussion of the piece of wax in the Second Meditation that "Descartes is primarily concerned to show that the *general* ideas of extension and of its essential properties are intellectual ideas, independent of the [corporeal] imagination. . . . Because imagination-ideas about physical objects logically presuppose intellectual ideas, the general ideas of extension are best analyzed by an investigation of intellectual ideas." See her "Descartes on Thinking with the Body," 376–77. In the last of these sentences—given that she writes about analysis of "the general ideas of extension"—replacing the phrase "are best" by "can only be" would, I think, do greater justice to Descartes's position.

poral and logical order-violating precedence over the intellect. Rule 4 emphasizes that if they attempt to play that leading role, the results are disastrous: beginning by concentrating on "imaginary figures," we end up resting "content in the knowledge of . . . trifles" (AT 10:375; CSM 1:18). These are the "haphazard studies and obscure reflections [which] blur the natural light and blind our intelligence" (AT 10:371; CSM 1:16). It is the pure intellect which must lead, for "the exclusive concern of mathematics is with questions of order or measure and . . . it is irrelevant whether the measure in question involves numbers, shapes, stars, sounds, or any other object whatever" (AT 10:377–78; CSM 1:19).

This "irrelevance" is indicated by the very place geometry occupies in the tree of knowledge: geometry or pure physics is the trunk of the tree leading up to the sciences which deal with the world in which we live and in which numbers, shapes, etc., are of prime concern. Geometry is the science which— to repeat the closing words of the French edition of the Fifth Meditation— gives us "demonstrations which have no concern [*n'ont point d'égard*] with whether that object exists." It *cannot*, that is, *is not allowed to*, have such concern as long as the science is being developed, for it can be developed only by reason aided by intellectual imagination. It *may only* be a matter of implementation of the method whose articulation is a functional definition of reason, of that "general science which explains all the points which can be raised concerning order and measure irrespective of the subject-matter."[24]

However, "irrelevance" and "no concern" are here themselves strictly relative. As long as we deal with the *development* of this science, visible illustrations may play no role; hence sense and corporeal imagination must be kept at bay. Once the science (or a distinct part thereof) has been developed, illustrations become crucially important. For since geometry is meant to be developed as a basis for the sciences which promise their dividends in their *utility*, it becomes necessary to illustrate the physical applicability of geometry to the extent that it has such applicability. The geometrically constructible diagram therefore is needed as intermediary between pure thought and practical application.

Corporeal imagination plays a crucial role when, in imaging the analytic relationships stated in an equation, it produces an item which is both intellectual and corporeal. It is therefore apt to speak about the corporeal imagination as "mediator."[25] It can play this mediating role be-

[24]   Here recall the point I made before: In this functional definition of reason the role of intellectual imagination is implicated in the phrase "by supposing some order even among objects that have no natural order of precedence" (AT 6:18–19; CSM 1:120).

[25]   In "The Cartesian Imagination," Veronique Foti alludes to both the mediating and the limiting roles of corporeal imagination when she writes that "the imagination . . . can be at the behest of the intellect and serve as both the medium and the limit marker of representation" (636). See here also the excellent discussion of corporeal imagination as "mediator"

cause (as we have seen) although both understanding and corporeally imagining are mental functions, they are quite different mental functions. "For in understanding the mind employs only itself, while in imagination it contemplates a corporeal form. And although geometrical figures are wholly corporeal, this does not entail that the ideas by means of which we understand them should be thought of as corporeal (unless they fall under the [corporeal] imagination)" (At 7:385; CSM 2:264).

This interpretation of the role of diagrams is supported by Descartes's theory about geometry in the *Regulae*. In rule 12 (at AT 10:416; CSM 1:43) we read that the intellect "cannot receive any help from" and would only be "hampered by . . . the senses . . . and the imagination." But as the immediate context of these phrases makes clear, this is only when "the intellect is concerned with matters in which there is nothing corporeal or similar to the corporeal." "If, however, the intellect proposes to examine something which can be referred to . . . body, the idea of that thing must be formed as distinctly as possible in the [corporeal] imagination." Given the place of geometry in the tree of knowledge, it is to be expected that it contains at least something relevant to the "corporeal or similar to the corporeal," that there will be "something which can be referred to body," and "the idea of *that* thing must be formed as distinctly as possible in the [corporeal] imagination." This is because "if we are to imagine something, and are to make use, not of the pure intellect, but of the intellect aided by images depicted in the imagination, then nothing can be ascribed to magnitudes in general which cannot also be ascribed to any species of magnitude." When, therefore, through the use of symbols we abstract from specific "geometrical figures," "numbers," and "from any matter whatever," and so transcend the boundaries of Euclidean space and deal with "magnitudes in general," there is nothing to prevent us subsequently from determining which of these "magnitudes in general" can "also be ascribed to" a specific "species of magnitude" (AT 10:457–58; CSM 1:68–69). The fact that nothing prevents us from this activity allows for the realization of the duty Descartes ascribes to those who develop pure science: they must make their abstract thought serviceable to achieving understanding of practical reality.

This task can be achieved because of the nature of corporeal imagination and the role which this nature makes it possible for it to play. When, through corporeal imagination, the mind images the relationships holding in an algebraic formula, the image which results is a generalized image and, as such, differs from the particular image received through sensation. In this

in E. van Leeuwen's *Descartes' Regulae: De eenheid van heuristische wetenschap en zelfbewustzijn* (Amsterdam 1986), especially 204–11.

process of imaging, the passivity and haphazardness of sensation have come to be replaced by the activity and scientific control of the intellect. Imagination now no longer represents what our eyes have fortuitously come across in the physical world, but presents what our intellect has inscribed from within. In both cases, the image is a physical entity, for this imagination is corporeal. In both cases, therefore, there is embodied extension. But what used to be (as in pre-Cartesian geometry) embodied extension over whose configurations the intellect had limited or no control, is now embodied extension over whose configurations the intellect—being its author—has full control. Its authorship consists in the fact that these now visible configurations arose through the intellect's imaging the relations holding in the algebraic equations which it itself both constructed and solved.

The preceding paragraphs indicate considerable coalescence of my position with Dennis Sepper's most recent thought on this subject in "The Problem of Figuration, or How the Young Descartes Figured Things Out."[26] They also indicate the point at which I go beyond the position he there adopts. We agree that diagrammatic instantiation allows the scientist passage from theory to practice and so provides the foundation for the relevance of theoretical solutions to problems of the world in which we live. For both of us, therefore, imagination becomes crucial to understanding Descartes's thought—both the young Descartes and Descartes the mature thinker. The point on which there is disagreement is that for Sepper, in both the *Regulae* and the *Geometry*, algebra remains subordinate to geometry as a memory aid which allows us schematically to keep track of geometrical problems.[27] This is no doubt one of the functions of algebra. But a more important function is that algebraic representations indicate *various* realms of possibility, while geometric or imagistic figuration indi-

---

[26]   This paper is forthcoming in a collection being edited by Stephen Gaukroger, John Schuster, and John Sutton, *Descartes' Natural Philosophy*.

[27]   Sepper here adopts the 1980 position of Emily Grosholz who argued that since, for Descartes, it is the geometric diagram which is "the source of discovery," "algebra alone, like logic, cannot lead to discovery, but merely record in orderly form information previously ascertained." Grosholz bases her position on rule 14. I do not see any grounds for drawing such a conclusion from rule 14. And rule 16 indicates the opposite position, the one for which I argue, when it states that "Accordingly, once we have investigated the problem expressed in general terms, we should re-express it in terms of given numbers, to see whether these might provide us with a simpler solution"; and "The purpose of this is that once we have found the solution in terms of these symbols, we shall be able to apply it easily to the particular subject we are dealing with . . . " (AT 10:457–58; CSM 1:68–69). Grosholz does take a step toward my position about the role of algebra, but not as it functions in Descartes: "In the work of succeeding generations, techniques for moving back and forth between the geometric graph and the algebraic equation gradually led to the accession of the equation to instrument of discovery in its own right." The quotations from Grosholz are from "Descartes' Unification of Algebra and Geometry," 160–61.

cates possibilities, or actualities, in the *specific* realm which constitutes the human sensible world. Sepper, in other words, has no room for the double role of relativization which I ascribe to Descartes's figuration.

Metaphysical questions about the trustworthiness of both intellectual and corporeal imagination are among those remaining for my final chapter. If we assume, for the moment, that these questions can be satisfactorily resolved, then we may take the *Geometry* as the work in which Descartes passed beyond the limits of the Fifth Meditation. For he is, here, in the process of achieving "full and certain knowledge . . . of that corporeal nature which is the subject-matter of pure mathematics"—but through his reason-sanctioned introduction of corporeal imagination, it is now no longer the case that this knowledge has "no concern with whether that object exists."

We have now arrived at the point where the exposition may be connected with various paragraphs of my fourth chapter. Through corporeal imagination Descartes believes he has passed from the glowing embers of the imaginatively possible to the blazing fire of the scientifically understood actual. The scientifically understood, physically actual image traced in the corporeal imagination is to guarantee that this image can be made actual as intelligible-sensible object in the physical context of the being in whose imagination this image exists. In the process, Descartes has taken a position far removed from that which allowed him admiration for the sparks which the sharp blows of enthusiastic poetic imagination force from the flint of human nature. For Descartes, these sparks are bound to grow pale once the flame of systematic truth begins to light humanity's path with its steady brilliance. This is the systematic truth which philosophers and scientists extract through reason aided by disciplined intellectual imagination and which is revealed as potentially useful through corporeal imagination. It is the truth of which, Descartes was convinced, his *Geometry* was the most blazing instance yet in the progress of philosophy and science.

4. Disciplining Intellectual Imagination

It needs no emphasis that Descartes assigned a crucial role to sensation in applied science. That role comes to the fore in his insistence on experimentation, an aspect of his thought which has been analyzed and emphasized in many an excellent study during the past two decades. Instead, what needs highlighting is the role of intellectual imagination in applied science, more specifically, the interplay between intellectual imagination and sensation: the former in its function of hypothesis formation, the latter as necessary for the kind of experimentation which leads to the achievement of the useful knowledge which Descartes expects from mechanics, medicine, and morals.

We know it to be Descartes's position that theory developed in geometry or pure physics on the one hand is necessary for achieving the useful knowledge of the applied sciences, and on the other hand gives us no immediate access to the world in which these sciences find application. It is therefore fair (in fact, Cartesian) to characterize pure geometrical thought as fictitious in the sense that it need not be about the kind of physical world which is in fact our world. A complication is that Descartes states that even the science which he developed about the world in which we live—such as that presented in his *Meteorology* and *Optics*—is founded on hypotheses and hence in a sense remains fictitious. Thus although Descartes characterizes the pure physics of the *Geometry* as well as the applied physics of the *Optics* as *science*, in both there is for him an element of fictitiousness. Since no science is possible except as a product of reason, it now appears that reason itself is responsible for our possession of scientific knowledge which in some sense is fictitious. If this is a correct conclusion to draw, then two questions are: How can we account for the fact that reason is responsible for fictions? (is not that the realm of imagination?), and how is it that reason's fictions equip us with the knowledge whose application ameliorates our condition in the physical world in which we find ourselves? (is not such amelioration dependent on scientific fact?).

Answers to these questions lie in part in the complex set of relations between and among reason, intellectual imagination, freedom, hypotheses, corporeal imagination, sensation, and the external world. The key notion now to be discussed was mentioned in the penultimate sentence of the preceding section; it is that of *discipline*.

Through the freedom which intrinsically attaches to intellectual imagination we can imagine anything we like, even that which is irrational (as is the notion of an evil genius), not accessible to intuition (as are negative roots), or incapable of finding instantiation in our sensible world (as are the equations of analytic geometry which go beyond the power of three). It is this freedom of imagination which introduces the fictitious element in science, whether that science be metaphysics, pure physics, or even (as we shall see) an applied science like mechanics. Now such irrational, nonintuitable, or noninstantiable notions do have their use; my discussion of the *Meditations* and the *Geometry* makes that clear enough for the pure sciences. But at certain stages in the development of the sciences whether pure or applied, intellectual imagination requires the kind of discipline which limits its freedom to imagine anything it can. At the stage where we look for power-bestowing knowledge in the development of science useful to us as beings composed of soul and body, this discipline comes from reason on the one hand and from corporeal imagination and sensation on the other.[28] First, some comments about the discipline which reason exerts on intellectual imagination in the context of the pursuit of this useful knowledge; after that, I can turn to the discipline exerted by corporeal imagination and by sensation through experimentation.[29]

Intellectual imagination generates hypotheses (proposes "causes"), but, as we saw in my third chapter, since the hypotheses must be relevant to the problem to be solved (to specific "effects" to be explained), not any hypotheses will do. How do we come to entertain the hypotheses which are in fact relevant? The general answer was that for any effect to be explained, the imagination will offer as simple a cause as possible or a number of the simplest possible alternative causes. These causes or hypotheses are conjectures, hence fictional in nature. If such a cause can be intuited to have a necessary connection with the effect to be explained, that reduces its hypothetical character and it becomes a true proposition which extends the deductive argument. The reduction of its hypothetical status is a shedding of some of its fictional character. Why Descartes maintains that it has not shed all of it will be clear later on.

The disciplinary action of reason enters in two distinct ways. One of these is related to intuition. It may be stated negatively, as follows. Suppose that a conjectured cause cannot be intuited to have a necessary relation to the relevant parts of the body of knowledge we have already developed, or that it cannot even be seen to be so related to some still only partially intelligible item which is thus only partially incorporated in that body of knowledge. Then such a cause is rejected as false and the hypothesis is dismissed.

---

[28] There is a long tradition stretching from Newton till our days which appears unaware of the discipline to which Descartes explicitly subjects imagination and which therefore gives a strong sense-based character to his applied science. We know Newton's explicitly anti-Descartes remark, *"hypotheses non fingo."* And Desmond Clarke (who quotes this Newtonian dictum) writes that "Descartes and his followers in France in the seventeenth century were almost profligate in imagining hypothetical models to explain natural phenomena. . . . It was this widespread and notorious dedication to unrestrained hypothesis construction that helps explain Newton's famous disclaimer." Whatever may have been the practice of Descartes's "followers" in this case hardly holds for Descartes himself. Later on in the article from which I just quoted Clarke implicitly acknowledges this point when he writes that "one cannot avoid the necessity of relying on experientially based evidence. Descartes acknowledges the need for this kind of evidence in natural philosophy and uses it extensively. . . . He says openly, in Part VI of the *Discourse*, 'regarding observations, that the further we advance in our knowledge, the more necessary they become' (AT 6:63; CSM 1:143)." Clarke's use of "openly" here seems to imply something unusual on Descartes's part, while in fact there is, for Descartes, nothing unusual in it. My quotations are from Desmond M. Clarke, "Descartes' Philosophy of Science and the Scientific Revolution," in Cottingham, *Cambridge Companion to Descartes*, 270 and 279.
[29] The following four paragraphs restate conclusions reached in my third chapter (section 2). For more on reason's discipline of imagination, see particularly my *Imposition of Method*, chap. 3, section 4.

The second way in which reason as disciplinarian enters is logically prior to that just stated. It is related to the fact that although the imagination presents causes for which it does not yet have any proof, these hypotheses are not presented without any justification at all beyond the fact of their simplicity. It is thus not by chance that certain conjectures are initially relevant: the introduction of possibly relevant causes is in part determined by the effect to be explained and in part by the knowledge we already possess. Some comments about each of these are in order, beginning with the latter.

The imagination's ability to introduce relevant hypotheses depends on suitable preparation, on the discipline of reason which requires thorough familiarity with the details of the argument as far as it has been developed. It is these details which help to set one context for the initial relevance of any proposed cause.[30] This role of reason as disciplinarian of intellectual imagination is behind a statement such as that from the Second Set of Objections and Replies: "Analysis shows the true way by means of which the thing in question was discovered methodically. . . . But this method contains nothing to compel belief in an . . . inattentive reader; for if he fails to attend even to the smallest point, he will not see the necessity of the conclusion" (AT 7:155–56; CSM 2:110). This role of disciplinarian is also behind the following statement from the end of the *Discourse*, where the implied discipline is more than that exercised by reason alone:

> Should anyone be shocked at first by some of the statements I make at the beginning of the *Optics* and the *Meteorology* because I call them "suppositions" and do not seem to care about proving them, let him have the patience to read the whole book attentively, and I trust that he will be satisfied. For I take my reasonings to be so closely interconnected that just as the last are proved by the first, which are their causes, so the first are proved by the last, which are their effects. It must not be supposed that I am here committing the fallacy that the logicians call "arguing in a circle". For as experience makes most of these effects quite certain, the causes from which I deduce them serve not so much to prove them as to explain them; indeed, quite the contrary, it is the causes which are proved by the effects. And I have called them "suppositions" simply to make it known that I can deduce them from the primary truths I have expounded. . . . (AT 6:76; CSM 1:150)

To "deduce them from the primary truths" is not to say that they immediately follow from such truths, for most of the time—and in the applied sciences all of the time—hypotheses enter quite some way removed from the "foundation." Those who want metaphysical certainty for the

---

[30] Note that in reason's disciplining imagination there is the assumption of a generally trustworthy memory through which the thinker is allowed access to the relevant doctrine already developed.

contents of the *Optics* or *Meteorology* (assuming for a moment the possibility of such certainty) will have to retrace their steps to the cogito and pay careful attention to all the intermediate steps. But even if that were to be done, more is needed in this case of applied sciences. Their suppositions or hypotheses are proved by the effects—though not, ultimately, either generated or validated by these effects. Their hypotheses are generated by intellectual imagination, and ultimately validated by reason; for their proving we need to turn to corporeal imagination and sensation in their relations to the effect requiring explanation.

About the discipline which corporeal imagination exerts on intellectual imagination I can be very brief, for all the relevant details were introduced when I considered the corporeal imagination's role as mediator. Through its imaging and construction of diagrams, corporeal imagination transcribes the intellectual imagination's and reason's ideas onto body. In this process of giving them their first bodily form, it helps to determine the possible linkage between pure and applied science. What I earlier called the relativization of analytic geometry through the use of diagrams can now also be seen as a matter of discipline: given that we want to develop useful knowledge which benefits us in this world, we must concentrate our attention on those deliverances of reason aided by intellectual imagination which promise such utility. Corporeal imagination as disciplinarian helps to determine the nature and extent of the possible linkage between pure physics and applied science.

It only *helps* in determining this, for both the actual existence of physical objects and the kinematic relationships which hold in the actual physical world elude the static diagram of solid geometry. For knowledge of them, reason, while continuing in its role as disciplinarian of intellectual imagination, now itself needs guidance or—a word used as legitimately here as earlier—discipline of sensation and experimentation. This is the second matter mentioned above which calls for some further comment.

Hypotheses originating with intellectual imagination and judged relevant by reason were often suggested to imagination by sensation, and sensation is always required to test them. We already mentioned sensation's suggestion of hypotheses when we discussed the discipline of reason over imagination: for any *effect* to be explained, the imagination proposes as simple a cause as possible, which reason then judges to have or not to have a connection with the effect. For the useful knowledge which is our concern throughout this section, access to the effect necessarily depends on sensation. What is involved here is that the hypotheses which reason judges were not entertained at random, for imagination proposed them because of their prima facie "fit" with the effect to be explained. And this effect was something given in our experience. Experience therefore was necessary as one stimulus which led the imagination to propose these particular hypotheses.[31] And in the realm of experience from which this stimulus originated we must also look for the test of the hypothesis to which the stimulus helped give rise.

This necessity of experience is no usurpation of the direction-setting and ultimately validating role of reason. Although sensation disciplines reason, it does not take ultimate precedence over it. Such usurpation of precedence would reintroduce the element of chance which Descartes found in the work of the ancients and against which he so strongly warned. There is, nevertheless, some element of chance in all of this. Specific historical conditions often determine the kind of effects for which we need causes, so that today we are less inclined to develop scientific explanations for, say, the rainbow or the circulation of blood in the human body, and more concerned with the restoration of the ozone layer or the treatment of AIDS. This aspect of historical relativity is of little importance to the issue at hand. More important is that though chance remains involved in the discipline through experiment, it is not simply the case that chance circumstances alone often bring about the requisite experiments we need in order to develop the applied sciences. Descartes indicates quite the contrary, as when he closes the preface to the French edition of his *Principles* with the words:

> [M]any centuries may pass before all the truths that can be deduced from these principles are actually so deduced. For the majority of truths remaining to be discovered depend on various particular observations which we never happen on by chance but which must be sought out with care and expense by very intelligent people.

For *some* of the truths remaining to be discovered, Descartes leaves it open that the relevant observations may well be hit upon by chance, as was perhaps also the case for some of the truths already established. What is not left open at all is the need for observation; in the case of the useful knowledge I am discussing, this need is absolute. In a letter to Jean-Baptiste Morin (12 September 1638) Descartes mentions the notion of *comparaison* (analogy) as necessary to settle questions about physical nature,

---

[31]   This holds for more than the physical sciences. In these, we experience phenomena such as the rainbow, or the decay of the human body, and we desire explanations for them so that we can direct nature through mechanics and the body through medicine. But a similar situation pertains in metaphysics and methodology. We are confronted by skeptics who, through their questions, make real for us the experience of doubt which challenges our very project to provide a firm foundation for the sciences and to build a lasting structure on that foundation. And so, stimulated through experience, reason and imagination begin their quest for truth and certainty in metaphysics.

and it is quite clear from the examples he uses that such *comparaisons* are in fact experiments. The need for experiment is here pronounced to be absolute: "[W]hen someone makes an assertion concerning nature which cannot be explained by any such analogy, I think I have demonstrated knowledge that the point is false" (AT 2:368; CSMK 3:122). Jointly with reason and each in its own domain, sensation and experimentation have absolute disciplinary power over intellectual imagination—absolute in the sense that, if their joint disciplinary action goes unheeded, systematic applied scientific truth cannot be achieved and hence power-giving knowledge cannot be developed.

Thus, for Descartes, useful knowledge requires that intellectual imagination be subjected to a triple discipline. It is to be disciplined by reason through its connection with whatever relevant systematic knowledge is already in place, by corporeal imagination through its ability of determining what is possible in our world, and by sensation or experimentation through their determination of what is actual in our world both as problems to be solved and as solutions relevant to those problems.

With this triple disciplinary control, how can that which for Descartes is both applied (experiment-confirmed) and scientific (reason-authenticated) still have any vestiges of fictitiousness? This question incorporates the two raised earlier in this section: How can we account for the fact that reason is responsible for fictions? and how can reason's fictions equip us with the power-bestowing knowledge which ameliorates our condition in this world? Reason is responsible for fictions in the sense that the scientific knowledge it is able to develop need not be about the world in which we in fact find ourselves. But reason's knowledge can come to be about this world if, for the sake of actualizing our desire for power over nature, we are willing to discipline reason as well as intellectual imagination through corporeal imagination and sensation. In that case, reason's products shed all but one aspect of fictitiousness, and the aspect it retains is for all practical purposes unimportant.

This practically irrelevant aspect arises as follows. Nature is indefinitely complex. To put this differently, God, for Descartes, could have brought about certain effects in various ways, and our human faculties cannot reveal the way they were in fact brought about. However, if our scientific theory has as a consequence that it explains the effects we want to explain, or produces the effects we want to produce, then that *may have been* the way God in fact made things to work, and it is certainly a way in which things can and do work. Since we cannot get rid of the *may have been*, we do, to that extent, retain the element of fictitiousness. But to such "fictions" there pertains nothing either nonrational or nonapplicable to our world.[32]

Is this a conclusion tantamount to pronouncing Descartes to be intellectually in the company of the classical pragmatists? To the extent that Descartes distances himself from a God's-eye view, the answer would have to be affirmative. Similarly to the extent that, throughout Descartes's works, from the most metaphysical to the most applied, there is the emphasis on utility. But there is a difference in that Descartes's "fictions" are applicable to the world because they are hypotheses which, though generated through imagination, are sanctioned through both reason and sensation; and in the background of reason's role in this context there is Descartes's commitment to the ancient view that we live in a rational world as rational beings created by a rational God. It is the rationality of all three of these which guarantees in an a priori manner a potential fit between "fiction" and "fact". The commitment underlying this notion of a fit between theory and practice keeps Descartes's position well removed from that of classical pragmatism.

There is, nevertheless, more of a resemblance between the two positions than the preceding paragraph might lead one to expect. For example, for C. S. Peirce as for Descartes it is doubt which leads to inquiry, and, for both thinkers, such inquiry depends for its success on the use of disciplined imagination. What such shared doctrine would seem to indicate is that, in spite of Descartes's outmoded metaphysics and his far too stringent reductionistic methodology, there are nevertheless aspects to his position which remain of lasting interest and importance. Among these

---

[32]   It is for this reason that, in spite of his statement about the "suppositions" ("at the beginning of the *Optics* and the *Meteorology*") where the effects are "proved" by the causes and the causes by the effect, Descartes does not withdraw the word "suppositions" in their case. It is for the same reason that Descartes calls his evolutionary account of the creation of the world a fable. And, finally, for this reason he writes in the *Principles* (3:46 and 47) about "[t]he assumptions that I am making here in order to give an explanation of all phenomena" that "We are thus free to make any assumption on these matters with the sole proviso that all the consequences of our assumption must agree with our experience," for "[t]he falsity of these suppositions does not prevent the consequences deduced from them being true and certain." Sometimes, Descartes assigns to his applied scientific reasoning a certainty greater than that sufficient for such practical purposes. See *Principles* 4:205 and 206. Passages such as these function in the valuable discussions of Desmond Clarke in "Descartes' Philosophy of Science and the Scientific Revolution" and of Daniel Garber in "Descartes' Physics," both in Cottingham, *Cambridge Companion to Descartes*. Clarke's and Garber's discussions are parallel to mine in this section, with the major differences that I consider Descartes's use of hypotheses to be more disciplined than does Clarke, and that I insist on a point which Garber neglects, namely, the disciplinary role of experiment throughout the development of a Cartesian deduction.

there would then be the use of doubt and, especially, of imagination in the scientific enterprise. Since this is a story which I have told before, I need say no more about it here.[33]

[33] See my "Peirce and Descartes: Doubt and the Logic of Discovery" in *Pragmatism and Purpose: Essays Presented to Thomas A. Goudge*, ed. L. W. Sumner, John G. Slater, and Fred Wilson (Toronto, 1981).

6

Human Nature
and the Possibility of Science

1. The Challenge

Is human nature such that it allows human beings to know, to develop knowledge, and to apply it? Can human beings be absolutely certain in matters both of pure science and of science applied to the circumstances of everyday life? The process of obtaining, developing, and applying human knowledge necessarily requires activity at some stages (as through the freedom exercised in the use of intellectual and corporeal imagination) and passivity at others (as in reason's encountering truth or the senses' confronting physical objects). We must be able to know that we are in fact capable of guiding the activity of imagination, for voluntarily guided and disciplined imagination is necessary for realization of the promises offered by scientific control. Similarly, we must be able to keep our reason and senses in a state of passive receptivity. Unless we are able to keep our senses, for example, passively receptive, we remain subject to chance and devoid of the impressions of controlled experimentation which in the end make scientific control of our environment possible.

Are human beings capable of being active and passive in these required ways, and are they capable of discerning when, or whether, they are so active or passive? Or could it be that they are really active when they experience passivity, or passive when they believe themselves to be active? If Descartes were unable to answer these questions, the first one positively and the second negatively, he would be like the architect who has demolished his insecure house but is incapable of building a new and solid structure because he cannot find the needed firm foundation (cf. AT 10:509; CSM 1:406–7).

Since Descartes holds that to be human is to be rational and free, these questions relate particularly to human rationality and freedom. They indicate the metaphysical problem whose satisfactory solution is to provide the metaphysical basis for the program set out in the preceding chapters. It requires a return to the *Meditations* for a final consideration of parts of its argument. In this reconsideration, the question about passivity and activity will be the Ariadne's thread leading my reading.

This guiding question is related to the one which led the reading in my first chapter. There I determined what was "mainline" and what was "spur" through asking whether the parts of the argument encountered concern human nature as it relates to the possibility of progress in science. We now know more clearly what Descartes's concept of human nature is meant to be. The question Descartes now needs to ask is whether he can be assured that human nature really is what, for the sake of pure and applied knowledge, he requires it to be. Focusing on activity and passivity will reveal an important feature of Descartes's answer which, in the preceding chapters as in the accounts of other commentators, has not been accorded its intended role. This feature concerns the role of human free will which, in their discussions of the *Meditations*, commentators tend not to allow center-stage presence until the Fourth Meditation. We shall see that Descartes assigns it this position much earlier.

First, through the following eight paragraphs, recall the salient facets of the argument so far presented, specifically, the roles played by the various aspects of human nature in the development and application of knowledge. We need to have these facets, and their relation to activity and passivity, firmly in mind in order to discern how, in the *Meditations*, Descartes believes he meets the challenge of providing their metaphysical grounding and epistemological justification.

In the process of this recapitulation, it is important that we remain aware of the restrictions which will continue to operate. Although I deal with human freedom, this treatment is limited to its presence as distinct from its nature. I can legitimately restrict my discussion of freedom in this way because this limitation allows me to say whatever needs to be said about freedom for my purposes here. Similarly concerning Descartes's idea of progress. That he advocates progress is clear enough; what he conceives progress to consist in and, more especially, how he believes it can be discerned is another matter which does not demand discussion now.[1]

With these restrictions in place, this might seem to have left reason and science as the focus of discussion. That, however, is too narrow a statement with respect to reason and too liberal for science. For when I dealt with the

---

[1] An extensive treatment of Descartes on the nature of freedom and of progress, and on the relationship he holds to exist between these two, would unnecessarily duplicate other work of mine, such as that in chapters 4, 5, and 6 of *Descartes and the Enlightenment*.

rational aspect of human nature, I focused on reason's aids: primarily on imagination, secondarily on sensation and memory. And when I dealt with science I took this term in the Cartesian sense of "systematic knowledge" and drew on Descartes's metaphysics and pure physics or geometry, but said little about his work in applied science—a restriction made legitimate through the considerable number of excellent recent studies on Descartes and applied science, for which this study intends to provide some crucial but still missing parts of their foundation. In sections 2 and 3 of this chapter I return to Descartes's metaphysical justification of this foundation, particularly to the extent that this justification concerns these missing parts.

For Descartes, as for many of his contemporaries and successors, the importance of his work derived from two of its aspects, from the articulation of a new method which is taken to be a functional definition of reason, and from a demonstration that reason is absolutely trustworthy and can establish the trustworthiness of its aids. Descartes believes that it is critical to establish such trustworthiness because he intends to show that, and how, as human beings we can "make ourselves, as it were, the lords and masters of nature" through applied sciences which have a firm basis in pure science, a basis which, in turn, is ineradicably fixed in human consciousness.

The actuality of human progress depends on the possibility of science, and the kind of progress Descartes has in mind is to come about as the results of applications of mechanics, medicine, and morals. I therefore introduced both Descartes's methodology and his ultimate foundation for the applied sciences in the form of the pure science of metaphysics in the first chapter; its introductory statements on both methodology and human nature (particularly in the form of reason and its aids) gained depth in chapters 2 through 5. There we discerned how Descartes's belief in progress is intrinsically related to the particular form of his dualism: There can be no progress in achieving greater freedom unless there are developments in science, no applied science can be developed except on the foundations of metaphysics and physics, no such foundations can be put in place unless the mind be taken as separate from nature, and therefore dualism is a necessary condition for the possibility of science. For if mind were not separate from nature, then mind, too, would be nothing but a mechanism, and that would preclude the possibility of acts of will through which a human being freely relates to nature in order (through developing science) to deal with nature for humanity's benefit. The mental pole of this dualism is therefore characterized by freedom and by reason, and possesses (among others) the powers of intellectual memory and intellectual imagination—to the latter of which I then paid special attention in the context of the other aids which Descartes pronounces to be necessary for developing applied science, namely, intellectual and corporeal memory, corporeal imagination, and sensation.

Intellectual imagination revealed itself as the mental power which introduces new material in the form of hypotheses to fit with what is already known. Thus it is, to begin with, through intellectual imagination that there can be developments in philosophy and science. Intellectual imagination accomplishes this task always in tandem with Descartes's principle of doubt and, depending on the science which is being developed, in the company of corporeal imagination (during certain stages of geometry or pure physics) and of sensation (in the applied sciences). The initially abstract discussion of imagination provided the platform for demonstrating its role in metaphysics and geometry.

With the emphasis in chapter 4 again on metaphysics, it was a matter of course to continue the focus on intellectual imagination, for that is the only aid of reason which is assigned a positive role in the first three of the Meditations. It is intellectual imagination which confronts reason with the hypothesis of the deceiving God. This hypothesis allows for progress in the attempt to find the secure metaphysical foundation for the sciences in Descartes's Archimedean point; it also forces reason to the acknowledgment that it must pass beyond the self if further knowledge is to become possible. Once intellectual imagination has led Descartes to his Archimedean point, he finds himself in the position from which he believes he can demonstrate the metaphysical trustworthiness of reason. With that demonstration in place he is ready to articulate a rule of which he states that, if adopted, it will make error a thing of the past. As well, he is now able to articulate conditions under which we can employ corporeal imagination, the senses, and memory. That, in turn, equips him to begin to develop the geometry which is to serve as the immediate foundation for the sciences of mechanics, medicine, and morals.

My discussion of Descartes's *Geometry* connected the metaphysical foundation with the sciences whose power-giving knowledge is to ameliorate the human condition. Intellectual imagination again looms large, but both corporeal imagination and sensation now appear on the scene in roles which they must play if improvement of humanity's condition is to become more than a utopian dream. For the sake of this human aspiration, scientific investigators must place their intellectual imagination and to some extent even their reason under the discipline of corporeal imagination and sensation. The discipline of corporeal imagination guides scientific investigation toward results of *possible* relevance to us in the world in which we find ourselves; through experimentation, the discipline of sensation secures *actual* relevance of some of these results and so places the sought-after power-bestowing knowledge in humanity's hands.

With the insight gained in earlier chapters thus recalled, I can now return to the theme which guides my study, to the human powers supposedly capable of performing the task of ameliorating humankind's situation. And I can now focus again on Descartes's attempt at answering the question: Are there grounds for this belief in human progress which can withstand the strongest assault of which skeptics might conceivably be capable? As we just saw, it is this question which can be interpreted in terms of activity and passivity. It is a formulation of Descartes's challenge which directs us once more to the beginning of the *Meditations*.

"I realized that it was necessary . . . to demolish everything completely and start again right from the foundations if I wanted to establish anything at all in the sciences that was stable and likely to last." Much has been written about these words from the opening paragraph of the *Meditations*, as commentators have paid attention to the grounds for the "necessity" of the "demolition," to the intended extent of the "demolition" (how inclusive is "everything" meant to be?), and to the "foundations" and the "sciences" to be (re)constructed on them. These are matters I will now explore from the vantage point of what we have seen to be Descartes's teachings about human nature. I will argue that the necessity and extent of the demolition, as well as the nature of the new starting point for (re)construction, are determined by his doctrine of human essence as this functions in his discussions of the development of science. For it is the capacities which humans are supposed to possess to make science and its progress possible which are going to be the targets of the attempted demolition: Do these capacities exist at all, and if they do, can they serve as the development and application of science requires them to serve?

In order to deal with these capacities and their attempted demolition, I will now organize my exposition under two headings: human reason and the argument of the *Meditations*, and human freedom and that argument. These will become the headings of the following two sections. Since my preliminary discussion of reason in the first chapter has already covered a good deal of the material now relevant, I here present no more of an argument than is sufficient to give the required depth which it would have been premature to enter earlier. In addition, I will as far as possible avoid duplication of the argument of chapter 4—that, too, I assume still to be before our minds. One consequence of these restrictions is that I will now give most of my attention to human freedom. Here, my argument will accomplish two things at once: it will offer a new slant for our reading of parts of the *Meditations*, and this reading will help to provide the grounds which are to make legitimate our trust in the human capacities Descartes believes are required for developing science. Much of the argument about freedom will be parallel and complementary to that about reason; in both cases I really present the same argument but from different vantage points. The argument is such that it requires as its main focus only the first three of the Meditations.

As a last preliminary matter before we enter upon the argument, an issue first broached in my second chapter needs further explication. It again concerns the matter of activity and passivity.

To Regius, Descartes writes, "There is only one soul in human beings,

the rational soul; for no actions can be reckoned human unless they depend on reason." This "rational soul" is thus "the first principle" of human
"actions" (May 1641, AT 3:371; CSMK 3:182). In the same letter he states
that "willing and understanding" "differ only as the activity and passivity
of one and the same substance," with "understanding . . . the passivity of
the mind and willing . . . its activity." At about the time of this letter,
Descartes composed the part of his *Principles of Philosophy* where we read:

> All the modes of thinking that we experience within ourselves can be brought
> under two general headings: perception, or the operation of the intellect, and
> volition, or the operation of the will. Sensory perception, imagination and
> pure understanding are simply various modes of perception; desire, aversion,
> assertion, denial and doubt are various modes of willing. (*Principles* 1:32)

The "passivity" of the intellect is clear enough in "sensory perception."
But it pertains also in "pure understanding" when, once we are confronted
with a truth which is clear and distinct to the intellect, there is no choice but
to accept this truth as long as one pays attention to it.[2] Thus, as *res cogitans*,
we are active and passive, creatures of intellect and will, and it is only when
intellect and will are co-present and co-operate (in a manner which will receive further illumination later on) that action, as distinct from mechanistic
behavior, ensues. The question about activity and passivity therefore concerns the very essence of what it is to be human. Hence my earlier translation
of Descartes's challenge in terms of questions about activity and passivity.
    The significance for the following argument is this. If "no actions can be
reckoned human unless they depend on reason," then there is no expression of human essence apart from reason. Similarly, there is no human
essence apart from exertion of will, for there is no action (as distinct from
mechanistically determined behavior) unless it be willed. If we doubt
whether there is reasoning (with its necessary moments of passivity) or
willing (the peculiarly human expression of activity), we doubt the existence of the human being with all characteristically human powers, including all those required for doing scientific work. Let me restate this
and bring out some of its relevant aspects more clearly.
    Once (in the part of the *Principles* where we find the counterpart to the
Meditations) the existence of the *res cogitans* is established, Descartes says
that we are still "supposing that everything which is distinct from us is
false," that is, unreal or nonexistent (as the French version has it, we are
"now thinking that there is nothing outside of our thought which truly is
or exists").[3] Thus that which can be doubted is counted as nonexistent un-

---

[2] Descartes wrote to Regius that "perception" is not, strictly speaking, an action; hence
willing is the only activity of the soul. See AT 3:454–55; CSMK 3:199.
[3] *Principles* 1:8.

less the doubt can be dispelled. Descartes then asks the question: Do we know anything about *res extensa*? which, once answered negatively, is followed immediately by the question: Is there a *res extensa*? But these questions presuppose another set of questions, a set which is the more fundamental one in that the very possibility of answering the first depends on the possibility of answering this second set. And the second set is: Do we know anything about the *res cogitans*? which, once answered negatively, is then followed by: Is there in fact a *res cogitans*? At a certain moment we do not know whether distant towers are round or square, and this leads us to question whether both towers and senses exist. Similarly, at a certain moment we do not know whether two and three make more or less than five, and this makes us wonder whether both sciences and *res cogitans* exist. Thus my reading of the *Meditations* is that it is an argument structured by the fundamental need to prove the existence of the *res cogitans* as an autonomous, passive and active, reasoning and willing being. I can now turn, first to *human reason*, next to *human will* and the argument of the *Meditations*.

2. Human Reason

To be human is to be free to reason and to act on one's reason's precepts. Implied is the individual's radical epistemic autonomy, an autonomy grounded in the nature which God has given human beings.[4] Perhaps the best-known early statement of this epistemic autonomy is the striking passage in the *Discourse* where Descartes writes of his "resolution to abandon all the opinions" which he "hitherto accepted," thus "uprooting [*ie déracinois*] from my mind any errors that might previously have slipped into it" (AT 6:15, 28; CSM 1:118, 125).[5] The doctrine requires that only such new opinions will be adopted (or only such old ones readopted) as can be "squared . . . with the standards of reason" (AT 6:13; CSM 1:117).[6]

---

[4]   See, e.g., the *Discourse* (AT 6:27; CSM 1:124). I shall deal with another passage (AT 7:60–62; CSM 2:42–43), which has the same import, when, in the third section, I consider aspects of the Fourth Meditation.

[5]   Other examples readily come to mind. The *Principles* we saw characterized as quite different from those of Aristotle (or, for that matter, of any other thinker) because of the way in which they are derived (AT 9B:20; CSM 1:190). In *The Search for Truth* he insists on beginning "by overturning all the knowledge acquired up to the present" because it is like "a badly constructed house, whose foundations are not firm," and there is "no better way to repair it than to knock it all down, and build a new one in its place" (AT 10:509; CSM 1:406–7). And in *The Passions of the Soul* he feels "obliged to write just as if I were considering a topic that no one had dealt with before me" (AT 11:328; CSM 1:328).

[6]   Thus with respect to the doctrines of his own scientific works like the *Geometry*, the *Dioptrics*, and the *Meteors*, Descartes writes that "I do not boast of being the first to discover

This gives us the first vantage point from which to approach the question why "it was necessary, once in the course of my life, to demolish everything completely and start again right from the foundations. . . . " It is human nature itself which dictates as much through human reason. If anything is to be an item of knowledge for me, it must be clear and distinct to me. Whatever experience initially gives is complex, hence not at first meeting clear and distinct, and therefore cannot then be grasped by the intellect as true even if it is true. With respect to any complex item, it will be *necessary*, at least once, to submit it to analysis until we reach the "foundations," where we have items which are absolutely simple and therefore self-evident, entities known per se rather than *per aliud*.[7] Ultimately, it is only from the simplest items that we can commence our scientific construction. But such items are never given to begin with; they must always be established by whoever comes to know them.

In the First Meditation we go beyond this statement from the *Discourse*, radical though it is: Now there are not just the questions whether what is given by the senses can be "squared with reason" and whether what we take to be constructed by the understanding does indeed come from the understanding. As we already saw in the first chapter, there are the further questions whether we can know that sensation usually or ever gives us materials which allow us to construct accurate knowledge of our surroundings and, more broadly, whether the understanding provides correct accounts of whatever can be an object of thought.[8] Hence my statement that one of the *Meditations'* grounds which made it "necessary . . . to demolish everything completely and start again right from the foundations" is located in what Descartes has all along accepted as part of human nature.

---

any of them, but I do claim to have accepted them not because they have, or have not, been expressed by others, but solely because reason has convinced me of them" (AT 6:77; CSM 1:150).

[7] As we read in the *Regulae* with respect to items which are simple and hence "self-evident" (*per se notas*): "[I]t is evident that we are mistaken if we ever judge that we lack complete knowledge of any one of these. . . . For if we have even the slightest grasp of it in our mind . . . it must follow that we have complete knowledge of it. Otherwise it could not be said to be simple, but a composite made up of that which we perceive in it and that of which we judge to be ignorant" (AT 10:420; CSM 1:45).

[8] Some commentators argue that the doubt in the First Meditation is one limited to the senses. Recent statements of this position are J. Carriero, "The First Meditation" (*Pacific Philosophical Quarterly* 68 [1987]: 222–48) and R. Smyth, "A Metaphysical reading of the First Meditation" (*Philosophical Quarterly* 36 [1986]: 283–303). Of these two, Carriero tells the more plausible story. He reads the First Meditation as only an anti-Aristotelian attack on the senses as a foundation for science. Interpretations alternative to his own he dismisses in part because (so he claims without offering support for the claim) they result in a reading of the First Meditation "as a loosely connected string of sceptical challenges" (243). My disagreement with a position like Carriero's concerns the extent of doubt rather than the suggestion that, in doubting the senses, Descartes attacks Aristotelian philosophers.

Justification of trust in the rational and then the sensuous aspects of human nature is accomplished through the journey which we traveled with Descartes in my first chapter, that on which he "led the mind from knowledge of its own existence to knowledge of the existence of God and to the distinction between mind and body." This distinction allows for expression of the mind's essence (AT 7:550; CSM 2:375); I will return to the most salient of the implications of this distinction in the next section of this chapter. Of importance now is the mind's "knowledge of its own existence" and "of the existence of God." This knowledge will reveal several additional facts about the *rational* aspect of human nature and the argument of the *Meditations*.

The manner of achieving this knowledge introduced the skeptic's most "excessive doubt" imaginable, the hypothesis that not only do we not know that God exists, but for all we know there exists instead an omnipotent deceiver.[9] It is that supposition which demolishes "everything" hitherto accepted as true or trustworthy. And since no doubt about rational human nature can be legitimate after that supposition has itself been demolished, it is "necessary . . . to demolish everything completely"—where "everything" includes both all objects of, as well as the most far-fetched ground for, the skeptic's doubt.

Demolishing this supposition itself is by way of proof of the existence of a veracious God. Once that proof is in place we are in the position to know that reason is the human being's self-authenticating capacity which establishes the stable foundation for science and authenticates sense. These revelations, given by reason to reason, in effect show the absolute validity of radical epistemic autonomy. Implicit is the doctrine that it is rational human nature which is necessary as the foundation of science.[10]

---

[9] In Robert Stoothoff's terminology ("Descartes' Dilemma," *Philosophical Quarterly* 39 [1989]: 294–307), I interpret the deceiver as allowing Descartes to entertain the possibility that he is subject to "natural deception," that is, to "deception or error resulting from Descartes' nature" (296). Stoothoff's juxtaposition of "natural deception" and "ad hoc deception" (which corresponds to deception by an omnipotent God in the first and by a powerful but less-than-omnipotent external agent in the second case) seems not fully plausible—both because of "problem texts" which he himself introduces and because of relevant texts which he fails to cite. For an example of the latter, see AT 7:195; CSM 2:136–37. I hold that Descartes entertains the possibility of an omnipotent deceiver's existence in order to push methodological doubt beyond its normal boundaries to become metaphysical doubt. Hence I am among those who believe Descartes to make this move "in order to counteract the force of habit . . . " (300). My question in a moment will be "Habit with respect to what?" And my suggestion will be that it is considerably more than "habit, which threatens to impede the application of the method by preventing him from withholding assent to opinions that reason renders doubtful" (ibid.).

[10] As we shall see later, though necessary it is not sufficient as the foundation of science. Something additional is required, but for this addition we need introduce nothing beyond the other aspect of human nature, namely, the human will. This (as we saw in my second chapter) is a will whose existence is possible because of "the distinction between the human soul and the body."

Since I have elsewhere[11] given close attention to the stages of this part of the journey, they need not be reconsidered here. However, in my earlier account I missed one important stage—a failure I shared with other commentators. I argued that Descartes submits both "basic principles" of sense and reason to metaphysical doubt, but in the case of reason I believed he doubted only its compositive and not its intuitive function. Thus I believed that Descartes exempted from doubt reason's capacity of grasping self-evident items. It was a mistake so to limit the extent of metaphysical doubt. There remains an additional stage to the journey, one adumbrated in the first chapter. It now requires our more careful attention for a moment.

With the introduction of the omnipotent deceiver, Descartes doubts the trustworthiness of reason even in its intuitive function. Recall the central sentence of the First Meditation's ninth paragraph:

> What is more, since I sometimes believe that others go astray in cases where they think they have the most perfect knowledge, may I not similarly go wrong every time I add two and three or count the sides of a square, *or in some even simpler matter*, if that is imaginable? (AT 7:21; CSM 2:14)

This "even simpler" matter extends the doubt to reason's ability of cognizing the absolutely simple foundational items of knowledge, those contextless items known per se. Descartes here imagines (*fingo*) that even self-evidence has lost its certainty.[12] As he puts this in *Principles* 1:5: "Our doubt will also apply to other matters which we previously regarded as most certain—even the demonstrations of mathematics and even the principles [*principiis*] which we hitherto considered self-evident [*per se nota*]."[13]

---

[11] See *The Imposition of Method*, chaps. 4 and 5.

[12] In "Descartes' First Meditation: Mathematics and the Law of Logic" (*Journal of the History of Philosophy* 26 [1988]: 407–38) M. A. Olson excludes "any 'common notion' or inference rule 'intuitively' or non-abstractly known" from being dubitable (433). He is correct when he does so in the context of the Third Meditation (or, for that matter, of the Second after we have reached the Archimedean point). But if my interpretation is correct, then Olson is wrong in doing so in the context of the First Meditation—and that pulls the rug from under the central thesis of his interesting article.

[13] In the letter to Clerselier which serves as reply to objections from Gassendi (printed as "Appendix to the Fifth Objections and Replies" in AT 9A:202–17; CSM 2:263–77) there is the following passage which, superficially, appears to contradict this clear statement from the *Principles*:

> The second objection which your friends note is that in order to know that I am thinking I must know what thought is; and yet, they say, I do not know this at all, since I have denied everything. But I have denied only preconceived opinions [*les prejugez*]—not notions like these, which are known without any affirmation or denial. (AT 9A:206; CSM 2:271)

Only if one were to identify "denial" with "doubting" would this passage pose a problem. But to doubt is not yet to deny, though doubt may lead to denial. It does, initially, lead to

154 Descartes and the Possibility of Science

The intellect's nature is to sense, imagine, remember, and understand. We have habitually believed these functions to be capable of giving us, or of leading us to, truth. Since these are *habitual* beliefs, they are prejudices. Our beliefs about the first three functions can become rational beliefs if our reason can validate our trust in them—provided, of course, that our trust in reason is itself no longer habitual but is itself validated. Thus we have now placed ourselves in the position where we recognize that all our intellectual functions need validation—a recognition which frees us from all prejudice about intellectual human nature, and places us in the position to see whether we can in fact discover incontrovertible truth about this human nature, first about its existence and then about its essence.

On this journey of discovery Descartes starts with establishing the mind's existence; this activity turns out to be the very same which validates trust in reason's ability to establish foundations; that is, it validates trust in reason's intuitive function. It is the focus of the Second Meditation where (says Descartes in its synopsis) "the mind . . . supposes the non-existence of all the things about whose existence it can have even the slightest doubt"—the human intellect and its objects and therefore human nature and human existence itself—"and in so doing the mind notices that it is impossible that it should not itself exist during this time." "*I am, I exist*, is necessarily true whenever it is . . . conceived [*concipitur*] in my mind"—as the first formulation in the third paragraph of the Second Meditation has it. It is an item *per se nota*, known without affirmation or denial.[14] This first certainty is achieved with the omnipotent deceiver supposedly on the scene. That is, reason in its awareness of absolutely simple items of knowledge has been shown to exist and to be unconditionally trustworthy, for it has withstood the test of metaphysical doubt greater than which cannot be conceived. Next he settles reason's absolute trustworthiness in its compositive function; this is the focus of the Third and, to an extent, of the Fourth Meditations. Finally, in the Sixth Meditation, he confirms the trustworthiness of the senses.

Reason in its compositive function is shown to be absolutely trustworthy by reason functioning intuitively, which recognizes the contradictoriness[15] of the supposition, and hence the impossibility of the existence, of an omnipotent deceiver and so removes the ground of doubt. This places

---

denial in cases which are not self-evident; in the *Meditations* and elsewhere, these are the cases of *praejudicia, les prejugez*.

[14] That we do not reach the Archimedean point through syllogistic argument is clear enough from Descartes's entire mode of procedure and, for those of his readers who missed this to Descartes elementary point, is spelled out also in the Second Set of Objections and Replies (AT 7:140; CSM 2:100).

[15] As we saw in Cottingham, *Descartes' Conversation with Burman*, 4, 9.

us again where we were in the *Discourse* (at AT 6:15, 28; CSM 1:118, 125): We may accept whatever the senses present provided we have determined that these givens can be "squared . . . with the standards of reason." But we now have metaphysical grounds for our acceptance of these givens.

3. HUMAN FREE WILL

To be human is to be free to use one's freedom to reason and to act on one's reason's precepts.[16] The passive intellect's reception of truth, and the subsequent further actualization of one's humanity through action on that truth, become possible only through acts of will.

For Descartes, to the extent that one's freedom is limited by external constraints there is less of an expression (and hence less of a presence) of a *res cogitans*, just as there would be if one were deprived of part of one's reason. Our freedom is limited to the extent that we are passive rather than active. Which is to say that we give greater or lesser expression to our humanity depending on whether we are more or less active.

One way in which passivity dominates is through habit, when the habit in question is uncritically contracted through one's exposure to one's environment. The First Meditation states that we have domineering habits of precisely this kind in our trust of sense and reason. It is (in the words of its eleventh paragraph) these "habitual opinions" which "keep coming back" and which "despite my wishes . . . capture my belief, which is as it were bound over to them as a result of long occupation and the law of custom." In this situation Descartes then adopts a strategy which promises escape from imprisonment in captivity:

> I think it will be a good thing to turn my will in completely the opposite direction and deceive myself, by pretending for a time that these former opinions are utterly false and imaginary. I shall do this until the weight of preconceived opinion [*praejudiciorum*] is counter-balanced and the distorting influence of habit no longer prevents my judgment from perceiving things correctly. (AT 7:22; CSM 2:15)

---

[16] There is more to Descartes's position than this sentence states, for in an important setting Descartes holds that to be human is also to be free not to reason and not to act on one's reason's precepts. These statements point to what I believe to be an unresolved tension in Descartes's writings between his doctrines of autonomous will and authoritative reason. I have highlighted this tension in *Descartes and the Enlightenment*, chap. 5, section 1, and will say no more about it in this chapter.

This undertaking to deceive oneself is an attempt at expressing the *res cogitans* as free being. In words from the synopsis of the Second Meditation: "the mind uses its own freedom [*propria libertate utens*] and supposes the non-existence of all . . . things. . . . " The synopsis of the First Meditation asserts the far-reaching consequences of persistence in this attempt: "The eventual result of this doubt is to make it impossible for us to have any further doubts about what we subsequently discover to be true." That (as we shall come to see in retrospect) is because this attempt at expressing human freedom inexorably will deliver us from the doubt we have imposed on ourselves through adoption of the belief that there may be an omnipotent deceiver. If there is such a deceiver, then we might be so malleable, so passive in his hands that we do not even know whether or not we are being imposed upon, whether or not what we take to be assertions of free will or experiences of passivity are so in fact. I may be active when I experience myself to be passive, and vice versa. Consider this example from the Third and Sixth Meditations. My experience tells me that "there is in me a passive faculty of sensory perception, that is, a faculty for receiving and recognizing the ideas of sensible objects," and this implies that there is "also an active faculty, either in me or in something else, which produced or brought about these ideas," and it is only my knowledge that "God is not a deceiver" which allows me to conclude that these ideas are not "transmitted from a source other than corporeal things" (AT 7:79–80; CSM 2:55). As long as I entertain the possibility of an omnipotent deceiver, then, although my experience tells me that "these ideas do not depend on my will," "it does not follow that they must come from things located outside me," for "there may be some . . . faculty not yet fully known to me, which produces these ideas without any assistance from external things" (AT 7:39; CSM 2:27). Hence I may be active when I experience myself as passive or imposed upon, and, conversely, I may be passive or imposed upon when I experience myself to be active or in control.

Two paragraphs before he comes to his first articulation of the cogito, strategically at the very opening of the Second Meditation, Descartes vividly portrays this situation of doubt about the efficacy, and even the existence, of free will:

> So serious are the doubts into which I have been thrown as a result of yesterday's meditation that I can neither put them out of my mind nor see any way of resolving them. It feels as if I have fallen unexpectedly into a deep whirlpool which tumbles me around so that I can neither stand on the bottom nor swim up to the top. (AT 7:23–24; CSM 2:16)

The experience described is one of passivity, of being helplessly "tumbled around" by a force external to oneself, a force so powerful that both certainty ("standing on the bottom") and the pursuit of certainty ("swimming to the top" and so looking for a place to stand and making one's way to that) seem equally impossible. Whether there is any efficacy to either attempt we do not know: there may be, there may not. The only way to find out (if there is such a way) is to assume that the experience of passivity is not our ultimate state of being. Therefore: "Nevertheless I will make an effort and once more attempt the . . . path. . . . " And so: "I have convinced [*persuasi*] myself that there is absolutely nothing in the world, no sky, no earth, no minds, no bodies. Does it now follow that I too do not exist? No: if I convinced [*persuasi*] myself of something then I certainly existed." Here, two sentences before what is traditionally taken as the first arrival at the Archimedean point, we have the first arrival at the Archimedean point, not in terms of intellection but in terms of willing: *if I convince (persuade) myself of something then I certainly exist*. The experience of passivity cannot be our ultimate state of being simply because, when I entertain this experience as my reality, it is an experience which I have created through my act of will. If I persuade myself, then I am as persuading, willing being. If focusing on the *res cogitans* expressing itself in "the perception of the intellect" leads us to *cogito ergo sum*, focusing on the *res cogitans* expressing itself in "the operation of the will" leads us to *volo ergo sum*.[17]

Thus we may take the attempt at universal doubt as a necessary step in revealing the truth about the essence of a human being and in actualizing this essence as completely as possible. This strategy forces the confrontation with the omnipotent deceiver which results in optimally active human presence, destroying the habitual acceptance of those beliefs which routinely are taken not as customary beliefs but as obvious truths (I mean the beliefs which express trust in the existence and veracity of the senses and their objects, and trust in the existence and veracity of reason and its objects). But in addition, through this strategy we reveal to ourselves the important point about our nature that there is no passivity of which we are not or cannot be aware, no passivity to which we need be subject if we do not want such subjection.[18] This strategy reveals that we can work at being as free, as active, as in control, as fully human as we choose to be.[19]

---

[17] I owe this formulation to Anthony Kenny, who offered it during the discussion of my first presentation of this position at a conference on Descartes organized under the auspices of the British Society for the History of Philosophy at the University of Reading (September 1991).

[18] I am speaking here of what is usually the case in the course of human life, and not about unusual situations like that of being bound and tortured.

[19] Free development of the sciences of mechanics, medicine, and morals may be seen as ways to overcome the passivity of involuntary subjection to afflictions of a physical, mental, or social kind. A fruit expected from the science of medicine was that human beings would become less and less passive because able to do away with the involuntary submis-

Earlier I mentioned Descartes's response to Regius that "no actions can be reckoned human unless they depend on reason." There is, as well, his statement from the *Discourse* that it is only "our thoughts" which lie "entirely within our power" (AT 6:25; CSM 1:123). My reading now suggests that the question from the First Meditation is not just whether reason (whether "pure," or in its employment of imagination or memory, or in its validation of and conjunction with the senses) is ever to be trusted. That question concerns the *intellectual* aspect of the *res cogitans*. There is also the question concerning the *volitional* aspect (and we know that without acts of will there can be neither imagining nor remembering). One way of stating it is whether anything ever "lies entirely within our power." Certainty on the impossibility of an omnipotent deceiver answers both questions affirmatively.

My reading of the *Meditations* is one in which we reach certainty through an argument in which reason disqualifies sense, corporeal imagination, corporeal and intellectual memory, and then attempts to disqualify itself. It is an argument forced to its radical conclusion through the operation of the will working in tandem with intellectual imagination, a will imposing doubt on reason and all its aids, *a doubt which then comes to be applied to the will itself*. This reading, which involves both aspects of the *res cogitans*, finds support in the "cogito passages" in the Second and Third Meditations, passages which have traditionally been taken as the only passages expressing the certainty of Archimedean point immovability.

In the first of these, Descartes gives both will and intellect their place: "*I am, I exist*, is necessarily true whenever it is put forward by me [through an act of will] or conceived in my mind [through its impression on the intellect]" (AT 7:25; CSM 2:17). And when a few paragraphs later the *res cogitans* is more fully characterized, five of its eight characteristics are in terms of will ("doubts," "affirms," "denies," "is willing," "is unwilling") and three in terms of intellect ("understands," "imagines," "has sensory perceptions"). Descartes offers a near-identical list in the opening paragraph of the Third Meditation. The fact that in both these passages will is mentioned before intellect indicates a parallel with the argument I have elucidated in section 2 of this chapter. There, that which was doubted last (the ability to understand items known per se), is shown to be indubitable first, while in this case our experience of free will is doubted after reason and is pronounced validated before reason.

When in part 1 of the *Principles* Descartes restates the first two of the Meditations, the same order of argument presents itself. In principles 4 and 5, reason offers grounds which are to disqualify sense and corporeal

---

sion to death (which would itself no longer be predictable in its inevitability). For himself, Descartes optimistically expected death already to have lost its three-score-and-ten inevitability; and the *philosophes* who followed in his footsteps anticipated the passivity of death only through the statistically inevitable accident.

imagination as well as reason. Principles 6 and 7 then turn to "free will" and articulate the cogito. Since we here get further support for my reading of the *Meditations*, it is instructive to focus on the latter two principles for a moment.

Although we meet the traditionally recognized formulation of the cogito in principle 7, it is principle 6 in which bounds are set to the omnipotent deceiver through the experience of freedom. It reads as follows:

> But whoever turns out to have created us, and however powerful and however deceitful he may be, in the meantime we nonetheless experience within us the kind of freedom which enables us to refrain from believing things which are not completely certain and thoroughly examined. Hence we are able to take precautions against going wrong on any occasion.

Thus we now possess the certainty that (in the words of the heading of principle 6) "We have free will, enabling us to withhold assent in doubtful matters and hence avoid error." This is knowledge that what we "experience" is ultimately valid (it withstands the force of the one who has "created us," "however powerful and however deceitful he may be") and useful ("we are able to take precautions against going wrong on any occasion"). At this point one might say—but, I believe, mistakenly—that the *next* "piece of knowledge" is that of principle 7. There Descartes writes: Because "it is a contradiction to suppose that what thinks does not ... exist," it follows that "*I am thinking, therefore I exist* . . . is the first and most certain of all to occur to anyone who philosophizes in an orderly way." And one might add—again, I believe, mistakenly—that, since the knowledge of principle 6 is stated before that of principle 7, Descartes is confused when he calls the latter's knowledge "the first of all to occur. . . . " I believe it would be wrong to charge Descartes with confusion here, because these two principles express different aspects of the same thing. In the face of the presumed existence of an omnipotent deceiver, both express the achievement of certainty, both state the existence of the *res cogitans*, the first in terms of will and the second in terms of intellect. And the order in which they do so is not peculiar to the *Principles*; we found the same order in the *Meditations*.

If we now return to the *Meditations* we can see that this co-presence of will and intellect, with the will preceding the intellect in an order of exposition which reflects the structure of the argument, is typical of the first three of the Meditations. There is, in fact, a primacy of free will over reason in that the willing aspect of the *res cogitans* is the driving force which leads to each epistemically differently qualified presence of the intellect.[20]

20 C. Wilson and C. Schildknecht ("The Cogito Meant 'No More Philosophy': Valéry's Descartes," *History of European Ideas* 9 [1988]: 47–62) suggest that the nineteenth-century

Since I have dealt with this in detail elsewhere,[21] I shall not repeat the argument but only indicate the points at which this primacy is very clear.

The primacy of free will is very clear in the introduction of the omnipotent deceiver, which on my reading is the ultimate tool enabling us to doubt all our beliefs, whether about sense, memory, imagination, reason, or will. It is not just the submission to this test which is self-willed. Also the subsequent awareness of the truth so basic that it can function as Archimedean point comes about through an act of will. It is only through the act of willing expressed in "paying attention" that we have the assurance of the truth of the cogito and, later on, of the truth that in the awareness of the cogito we are necessarily aware of the existence of a veracious God.[22]

From that point on, will and intellect continue to operate in tandem, but it remains the case that in all the moves of the argument, both in the ones that constitute progress and in those that do not,[23] the will is primary to the intellect. Once we have established the existence of the *res cogitans* as characterized by will and intellect, we know that ideas or thoughts exist, but we also know that nothing will get us beyond this point unless we *will* to use "thoughts." And before the full powers of reason have been validated and all of reason has been shown to be autonomous, we already know that the will is autonomous, that we really are active when we experience ourselves to be so, and that we do not have such experiences un-

poet and critic Paul Valéry was the first to maintain that "Descartes was first and foremost a will" (49). That position led him to the conclusion that "Descartes' doubt [is] directed in the main not against the 'knowledge' proffered by the outer world, but against that making its appearance from within. It reflects an effort to contain and suppress a radical uncertainty: was the revelation of unlimited intellectual power truly a vision sent by God? Or was it fantasy generated by the dreaming idea-producing self which generates such other realistic fantasies, or even a temptation staged by a demon?" Though congenial to me, the statement goes both too far and not far enough. I would be able to support it fully were the phrase "was the revelation of unlimited intellectual power truly . . . " replaced by "was the experience of limited intellectual and unlimited volitional power truly. . . . "

21   See *Descartes and the Enlightenment*, chap. 2, section 1.
22   See the Third Meditation's statements on this paying attention to the cogito: "If one concentrates carefully [*Quod diligenter attenditi*], all this is quite evident by the natural light. But when I relax my attention [*Sed quia, cum minus attendo*] . . . it is not so easy . . . " (AT 7:47; CSM 2:32); and "the more carefully I concentrate . . . [*quo diligentius attendo*]" (AT 7:45; CSM 2:32). See as well Descartes's letter to Gibieuf, written one year after the publication of the *Meditations* (AT 3:474–76; CSMK 3:201–2); and note his statement in the Fourth Set of Objections and Replies (AT 7:246; CSM 2:171). That "paying attention" is an act of will Descartes states explicitly, for example, in a letter to Mesland (AT 4:116; CSMK 3:233–34). On this role of "attention" and its relation to the will, see as well Schouls, *Descartes and the Enlightenment*, chap. 4, section 2.
23   As we saw in my first chapter, there are several moves in the *Meditations* which do not so much constitute progress in the answering of Descartes's basic questions as prepare the ground for such progress through their breaking of the habit of trusting sense and trusting reason. So we saw that the Second Meditation's paragraphs 10–16 are meant to break trust in the senses and the Third Meditation's paragraphs 7–12 are meant to break trust in the compositive function of reason.

less we will to have them.[24] Hence, when we will to use our thoughts, we know that we are not externally determined to such willing by either omnipotent deceiver or veracious God. We can, *if we will*, "start again right from the foundations" and "establish" "sciences" which are "stable and likely to last."

Autonomous human nature therefore dictates, for both theoretical work and practical experience, that activity precede passivity. As the Fourth Meditation makes explicit, that is how God has made human beings: on their own capable of pursuing truth and continuing activity through implementation of the dicta of reason, but equally capable of avoiding truth and committing themselves to error and so binding themselves into the passivity which characterizes the mechanistic behavior which such nonrational deeds entail.[25] When the Fourth Meditation states this relationship between activity and passivity, between will and intellect, it lends further support for my reading of the first three Meditations:

> God could easily have brought it about that without losing my freedom, and despite the limitations in my knowledge, I should nevertheless never make a mistake. He could, for example, have endowed my intellect with a clear and distinct perception of everything about which I was ever likely to deliberate; or he could simply have impressed it unforgettably on my memory that I should never make a judgment about anything which I did not clearly and distinctly understand. (AT 7:61; CSM 2:42)

God has not imposed on me in either of these ways. Had he done so that would have been "without losing my freedom" in the sense that it would still have required willingness to act in accordance with my intellect's clear and distinct ideas or with my memory's forceful impression. Nevertheless, there would have been loss of autonomy at a different level, passivity where now there is activity. Instead of making me inescapably aware of ideas in my understanding or impressions in my memory, God has given me the power to "avoid error in the second way, which depends merely on my remembering to withhold judgment on any occasion when the truth of the matter is not clear." It is, then, my own activity which creates in me "the

---

24   Which is not to say that we really are passive when we experience ourselves to be passive. That matter will not be settled until the Sixth Meditation.

25   If they follow the latter course of action, this is a "misuse" of "freedom" resulting in the "privation" which constitutes "the essential definition of falsity and wrong" (AT 7:60–61; CSM 2:42). It results in a "privation" because, for Descartes, ignorance and error are not "real," just as blindness is not "real." Both error and blindness indicate a lack of power as distinct from the actualization of a human faculty. This "misuse" of freedom becomes compounded when action ensues on that of which one is ignorant or with respect to which one is in error, for such action is then really no more than nonrational, hence nonhuman, behavior. It results in ever-decreasing control over nature as it tends to incorporate one into the mechanism of nature.

habit of avoiding error," a critically acquired habit which supplants the un-critical habits suspended in the First Meditation and in the opening para-graph of the Second—those of unquestioning trust in sense, reason, and the competence of its aids (corporeal and intellectual memory and corporeal imagination) and in the efficacy of the will and, consequently, in the exis-tence of these faculties and their objects. It is, then, no wonder to see Descartes stating at this point that it is in the exercise of this power that my "greatest and most important perfection is to be found" (AT 7:62; CSM 2:43).

This "perfection" consists in being true to my nature through the right use of freedom. It is a perfection which allows for more than keeping from error; it is in fact one of the conditions necessary for the pursuit of truth. This is because of Descartes's position—again exemplified in the structure of the argument of the first three Meditations—that we cannot reason ex-cept through acts of will like those involved in suspending judgment, im-plementing doubt, determining the imagination to propose hypotheses, and determining the intellect to be attentive. Reason performs none of these tasks as it were automatically; strictly speaking, reason cannot per-form any of these on its own, for to each it has to be determined by the will. No action can be called human unless it be rational, but there can be no ac-tion called "reasoning" unless it be willed. Thus it is not God who has "en-dowed my intellect with a clear and distinct perception of everything about which I was ever likely to deliberate," but it is I who give myself such perceptions whenever they are possible through willing attentive awareness. Hence the *res cogitans'* passive cognition of truth depends not on the action of God on its intellect but on that of its will on its intellect.

We can now see that it makes sense to say about the opening paragraph of the *Meditations* that "everything" in the phrase "it was necessary . . . to demolish everything completely" covers whatever we are or perhaps might be passive in. We are passive in sensory perception but also in intel-lection when the mind is confronted with a truth which is clear and distinct to it. And with the presumed presence of an omnipotent deceiver, we are, for all we know, passive in what we experience as acts of self-determination when we exercise doubt, suspend judgment, propose hypotheses through intellectual imagination or contemplate images through corporeal imagina-tion, and focus attention on what appears as given in memory or intellect.

This necessary demolition, as well as the necessity and nature of the new starting point, is determined by Descartes's doctrine of human essence and its two aspects of reason and freedom. Both are traditionally assumed to be autonomous but, given the questioning of all tradition, Descartes asks whether they are in fact autonomous. Descartes's most fundamental question then becomes: Does anything ever lie "entirely within our power"? Once he knows that he really is active when he expe-riences himself to be so, and knows that he will not have such experiences unless he wills to have them, he turns to the next question, to the other aspect of human essence: Can reason ever be trusted? and through exercise of a will now known to be autonomous he shows that reason is absolutely trustworthy. Once that point has been established, he is ready to show the (extent of the) trustworthiness of the senses, the distinction in nature and function between sense and imagination, and the test (coherence) which is indicative of the trustworthiness of memories.

With these various items secured to his satisfaction, Descartes takes the question of the First Meditation to be fully and satisfactorily answered: Human beings are indeed capable of the requisite activity which allows their achievement of absolutely certain knowledge in pure science and, on its foundation, of the knowledge useful in daily life. It is an activity which—through mechanics, medicine, and morals—is to lead humanity to ever-expanding mastery over nature with its dividends of ever-increasing freedom from labor, pain, and anxiety.

Bibliography

PRIMARY SOURCES

Adam, C., and P. Tannery, eds. *Œuvres de Descartes*. 11 vols. Vols. 8 and 9 in two parts. Paris, 1965–75.
Cottingham, John; Robert Stoothoff; and Dugald Murdoch. eds. and trans. *The Philosophical Writings of Descartes*. Vols. 1 and 2. Cambridge, 1985.
Cottingham, John, Robert Stoothoff, Dugald Murdoch, and Anthony Kenny, eds. and trans. *The Philosophical Writings of Descartes*. Vol.3. Cambridge, 1991.
Olscamp, Paul J., ed. and trans. *Discourse on Method, Optics, Geometry, and Meteorology*. New York, 1965.

SECONDARY SOURCES

Ariew, Roger, John Cottingham, and Tom Sorell, eds. *Descartes' Meditations: Background Source Materials*. Cambridge, 1998.
Baker, Gordon, and Katherine J. Morris. *Descartes' Dualism*. New York, 1996.
Barber, Kenneth F., and Jorge J. E. Gracia, eds. *Individuation and Identity in Early Modern Philosophy: Descartes to Kant*. New York, 1994.
Beck, L. J. *The Method of Descartes: A Study of the Regulae*. Oxford, 1952.
Bennett, Jonathan. "Descartes's Theory of Modality." *Philosophical Review* 103, no. 4, (1994): 639–67.
Blom, John J. *Descartes: His Moral Philosophy and Psychology*. Hassocks, Sussex, 1978.
Broughton, Janet, and Ruth Mattern. "Reinterpreting Descartes on the Notion of the Union of Mind and Body." *Journal of the History of Philosophy* 16 (1978): 23–32.
Carriero, J. "The First Meditation." *Pacific Philosophical Quarterly* 68 (1987): 222–48.

Caton, Hiram. *The Origin of Subjectivity: An Essay on Descartes*. New Haven, 1973.
Chávez-Arvizo, Enrique. "The Utrecht Controversy and the Descartes–Regius Affair: A Historical Note." *British Society for the History of Philosophy Newsletter*, n.s. 3, no. 1 (1998): 1–5.
Clarke, Desmond M. "Descartes' Philosophy of Science and the Scientific Revolution." In Cottingham, *Cambridge Companion to Descartes*, 259–85.
Cottingham, John. *Descartes*. Oxford, 1986.
——. *The Rationalists*. Don Mills, Ont., and New York, 1988.
——, ed. *The Cambridge Companion to Descartes*. Cambridge, 1992.
——, ed. *Descartes' Conversation with Burman*. Oxford, 1976.
——, ed. *Reason, Will, and Sensation: Studies in Descartes's Metaphysics*. Oxford, 1994.
Davis, Philip J., and Reuben Hersh. *The Mathematical Experience*, Boston, 1981.
de Jong, Willem R. "How Is Metaphysics as a Science Possible? Kant on the Distinction between Philosophical and Mathematical Method." *Review of Metaphysics* 48 (1995): 235–74.
Des Chene, Dennis. *Physiologia: Natural Philosophy in Late Aristotelian and Cartesian Thought*. Ithaca, 1996.
Dicker, Georges. *Descartes: An Analytical and Historical Introduction*. New York and Oxford, 1993.
Foti, F. M. "The Cartesian Imagination." *Philosophy and Phenomenological Research* 46, no. 4, (1986): 631–42.
Garber, Daniel. "Descartes and Experiment in the *Discourse* and *Essays*." in Voss. 288–31.
Garber, Daniel. *Descartes' Metaphysical Physics*. Chicago, 1992.
——. "Descartes' Physics." In Cottingham, *Cambridge Companion to Descartes*, 286–334.
——. "Understanding Interaction: What Descartes Should Have Told Elizabeth." *Southern Journal of Philosophy* 21 (1983): 15–32, Supplement.
Gaukroger, Stephen. *Descartes: An Intellectual Biography* . Oxford, 1995.
——. "The Nature of Abstract Reasoning: Philosophical Aspects of Descartes' Work in Algebra." In Cottingham, *Cambridge Companion to Descartes*. 91–114.
——, ed. *Descartes: Philosophy, Mathematics and Physics*, Brighton, Sussex and Totowa, N.J., 1980.
Gaukroger, Stephen, John Schuster, and John Sutton, eds. *Descartes' Natural Philosophy*. Routledge, 2000.
Gay, Peter. *The Enlightenment: An Interpretation*. Vol. 1: *The Rise of Modern Paganism*. London, 1966.
Glouberman, M. *Descartes: The Probable and the Certain*. Amsterdam, 1986.
Glymour, Clark, and Kevin Kelly. "Thoroughly Modern Meno." In *Inference, Explanation, and Other Frustrations in the Philosophy of Science*, ed. J. Earnan. Berkeley, 1992. 3–22.
Graham, George. *Philosophy of Mind: An Introduction*. Oxford, 1993.
Grosholz, Emily. *Cartesian Method and the Problem of Reduction*. Oxford, 1991.
——. "Descartes' Unification of Algebra and Geometry." In Gaukroger, *Descartes: Philosophy, Mathematics and Physics*. 156–68.
Haldane, E. S., and G. R. T. Ross, eds. and trans. *The Philosophical Works of Descartes*. Vols. 1 and 2. Cambridge, 1911.

Imlay, Robert. Review of John Cottingham, *The Rationalists*. In *Canadian Philosophical Review* 10, no. 1, (1990): 6–8.

Jolley, Nicholas. "The Reception of Descartes' Philosophy." In Cottingham, *Cambridge Companion to Descartes*, 393–423.

Judovitz, Dalia. "Derrida and Descartes: Economizing Thought." In *Derrida and Deconstruction*, ed. Hugh J. Silverman, 20–58. New York, 1989.

Lachterman, David Rapport. *The Ethics of Geometry: A Genealogy of Modernity*. New York, 1989.

MacIntosh, J. J. "Perception and Imagination in Descartes, Boyle and Hooke." *Canadian Journal of Philosophy* 13, no. 3 (1983): 327–52.

Mahoney, Michael S. "The Beginnings of Algebraic Thought in the Seventeenth Century." In Gaukroger, *Descartes: Philosophy, Mathematics and Physics*, 141–55.

Marshall, John. *Descartes's Moral Theory*. Ithaca, 1998.

Olson, M. A. "Descartes' First Meditation: Mathematics and the Laws of Logic." *Journal of the History of Philosophy*, 26, (1988): 407–38.

Owen, Joseph. "Faith, Ideas, Illumination, and Experience." In *The Cambridge History of Later Medieval Philosophy*, ed. Norman Kretzmann, Anthony Kenny, Jan Pinborg. Cambridge, 1982.

Radner, Daisie. "Descartes' Notion of the Union of Mind and Body." *Journal of the History of Philosophy* 9 (1971): 159–70.

Rodis-Lewis, Geneviève. *Descartes: His Life and Thought*. Trans. Jane Marie Todd. Ithaca, 1998.

Rogers, G. A. J. *Locke's Enlightenment: Aspects of the Origin, Nature, and Impact of His Philosophy*. Zürich and New York, 1998.

Rorty, Amélie Oksenberg. "Descartes on Thinking with the Body." In Cottingham, *Cambridge Companion to Descartes*, 371–92.

Rozemond, Marleen. "The Role of the Intellect in Descartes's Case for the Incorporeity of the Mind." In Voss, 97–114.

Russell, Bertrand. *The Analysis of Mind*. London, 1921.

——. *Human Knowledge: Its Scope and Limits*. New York, 1948.

Ryle, Gilbert. *The Concept of Mind*. London, 1949.

——. *On Thinking*. Ed. Konstantin Kolenda. Oxford, 1979.

Schouls, Peter. "Arnauld and the Modern Mind (the *Fourth Objections* as Indicative of Both Arnauld's Openness to and His Distance from Descartes)." In *Interpreting Arnauld*, ed. Elmar Kremer. Toronto, 1996.

——. *Descartes and the Enlightenment*. Edinburgh and Montreal, 1989.

——. "Descartes and the Idea of Progress." In *History of Philosophy Quarterly* 4, no. 4, (1987): 423–33. Republished in *René Descartes: Critical Assessments*, ed. G. J. D. Moyal, 276–91. New York, 1991.

——. *The Imposition of Method: A Study of Descartes and Locke*. Oxford, 1980.

——. "Locke, 'the Father of Modernity'?" *Philosophia Reformata* 61, no.2, (1996): 175–95.

——. "Peirce and Descartes: Doubt and the Logic of Discovery." In *Pragmatism and Purpose: Essays Presented to Thomas A. Goudge*, ed. L. W. Sumner, John G. Slater, and Fred Wilson. Toronto, 1981.

Schuster, John. "Whatever Should We Do with Cartesian Method?—Reclaiming Descartes for the History of Science." In Voss, 195–223.

Sepper, Dennis L. "Descartes and the Eclipse of Imagination, 1618–1630." *Journal of the History of Philosophy* 27, no. 3, (1989): 379–403.
——. *Descartes's Imagination: Proportion, Images, and the Activity of Thinking*. Berkeley, 1996.
——. "Imagination, Phantasms, and the Making of Hobbesian and Cartesian Science." *Monist* 71 (1988): 526–42.
——. "Ingenium, Memory Art, and the Unity of Imaginative Knowing in the Early Descartes." In Voss, 142–61.
Skinner, Quentin. " 'Scientia civilis' in Classical Rhetoric and in the Early Hobbes." In *Political Discourse in Early Modern Britain*, ed. Nicholas Phillipson and Quentin Skinner. Cambridge, 1993.
Smyth, R. "A Metaphysical Reading of the First Meditation." *Philosophical Quarterly* 36 (1986): 283–303.
Stoothoff, Robert. "Descartes' Dilemma." *Philosophical Quarterly* 39 (1989): 294–307.
Thomas, Bruce M. "Cartesian Epistemics and Descartes' Regulae." *History of Philosophy Quarterly* 13, no. 4 (1996): 433–49.
Van De Pitte, Frederick. "The Dating of Rule IV–B in Descartes' *Regulae ad directionem ingenii*." *Journal of the History of Philosophy* 29, no. 3 (1991): 375–95.
Van Leeuwen, Evert. *Descartes' Regulae: De eenheid van heuristische wetenschap en zelfbewustzijn*. Amsterdam, 1986.
——. "Method, Discourse, and the Act of Knowing." In Voss 224–41.
Vartanian, Aram. *Diderot and Descartes: A Study of Scientific Naturalism in the Enlightenment*. Princeton, 1953.
Voss, Stephen, ed. *Essays on the Philosophy and Science of René Descartes*. New York and Oxford, 1993.
Watson, Richard. "What Moves the Mind: An Excursion in Cartesian Dualism." *American Philosophical Quarterly* 19 (1982): 73–81.
White, Alan R. *The Language of Imagination*. Oxford, 1990.
Williams, Bernard. *Descartes: The Project of Pure Enquiry*. Hassocks, Sussex, 1978.
Wilson, C., and Schildknecht, C. "The Cogito Meant 'No More Philosophy': Valéry's Descartes." *History of European Ideas* 9 (1988): 47–62.
Wilson, Margaret Dauler. *Descartes*. Boston, 1978.
Wolterstorff, Nicholas. *John Locke and the Ethics of Belief*. Cambridge, 1996.
Yandell, David. "What Descartes Really Told Elizabeth: Mind-Body Union as a Primitive Notion." *British Journal of the History of Philosophy* 5, no. 2 (1997): 249–73.

Index

Activity, 144–45, 148–49, 155–57, 160–61
Algebra, 119
Analytic geometry, 39, 64, 115–16
   and corporeal imagination, 128–35
   and intellectual imagination, 119–28
   as link between pure and applied science, 131–34
Ancient Greek geometry, 39, 59n, 112, 118–19, 123, 125, 127, 129–31
Animal spirits, 50, 53, 57
Anselm, 5n
a priori, 82, 103
Aquinas, 2, 5n
Archimedean point, ix, 2, 15, 29, 76, 103, 106, 153, 157–60
Aristotle, 43n, 65, 150n, 151n
Arnauld, Antoine, 4n, 30n
Atomism
   epistemic, 34–35, 151
   physical, 35n
Augustine, 2, 5n
Autonomy, epistemic, 7, 11, 150, 152, 161

Baker, Gordon, 32n
Barber, Kenneth, 5n, 116n
Beck, L. J., 119n
Bennett, Jonathan, 116n
Berkeley, George, 4n
Blom, John J., 30n, 55

Boethius, 82
Bonaventure, 5n
Brain traces, 40, 50–53, 113
Broughton, Janet, 32n

Cambridge Platonists, 5n
Caton, Hiram, 55n, 119n, 127n
Chavez-Arvizo, Enrique, 4
Circularity, 98, 102, 105, 138
Clarke, Desmond, 137n, 142n
Clear and distinct ideas, 7, 99, 151
Clerselier, 153n
Cogito, 15, 76, 103, 158–59
Copernicus, 2
Corporeal imagination, 36–42, 47, 56–8, 73, 85, 105–6, 118, 128–35
   as mediator between reason and sensation, 132–35
Corporeal memory, 36–42, 47, 49–51
Cottingham, John, 2, 30, 32
Cudworth, Ralph, 5n

Daydreams, 57, 111
De Jong, Willem R., 120n
Des Chene, Dennis, 55n
Determinism, 31–45
Diagrams, 63, 65, 118, 123, 128–35, 130–31
Dicker, Georges, 10n, 14n, 30n, 31n, 43n, 55n

169